Backfield in Motion

End Times Events Take Center Stage . . .

Behind the Scenes

MICHAEL J. RILEY

Backfield in Motion

End Times Events Take Center Stage . . .
Behind the Scenes

Revelation 13

MICHAEL J. RILEY

Derek Press

Printed by Derek Press, Cleveland, Tennessee

BACKFIELD IN MOTION: END TIMES EVENTS
TAKE CENTER STAGE . . . BEHIND THE SCENES by
Michael J. Riley

Unless otherwise noted, all Scripture quotations are from the
King James Version of the Bible. Copyright © 1999 by Thomas
Nelson, Inc.

Unless otherwise noted, all illustrations of the Dragon, the
Beast Coming Out of the Sea, and the Beast Coming Out of the
Earth are excerpted from the Revelation Illustrated series by
Pat Marvenko Smith.

ISBN: 978-1-59684-318-9

Printed by Derek Press, Cleveland, TN
Printed in the United States of America
www.derekpress.com

TABLE OF CONTENTS

Foreword: Things are Not as They Seem   vii

Rise of the Antichrist

Chapter 1:   The Beast Rising from the Sea................................   1

Chapter 2:   The Beast in Global Economics   13

Chapter 3:   The Beast in Global Politics   29

Chapter 4:   The Event that Changes the World........................   43

Chapter 5:   A Star is Born........................   61

Chapter 6:   New World Disorder   79

Rise of the False Prophet

Chapter 7:   The Beast Coming Up Out of the Earth....................   87

Chapter 8:   A Spiritual Blur Occurs........................   103

Chapter 9:   The Beast in Global Religion........................   113

Chapter 10:   Harmony in Motion........................   131

Chapter 11:   Signs and Wonders   149

Chapter 12:   Image is Everything   161

Chapter 13:   The Mark of the Beast........................   181

Here is Wisdom

Chapter 14:   The Number of a Man........................   195

Chapter 15:   The Good News........................   211

References   217

FOREWORD

Things are Not as They Seem

"Blessed is he that readeth, and they that hear the words of this
prophecy, and keep those things which are written therein: for the
time is at hand." – John the Apostle, Revelation 1:3

Revelation 13 is truly one of the Bible's centerpieces of symbolic end-
times prophecy. Meditate for a moment on this portrait of the imagery that
John, through the inspiration of the Holy Spirit, paints for us here:

Snapshot of
Revelation 13

The Mark
v. 16, 17

Image of the Beast
v. 14, 15

Miracles
v. 14

Heads, Horns, Crowns
v. 1, 3

The Beast of the Earth
v. 11, 12, 14, 15, 17, 18

The Dragon
v. 2, 4, 11

The Beast of the Sea
v. 1, 2, 3, 4

Throughout the Scriptures, the number 13 always represents a spiritual symbol that identifies *depravity* and *rebellion*. This means the imagery behind each major event described within Revelation 13 symbolizes a sinister, depraved situation of rebellion toward God that will take place in the last days of time before the Second Coming of Jesus Christ.

The first event involves the rise of an ugly and powerful beast, having seven heads and ten horns and wearing many crowns, that comes up out of the sea to take control over the world. The source of power and authority found in this horrible beast is derived from a great dragon, a creature of intense evil that orchestrates all of these events from behind the scenes, hidden from the natural human eye.

Next, another terrible beast rises up out of the earth, working great miracles that deceive the world into worshipping an image of the first beast. Though it deceptively resembles a harmless lamb, it speaks as the dragon and causes the entire world to accept a mark of slavery and bondage under the authority of the first beast. This means its power also comes from the same evil source that is hidden behind the scenes.

What is really going on here? What do all of these symbols mean? Also, why are all of these events, or things that appear to be related to these events, being frequently discussed today *outside of the church*, outside of religious circles?

It seems everyone these days is familiar with the terms *antichrist*, *false prophet*, the *mark of the beast* and *666*. It doesn't matter whether you are a religious person or not. These terms are familiar because they are all popular themes that are continually being explored throughout many computer games played by our youth, movies seen by millions of people, music listened to by millions more, personal conversations between friends at the office water cooler, public seminars and debates about conspiracy theories, and of course, spiritual discussions on end-times prophecy. Why are these themes so popular?

Because today, more than ever before, there seems to be some sort of tension building inside everybody that things are not really as they seem anymore. Everyone you talk to feels it. There *appear* to be major events happening all around us that do not seem or feel right, events that do not *appear* to target our common good as a collective people. They *appear* to be happening . . . yet we don't always know for sure whether or not they are all real, because many of these events apparently happen behind the scenes and are not publicly reported in the news. Furthermore, what *is* actually reported in the news often *appears* instinctively to be filtered in many respects.

For whatever reason, we simply can't get our minds around this sense of tension that is building – except for an unnerving notion of absolute certainty that we have no control or influence over what is happening. What makes all of this so weird is that we *do* know that something really is happening, because we see, feel and live the results that these situations are creating.

There are definitely some strange political and economic events of a grand scale taking place around us – and they all *appear* to be crafting some sort of unspoken global policy that points toward the entry of the Antichrist. At the very same time, vastly different religions *appear* to be aligning together along some sort of ecumenical undercurrent of this same unspoken global policy – and they are sounding a very strange religious voice that *appears* poised to announce the presence of the false prophet.

That's not all. Embedded in the middle of our fast-paced, busy world of change is the astonishing growth of technology that we all use within our own personal lives – credit and debit cards, Internet access, email, text messaging, etc. – that, in many very real ways, inject this same unspoken global policy directly into the space we live in at a local level, through transactions that *appear* instinctively to model the acceptance and use of some sort of mark; transactions that inherently *appear* to point us toward that evil number 666.

All of these situations provoke people to ask, "Are these things really happening? What is going on?"

The current events of our day are the reasons why everybody is familiar with these terms, all of which are found in and line up with Revelation 13. In other words, lots of people – both religious and secular – are talking about Revelation 13 in one way or another, formally or informally, whether they know it or not. Often, we may not even realize that many of the current events happening around us actually reveal some deeper insights into the imagery of Revelation 13.

For example, if you view the current events of our day as though they are all smaller components of a large critical mass of activities needed to produce a particular result, then suddenly these events *appear* to fall into some sort of sequence that really does resemble a *new world order*.

Rise of the New World Order?

The Dragon	The Beast of the Sea	The Beast of the Earth
SATAN	ANTICHRIST	FALSE PROPHET

- Character
  - Rebellion
  - Anarchy

- Global Economics
- Global Politics
- Shadow Government

- Religious Pluralism
- Interfaith Ecumenism
- Shadow Government

Globalization – One World System

Think this concept through for a moment. We are all witnessing the obvious overall decline of the moral character and discipline of mankind. While volumes have been written about the variety of reasons for this decline, they all inevitably point toward a society that is coming unraveled by personal depravity and rebellion (symbolized by 13). We are evolving into a culture of personal anarchy that dilutes and weakens every level of authority. This rebellious culture redefines our values so that we shift our collective basis of fundamental understanding from a Christian worldview to a secular humanist worldview.

In other words, the overall moral character and discipline of mankind is shifting from a philosophy of values based upon core beliefs in the Christian God to a different philosophy based upon no belief in God. Because these non-theistic values are deeply antagonistic toward traditional religious beliefs, they manifest themselves in different degrees of depravity, rebellion and anarchy that occur at various levels of social interaction.

These social acts of depravity, rebellion and anarchy are the roots of great tensions that shape and influence global economics and global politics. These social roots of tension are subtly merging our political and economic sciences into some sort of world union, a one-world unity that is actually being promoted by religious pluralism and interfaith ecumenism that emphasizes an ultimate shift away from the Christian worldview.

From this perspective, we begin to see that each symbol of Revelation 13 resembles an individual piece of a larger spiritual jigsaw puzzle. Each piece of the puzzle is interpreted by its own uniquely-shaped influence of great social tension. For example, great social tension is the root of our shift in core beliefs, as people turn away from values of good to influences of evil (symbolized by the dragon as Satan). Great social tension is the root of globalization, the enormous political and economic convergence of a one-world system (symbolized by the first beast as the Antichrist) that is being oddly woven together through threads of different religions (symbolized by the second beast as the False Prophet).

Many people often isolate each of these events as separate situations that *appear* to occur by simple chance or coincidence. But when viewed as a whole, all of these events happening around us construct a continual progression of things that are changing in an *intelligent* pattern. They point us toward a deliberate direction that is being followed, a certain end or goal.

For instance, the mark of the beast is usually interpreted to mean anything from a social security number (40 years ago), to an ATM pin number (20 years ago), to a computer chip being surgically implanted in the hand or forehead today. The lesson here is that although technology continues to change in complexity, its direction remains unchanged – it is definitely evolving toward one ultimate goal: the *control* of the masses.

Revelation 13 explains how each of these pieces of imagery relates to the current events happening around us. The Scriptures help us to understand where and why they are interrelated, so that we may concentrate our thoughts on how all of this fits together for God's purpose in our lives.

That is truly a blessing.

The Beast of the Sea

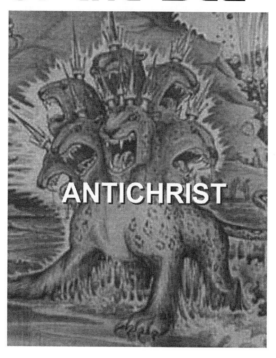

ANTICHRIST

The Rise of the Antichrist

CHAPTER 1

The Beast Rising From the Sea

"We're from the government and we are here to help you."

Talk about help. Governments around the world are helping international financial institutions such as JP Morgan Chase use debit and credit cards to usher in the cashless society. As the second largest financial institution in the world (behind Citigroup), JP Morgan Chase to date has issued more than 87 million credit cards.[1]

Governments are helping Hitachi and other companies implant microchips with RFID (radio frequency identification) technology into paper, watches, cell phones, money and other products to track their authenticity and transaction history.[2]

Governments are helping Digital Angel and other firms test under-the-skin implants of other microchips that use biosensor technology and Web-enabled wireless telecommunications linked to Global Positioning Systems (GPS) to monitor key body functions – such as temperature and pulse – and transmit that data, along with accurate location information, to a ground station or monitoring facility.[3]

With governments providing all of this "help," it's no wonder that *the mark of the beast* is the one of the most frequent subjects being discussed today. The mark is a tool that the Apostle John connects to a huge, evil entity that he describes as a rising beast in the opening verse of his vision in Revelation 13:

> "And I stood upon the sand of the sea, and saw a beast rise up out of the sea, having seven heads and ten horns, and upon his horns ten crowns, and upon his heads the name of blasphemy."
> – Revelation 13:1

1

Notice that the description of this beast starts by immediately establishing where it is coming from. Why? In his study *Revelation 13: Closer Home Than We Think*, David A. DePra explains that "the *sea* here represents the masses of humanity, the 6.5 billion people that inhabit our planet. John announces that this beast *rises* up out of the sea . . . in other words, this beast is *of* the sea. It is *of* the people." [4]

So this beast is actually a reflection of the people; a broader reflection of mankind itself. It reflects their characteristics – their character traits. This beast reflects the broader character of mankind, but John also explains that the power of this beast comes directly from the dragon, which is the symbol for Satan. In fact, throughout all of Revelation 13 we discover that Satan is the real power behind this beast. So the power of this beast is rooted in satanic evil.

If Satan is giving this beast its power, and this beast reflects the character of man, then the satanic power of this beast to rise represents Satan giving power to the fallen character – the evil immorality – of man. As evil immorality gains more power and visibility, moral authority weakens and fades from view.

This is the sinister paradox of the last days. The rising beast of the sea reflects the falling character of mankind, the moral decline of society. The rising beast of the sea is the growing satanic immorality of an evil world.

Isn't this true? Don't we see rampant moral decline happening everywhere? Acts of profanity, violence, pornography, public immorality, rape and murder are now commonplace in our world today. Some of these acts are even *socially acceptable* in certain circles. Mankind is unraveling at the very seams of society.

That's not all. The term *beast* here in the ancient Greek really has two meanings – *a dangerous animal* and *destruction*. These meanings speak volumes about how this beast, rising out of the sea, represents the rising danger found in the destructive evil of the fallen man, an otherwise intelligent being that is governed purely by his lower nature of animal instinct and survival.

In other words, we are witnessing the baser instincts of mankind rise to prominence. Fleshly perversion is destructively permeating every facet of our society's mental, emotional, physical, and economical health. This creates the dangerous mental, emotional, and physical condition of fallen man that fuels moral confusion behind many global economic and political events that are happening in the world.

Rising up out of the sea not only explains that this beast is coming about as an agency of the enemy, but according to DePra, "this rising also implies a *rising up*, or progression, as opposed to being there all of a sudden. Everything that this beast represents is *progressive in nature.*" [5]

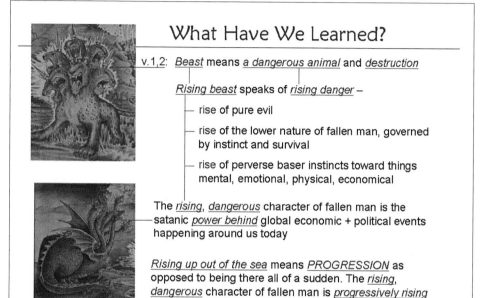

What Have We Learned?

v.1,2: *Beast* means <u>a dangerous animal</u> and <u>destruction</u>

Rising beast speaks of <u>rising danger</u> –

- rise of pure evil
- rise of the lower nature of fallen man, governed by instinct and survival
- rise of perverse baser instincts toward things mental, emotional, physical, economical

The <u>rising, dangerous</u> character of fallen man is the satanic <u>power behind</u> global economic + political events happening around us today

Rising up out of the sea means <u>PROGRESSION</u> as opposed to being there all of a sudden. The <u>rising, dangerous</u> character of fallen man is <u>progressively rising</u> around us in the form of global economic + political events

John points out that this beast has seven heads and ten horns, and that there are ten crowns upon its ten horns. These details immediately associate the beast with the dragon, which John describes in the previous chapter of Revelation:

> **"And there appeared another wonder in heaven; and behold a great red dragon, having seven heads and ten horns, and seven crowns upon his heads." – Revelation 12:3**

DePra notes the similarities between this beast and the dragon, pointing out that "the dragon also has seven heads and ten horns. This signifies that the first beast is birthed *of* the dragon, because parent and child both have seven heads and ten horns. But notice that the dragon wears its crowns upon its seven heads, not upon its horns." [6]

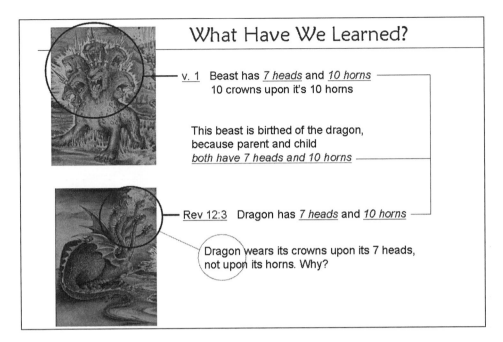

What Have We Learned?

v. 1   Beast has *7 heads* and *10 horns*
10 crowns upon it's 10 horns

This beast is birthed of the dragon,
because parent and child
both have 7 heads and 10 horns

Rev 12:3   Dragon has *7 heads* and *10 horns*

Dragon wears its crowns upon its 7 heads,
not upon its horns. Why?

We'll explore the reason for this difference in a moment. Why does the Bible go into such detail about the number of heads, the number of crowns, etc.? Throughout the Scriptures, numbers not only indicate physical *amounts* in the natural realm, they also indicate spiritual *character* in the supernatural realm. From this perspective, what does having seven heads indicate about this beast?

Heads here denotes *authority, direction, guidance*, which refers to seven physical authorities, directions or paths of guidance. At the same time, the number *seven* spiritually symbolizes a character of *completion* or *perfection*. Seven numerically denotes the spiritual authority that is rooted in a completely perfect life lived here on earth. Jesus is the only human to ever live a completely perfect life in this world. For this reason, Jesus is the only Man with complete spiritual authority.

Because Jesus has a perfect relationship with God, in complete spiritual union with Him, this means the number seven shadows Jesus' life as the only model to follow for a perfect relationship that is in complete union with God.

We can also achieve this perfect union with God through Jesus, because Acts 4:12 explains that "there is none other Name under heaven given among men, whereby we must be saved." Philippians 2:9-12 explains His perfect, complete authority in this way: "God also hath highly exalted Him, and given Him a Name which is above every other name: That at the Name of Jesus every knee should bow . . . and every tongue should confess that Jesus Christ is Lord, to the glory of God the Father."

In this context, seven numerically signifies the complete, perfect authority that Jesus has over the earth. When we are in union with God, seven represents the spiritual stamp of His complete guidance for our lives through Jesus, His perfect direction for our lives through the Light of His Holy Spirit.

We know this is true because the perfect direction that God provides to us through the Light of His Holy Spirit is numerically designated by seven in the spiritual structure of the Menorah – the seven-lamped candlestick that lit up the Temple of the Most High God in the Old Testament.

In Exodus 25:31-40, the Bible describes how all of the Menorah candles or lamps are arranged so as to "give light in front of it."

In *The Menorah from a New Angle*, Eliezer Ben Moshe explains that each of the six outer candles are arranged to face inward toward the center candle, in a pattern that is contrary to the normal method of diffusing light in as wide an area as possible. This arrangement actually concentrates all light toward the center, making the individual lights shine together as one single large unified light.[7]

What does this arrangement tell us?

First of all, it shows us that the Menorah is not designed to merely broadcast light over as large a space as is practical. Its unique structure causes it to concentrate its light, as from a single source, with all the candles or lamps shining forth in union, together as one. This means the Menorah's unique structure is designed more for a spiritual purpose than for a physical or practical purpose. The seven individual lamps of the Menorah therefore represent the spiritual union of the seven Spirits (representing natures of character) that are the Person of the Holy Spirit, as John describes in other sections of Revelation, such as:

> **"John to the seven churches which are in Asia: Grace be unto you, and peace from Him which is, and which was, and which is to come; and from the *seven Spirits* which are before His throne . . ."**
> **– Revelation 1:4**

> **"And I beheld, and, lo, in the midst of the throne and of the four beasts, and in the midst of the elders, stood a Lamb as it had been slain, having seven horns and seven eyes, which are the *seven Spirits of God* sent forth into all the earth." – Revelation 5:6**

So each individual lamp represents an individual Spirit, or character nature, of the unified Holy Spirit that describes the character of the coming Messiah, as prophesized in the Old Testament:

> "And *the Spirit* of the Lord shall rest upon Him, *the Spirit* of wisdom and understanding, *the Spirit* of counsel and might, *the Spirit* of knowledge and of the fear of the Lord; And shall make Him of quick understanding (obedience) in the fear of the Lord: and He shall not judge after the sight of His eyes, neither reprove after the hearing of His ears: But with righteousness shall He judge the poor, and reprove with equity for the meek of the earth: and He shall smite the earth with the rod of the mouth, and with the breath of his lips shall He slay the wicked. And righteousness shall be the girdle of His loins, and faithfulness the girdle of His reins." – Isaiah 11:2-5

Just as the physical Menorah was used to light the innermost sanctuary of the Temple of God, the seven Spirits of the Holy Spirit light the very Throne Room of God in heaven today. Furthermore, 1 Corinthians 6:19 explains that everyone who believes in Jesus Christ as their Lord and Savior is a living temple of the Holy Spirit, so the Light of the Holy Spirit also enlightens us today as living temples of God. The Holy Spirit brings Light into the innermost darkness we harbor in our hearts.

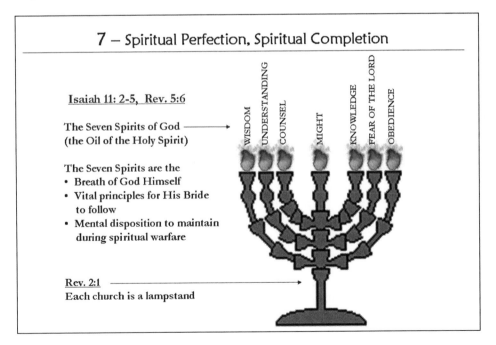

7 – Spiritual Perfection, Spiritual Completion

Isaiah 11: 2-5, Rev. 5:6

The Seven Spirits of God ──→
(the Oil of the Holy Spirit)

The Seven Spirits are the
- Breath of God Himself
- Vital principles for His Bride to follow
- Mental disposition to maintain during spiritual warfare

Rev. 2:1
Each church is a lampstand

WISDOM · UNDERSTANDING · COUNSEL · MIGHT · KNOWLEDGE · FEAR OF THE LORD · OBEDIENCE

This means the Holy Spirit's Menorah concentration of Light is spiritually designed to cut through darkness, just like a sword. This explains how His Truth cuts through lies, His Counsel cuts through confusion, His Healing cuts through sickness, His Love cuts through fear, His Hope cuts through insecurity, His Life cuts through death, hell and the grave.

In this context of the spiritual realm, the power behind the Menorah concentration of Light prophetically represents the sword of the Spirit constructed from the Word of God, an important piece of the whole armor of God that the Apostle Paul refers to in Ephesians as a weapon of spiritual warfare:

> **"Wherefore take unto you the whole armour of God, that ye may be able to withstand in the evil day, and having done all, to stand . . . and take the helmet of salvation, and the sword of the Spirit, which is the Word of God . . ." – Ephesians 6:13, 17**

The New Testament describes how the power within the sword of the Spirit enables the Christian to successfully wage battles in spiritual warfare:

> **"For the Word of God is quick, and powerful, and sharper than any twoedged sword, piercing even to the dividing asunder of soul and spirit, and of the joints and marrow, and is a discerner of the thoughts and intents of the heart." – Hebrews 4:12**

All of these insights signify that the seven heads of this dangerous and destructive beast represent a complete paradox in spiritually perfect headship or leadership.

On the surface, all of these insights indicate that each *head* of this beast is somehow *spiritually complete* or *perfect*. In other words, the authority that this beast serves under, and the source of all that directs it, is spiritually perfect in some form. All seven separate heads, all seven separate authorities, each of the seven separate directions, each of the seven separate paths of guidance – all of this is working together as a *system*, an organization that is in union, towards some form of spiritual completion or perfection.

But underneath the surface, it is important to recognize the sheer magnitude of evil being framed here in this paradox, because the end of the first verse of Revelation 13 clearly states that this system is pure evil: ". . . and upon his heads the name of blasphemy." This reveals the *nature* of each of the heads. These seven heads represent a form of spiritual perfection, but upon each head is the name of blasphemy – meaning this system actually symbolizes *the perfection of spiritual blasphemy.*

Digest that for a moment by studying the seven natures represented by these seven heads.

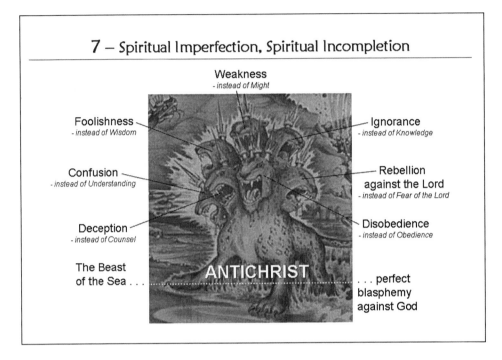

7 – Spiritual Imperfection, Spiritual Incompletion

Weakness
- instead of Might

Foolishness
- instead of Wisdom

Ignorance
- instead of Knowledge

Confusion
- instead of Understanding

Rebellion against the Lord
- instead of Fear of the Lord

Deception
- instead of Counsel

Disobedience
- instead of Obedience

The Beast of the Sea . . . ANTICHRIST . . . perfect blasphemy against God

Blasphemy is irreverence and rebellion toward God. DePra explains that "blasphemy can be manifested in a number of ways, but irreverence for God, and rebellion against God, are really all about refusing God's rule over me, in favor of my own rule. Instead of "Thy will be done . . .," I say, "*my will be done.*" [8]

This means the seven heads of this evil system represent *perfectly irreverent* and *perfectly rebellious behavior* toward God. That's the paradox. Rather than representing spiritual completion, they signify spiritual *incompletion*. Rather than perfection, this is total *imperfection*. In other words, *seven* here paradoxically denotes the irreverence manifested from an incomplete life that is in total rebellion against God. This incomplete, rebellious life is authorized through confusion and deception – the spiritual darkness of Satan.

The irreverent and rebellious authority, direction, and guidance of this system acts in perfect opposition to the Holy Spirit of God. Darkness

8

opposes Light. Each of the seven heads of darkness in this system signifies perfect opposition to each of the seven Spirits of Light in the Holy Spirit. Rather than acquiring the wisdom of the Holy Spirit, this system acts in irreverent, rebellious foolishness; instead of learning the knowledge of the Holy Spirit, this system dwells in irreverent, rebellious ignorance; rather than being obedient to the Holy Spirit, this system acts in irreverent, rebellious disobedience; and so on for each of the seven Spirits.

Does any of this sound familiar in our world today?

What better way to portray the progressive rise of the irreverent, rebellious, fallen man against God than to show a system that is ruled and directed by an authority that guides fallen man toward perfect blasphemy against God – specifically against the rule, guidance and direction of God Himself.

The beast of the sea represents a system that is organized in total independence from God, through irreverent behavior and rebellion. Instead of following Jesus Christ as its perfect authority, this organization follows an enemy that is the perfect opposite of Jesus Christ. Irreverence and rebellion are the spirits of an *antichrist*. They represent acts of perfect spiritual blasphemy, the outcome and summation of independence from Almighty God.

The Scriptures explain that the culture of irreverence and rebellion we see rising around us today represent serious spiritual issues with satanic roots:

> **"Behold, to obey is better than sacrifice . . . for rebellion is as the sin of witchcraft, and stubbornness is as iniquity and idolatry." – 1 Samuel 15:22, 23**

We should expect nothing less from an antichrist which has the motivation and power of Satan behind it. Satan is the source of *all* rebellion against God. Any antichrist which comes from Satan will look like Satan, carry the same anti-Christian spirit of Satan, and be used for the same purpose as Satan. Jesus describes the Antichrist to us this way:

> **"Ye are of your father the devil, and the lusts of your father ye will do. He was a murderer from the beginning, and abode not in the truth, because there is no truth in him. When he speaketh a lie, he speaketh of his own: for he is a liar, and father of it." – John 8:44**

Remember that this system of the Antichrist *rises* from the sea, which indicates a *progression*. In other words, this system of the Antichrist has been rising for a period of time. More specifically, this means the person of *the* Antichrist will be found in a system which is coming to maturity, a massive entity being formed *by* Satan.

Notice the horns and crowns in Revelation 13:1. Just as the heads here denote headship, the *horns* upon the heads denote *power*, as in *might*. The *crowns* upon the horns denote *authority*, as in *privilege* or *right*. This antichrist system, operating within all of its spiritually perfect blasphemy, has the *right* and *might* to execute its purpose – all privileges given, of course, by Satan, the dragon.

There is a lot to think through here and meditate upon.

First of all, Jesus tells us as Christians to seek first the kingdom of God in heaven. Our Lord teaches us to search for the spirit-filled life of abundance found only in an obedient relationship with Him.

> **"But seek ye first the kingdom of God, and His righteousness, and all these things shall be added unto you." – Matthew 6:33**

In contrast, Satan – the father of lies – leads the fallen man to first seek the natural kingdom here in this world. Satan guides the fallen man to crave a life of worldly abundance that he claims is found only in the power, wealth and perversion of the carnal things that the Bible warns against and condemns:

> **"For all that is in the world, the lust of the flesh, and the lust of the eyes, and the pride of life, is not of the Father, but is of the world." – 1 John 2:16**

So this system represents a rising danger in the world, an increase of the pure evil of Satan himself being executed through the rise of sinful man, a fallen being that is increasingly governed by his carnal instinct not only to survive, but ravenously driven by and envious of the privileges of power, wealth and perversion.

This evil system is being directed and guided by seven heads that represent the imperfect mind and spiritual nature of the Antichrist. John emphasizes this fact in the second verse by explaining that the dragon gives the beast power and his *seat*.

Seat here points to *position*, to the *role of authority*. This beast is being guided by fallen men in high places, in roles of authority. These seven heads and ten crowns speak of authorities who not only desire the privileges of power, wealth and perversion, they point toward *ultimate*

10

privileges – in other words, these authorities want *all* power, *all* wealth, *all* perversion for themselves. This is the all-consuming purpose of the Antichrist: *control*. Control of all things, everything, everybody.

These authorities cannot accomplish this purpose openly, not yet anyway – because we the people, especially Christians not yet taken in the Rapture, will all reject and fight them. So these authorities excel in deception. They are doing things *behind the scenes*, even though in some areas they are becoming more blatant. This evil deception involves many economic and political activities occurring on a global scale.

Behind the Scenes – The Beast of the Sea

The Dragon   The Beast of the Sea

SATAN   ANTICHRIST

- **Global Economics**
  - Currency manipulation
  - Federal Reserve
  - World Bank, IMF
  - WTO

- **Global Politics**
  - Council on Foreign Relations
  - United Nations
  - Bilderbergers, Club of Rome
  - Trilateral Commission

- Character
  - Rebellion
  - Anarchy

Globalization – One World System

- **Shadow Government**

Let's explore some of these deceptive activities that are going on behind the scenes, the ones that we can verify.

CHAPTER 2

The Beast in Global Economics

We have established that these authorities, filled with the spirit of an antichrist, are paving the way for the future introduction of an individual who is *the* Antichrist.

Consumed with the lust for power, they ultimately desire *all* the wealth that exists in this world. To control all the wealth in the world, they must control all of the currencies in the world. This is difficult, because many currencies are designed around the character of the nation they represent.

For example, pull out a $20 bill. It has the face of Andrew Jackson on the front. Jackson was a national hero during the War of 1812, he was a Congressman, a U.S. Senator, a Judge on the Tennessee Supreme Court and the seventh President of the United States. On the back is a picture of the White House, home of our president. Now think back for a moment. This is not the same $20 bill design that you held in your hands in 1997. Do you remember when the $20 bill, and other currency later on during the last few years, was redesigned? Behind every redesign is a purpose. Let's interpret the purpose behind the redesign of our currency.

Viewed as an isolated event, the $20 bill *had* to be redesigned to prevent counterfeiting – particularly counterfeiting throughout the Middle East, according to public news reports. So the new bill came out in 1998 under the pretense of financial protection and as a security measure.

But now consider this same event from a global perspective. Gary Kah, a Christian author from Indiana, was a high-ranking government liaison in the Reagan administration Treasury Department during the early-to-mid 1980s. Kah was touring a certain plant on other official Treasury Department business when he accidentally came upon the die sets designed to print the new currency. He and the others in his federal group knew nothing about any *plans* for new currency, much less the currency itself.[9]

So here you have a group of U.S. government officials learning about the planned new currency through the grapevine, from a non-governmental plant that already has the equipment and tooling to print the currency. Kah and Congressman Ron Paul of Texas began investigating the new currency and the purpose behind it.

They learned that the plans to issue a new currency were international in scope. At least a dozen major countries were already planning to come out with new money – and this was in the early-to-mid 1980s, almost 20 years before the redesigned $20 bill you have in your hand actually appeared. Countries that redesigned and issued new currencies included Switzerland, the United Kingdom, Japan, Canada, France, Germany, Australia, Brazil and others.[10]

Follow the logic being applied here as we explore each of these global areas of activity. We're assembling the pieces of the jigsaw puzzle that create this beast – this evil system – rising out of the sea. These authorities blindly crave power. They understand that to achieve all power they must control all the wealth there is in the world. To control all the wealth in the world, they must control all of the currencies in the world.

To control world currencies, these authorities must manipulate currency. There are ultimately two pillars of currency manipulation: tracking the currency being used, and dictating the value of the currency being used at any given time.

To track your money with new technology, the existing currency must be redesigned for release into financial transactions. As noted earlier, openly redesigning currency is a difficult feat because individual currencies are designed around the character of the nation they represent.

To overcome this redesign issue, the basic characteristics of the currency must remain intact, but *security* features are deceptively added under the auspice of preventing international counterfeiting. How is the money you have today being tracked?

Study closely the nine redesigned features of the new $50 bill that are shown on the next page. Of particular interest is the embedded strip noted in Feature 3. The initial purpose of this strip was to enable special devices to detect this currency as it passes through airports or across international boundaries. Could this currency be tracked by the GPS satellites today?

14

The ability to track specific currency implies the broader capability of specifically tracking anyone who carries that currency, a means of identifying the location of a person. Could something sinister lurk beneath this auspice of security?

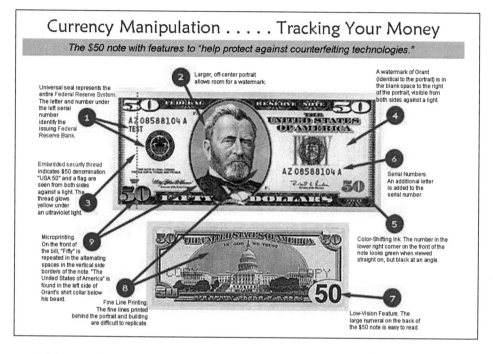

Currency Manipulation . . . . . Tracking Your Money

The $50 note with features to "help protect against counterfeiting technologies."

2 Larger, off-center portrait allows room for a watermark.

A watermark of Grant (identical to the portrait) is in the blank space to the right of the portrait, visible from both sides against a light.

1 Universal seal represents the entire Federal Reserve System. The letter and number under the left serial number identify the issuing Federal Reserve Bank.

3 Embedded security thread indicates $50 denomination. "USA 50" and a flag are seen from both sides against a light. The thread glows yellow under an ultraviolet light.

6 Serial Numbers. An additional letter is added to the serial number.

9 Microprinting. On the front of the bill, "Fifty" is repeated in the alternating spaces in the vertical side borders of the note. "The United States of America" is found in the left side of Grant's shirt collar below his beard.

5 Color-Shifting Ink. The number in the lower right corner on the front of the note looks green when viewed straight on, but black at an angle.

8 Fine Line Printing. The fine lines printed behind the portrait and building are difficult to replicate.

7 Low-Vision Feature. The large numeral on the back of the $50 note is easy to read.

This question reminds us that it was Congressman Paul who had the courage a couple of years ago to denounce the national ID card provisions that were contained in HR 418 (the REAL ID Act) an intelligence bill voted upon in the U.S. House of Representatives.[11]

Paul urged his colleagues to reject the bill and its new layers of needless bureaucracy. "National ID cards are not proper in a free society," he stated. "This is America, not Soviet Russia. The federal government should never be allowed to demand papers from American citizens, and it certainly has no constitutional authority to do so. A national identification card, in whatever form it may take, will allow the federal government to inappropriately monitor the movements and transactions of every American."

He continued, "History shows that governments inevitably use such power in harmful ways. The 9-11 commission, whose recommendations underlie this bill, has called for *internal* screening points where identification will be demanded. Domestic travel restrictions are the hallmark of authoritarian states, not free nations. It is just a matter of time until those who refuse to carry the new licenses will be denied the ability to drive or board an airplane."[12]

Congressman Paul further argued, "Nationalizing standards for drivers licenses and birth certificates, and linking them together via a national database, creates a national ID system pure and simple. Proponents of the national ID understand that the public remains wary of the scheme, so they attempt to claim they're merely creating new standards for existing state IDs. Nonsense! This legislation imposes federal standards in a federal bill, and it creates a federalized ID, regardless of whether the ID itself is still stamped with the name of your state."

He concluded, "Those who are willing to allow the government to establish a Soviet-style internal passport system because they think it will make us safer are terribly mistaken. Subjecting every citizen to surveillance and screening points actually will make us less safe, not in the least because it will divert resources away from tracking and apprehending terrorists and deploy them against innocent Americans! Every conservative who believes in constitutional restraints on government should reject the authoritarian national ID card and the nonsensical intelligence bill itself."[13]

Even though Congressman Paul argued vehemently against this national ID system, HR 418 (the REAL ID Act) was voted into law by Congress on May 10, 2005. Under this context, let's revisit our jigsaw puzzle, where Kah and Paul learned that the plans to issue a new currency went far beyond American money. They discovered that these plans were international in scope, because at least a dozen major countries had already planned to come out with new money. Remember, too, that this was in the early-to-mid 1980s – almost 20 years before the redesigned $20 bill we now have actually appeared.

As isolated events, these countries appear to simply have released their new currencies by chance, again under the pretense of financial protection and as a security measure. But viewed from a global perspective, we see that the respective currencies of the world's top *industrialized* nations – read that top *economic* nations – were redesigned 20 years ago to share many of these same "security" features – features that apparently weren't needed until the mid-to-late 1990s. Huh?

This suggests that the leaders of the top economic nations in the world were *collaborating* on currency redesign for a threat that didn't fully exist *for another ten years*. In other words, the "security" features of global currency redesign were being aggregated along the lines of the world's top economies – an economic aggregation of currency redesign. None of this was ever reported on the nightly news, and it doesn't stop there.

This economic aggregation of currency is being aligned even further. You need look no further than the G-8, the group of the world's eight top industrial nations, to see how this alignment is transitioning into place.

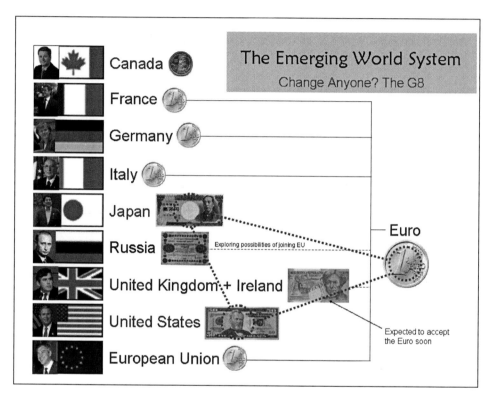

The member nations of the G-8 currently account for about two-thirds of the world's total economic output. A cursory glance of the G-8 reveals that the very name of this group harbors some sort of deceptive nature, because the actual number of nations involved here really forms the *G-9*, not the G-8.

This is interesting because Russia joined this club (in the early 1990s) after the downfall of the Soviet Union, yet the Russian ruble remains essentially worthless in comparison with the other currencies represented by the countries in the G-8. Furthermore, though the primary agendas of the G-8 discuss global economic, political and environmental issues, Russia does not participate in financial or economic issues. So why is Russia included as an "economic leader"?

A closer review of the G-8 shows that four countries already use the euro as their default currency, while England continues to debate whether to switch from their pound (based upon sterling) to the euro. Japan uses the yen. Canada uses the Canadian dollar, which is really a derivative the U.S. dollar.

Notice how this economic currency aggregation is inherently building the other pillar of currency manipulation – the ability to set the value of all currencies being used at any given time. Check out the three pegs of triangulation that establish currency valuation across the globe: the euro, the dollar and the yen. Virtually all of the currency valuation and exchange rates in the world are pegged to the dollar, the euro and the yen – the three-legged stool of currency exchange.

It is important to understand how this three-legged stool of currency exchange connects the dots within the operations of the G-8. In fact, the importance of this exchange cannot be overemphasized, because currency control has been recognized for years by those in banking as the absolute pillar of power in this world:

> **"Give me control of a nation's money and I care not who makes the laws."**
>
> **Mayer Amschel Bauer Rothschild (1744 – 1812)**
> **Godfather of the Rothschild banking cartel of Europe**

Currency control anchors the agenda of the G-8, which revolves around the *macroeconomic* management of economic and financial issues, including international trade, international financial institutions and relations with developing countries.

But by using currency aggregation to align regional economies, the international economic agenda of the G-8 has expanded considerably deeper into *microeconomic* issues, ranging from local employment to electronic commerce. In fact, the footprint of the G-8 now penetrates into the *political* issues surrounding terrorism, financial crime, nuclear safety and security, non-proliferation, human rights, arms control and regional security.

The use of regional currency aggregation enables the economic power behind currency control to bleed directly into the political management of deeper, broader security issues on a global scale. For this reason, the *globalism* that is rapidly expanding around us is, in a very real sense, being driven by currency aggregation that uses economic and security decisions – all made behind the scenes – to frame national policies that treat the whole world as a proper sphere for *political* influence.

This is very interesting when you note (from the following chart) that the representatives of the nations involved here do not necessarily represent the interests of their individual countries per se, as revealed through the fact that central bank governors are an influential part of this group.

The Group of Eight . . . . . Connect the Dots

- Members account for about *two-thirds of the world's total economic output.*

- G-8 discusses *global economic, political* and *environmental issues.* Russia does not participate in financial or economic issues.

- Leaders are heads of state or government, central bank governors, and finance ministers.

- Original focus was economic and financial issues — *macroeconomic* management, international trade, international financial institutions and relations with developing countries.

- Economic agenda has expanded considerably into *microeconomic* issues ranging from employment to electronic commerce.

- Focus now on *terrorism, financial crime,* nuclear safety and *security,* non-proliferation, human rights, arms control and *regional security.*

While government heads of state and finance ministers typically represent their respective national *interests* (which are typically driven by constituent desires and needs), central bank governors effectively represent national *economies . . .* not individual nations.

From all of this we suddenly begin to understand that a small group of individuals is making decisions that affect the economic conditions and security of billions of people worldwide. In other words, global economic policies and global security decisions are being made by a consolidated group of individuals, many of whom are not elected officials.

While the names that occupy the roles within this group may occasionally change, the functions of the roles themselves – particularly of the central bankers – do not.

The primary functions of the central bankers are to monitor government debt, set interest rates, monitor and manage deposit requirements, and

19

monitor and manage foreign exchange markets. To accomplish this role, central bankers work closely with commercial banks, pension funds, hedge funds, and private equity.

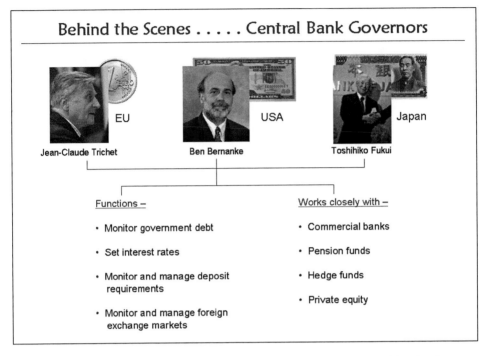

Behind the Scenes . . . . . Central Bank Governors

EU — Jean-Claude Trichet

USA — Ben Bernanke

Japan — Toshihiko Fukui

Functions –
- Monitor government debt
- Set interest rates
- Monitor and manage deposit requirements
- Monitor and manage foreign exchange markets

Works closely with –
- Commercial banks
- Pension funds
- Hedge funds
- Private equity

Viewed as isolated banking systems, each of these financial institutions *just happens* to take the same shape, *coincidentally* with the same structure, but over entirely different cultures, i.e. Japanese, European, or American. But when the dots are connected to view this same banking system from a global perspective, the functions of these central bank governors obviously play a critical role within a larger consolidation of global policy and decision-making, because these central bankers do not have formal accountability to any of the government heads of state or finance ministers of the G-8.

Instead, oversight of their roles in the G-8 (and elsewhere) actually resides in a powerful private financial organization called the Bank for International Settlements (BIS), a self-described "central bank for central bankers" that controls the vast global banking system with the precision of a Swiss watch.[14]

Patrick Wood, the editor of *The August Review*, explains that few people know anything about the BIS because it is surrounded in secrecy. "Even though the BIS is the oldest international banking operation in the world, it is a low profile organization, shunning all publicity and notoriety. As a result, there is very little critical analysis written about this important financial organization. Further, much of what has been written about it is tainted by its own self-effacing literature." [15]

Wood compares the BIS "to a stealth bomber. It flies high and fast, is undetected, has a small crew and carries a huge payload. By contrast, however, the bomber answers to a chain of command and must be refueled by outside sources. The BIS is not accountable to any public authority and operates with complete autonomy and self-sufficiency." [16]

The stated objectives of the BIS are to promote the cooperation of central banks, provide additional facilities for international operations, and act as trustees or agents in regard to international financial settlements entrusted to it under agreements with the parties concerned. [17]

Wood notes that "virtually every in-print reference to the BIS, including its own documents, consistently refer to it as "the central banker's central bank." Acting as a central bank, the BIS has sweeping powers to do anything for its own account or for the account of its member central banks. It is like a two-way power-of-attorney – any party can act as agent for any other party."

He explains that "the BIS was established in 1930 by an international charter and headquartered in Basle, Switzerland. According to James C. Baker, pro-BIS author of *The Bank for International Settlements: Evolution and Evaluation*, "The BIS was formed with funding by the central banks of six nations, Belgium, France, Germany, Italy, Japan, and the United Kingdom. In addition, three private international banks from the U.S. (J.P. Morgan & Company, First National Bank of New York and First National Bank of Chicago) also assisted in financing the establishment of the BIS."" [18]

So there is no coincidence that most of the original BIS charter member central banks are now influential members of the G-8. Behind the scenes, these influences enable the BIS to work through the International Monetary Fund (IMF) and the World Bank, the two primary financial organizations of the United Nations (UN). "Essentially removed from public view, the detailed interoperation between these three entities is understandably confusing to most people, so a little clarification will help," says Wood. [19]

"The IMF interacts with governments, whereas the BIS interacts only with other central banks," states Wood. "The IMF loans money to national governments, and often these countries are in some kind of fiscal or monetary crisis. Furthermore, the IMF raises money by receiving "quota"

21

contributions from its 184 member countries. Even though the member countries may borrow money to make their quota contributions, it is, in reality, all tax-payer money."[20]

He continues, "The World Bank also lends money and has 184 member countries. Within the World Bank are two separate entities, the International Bank for Reconstruction and Development (IBRD) and the International Development Association (IDA). The IBRD focuses on middle income and credit-worthy poor countries, while the IDA focuses on the poorest of nations. In funding itself, the World Bank borrows money by direct lending from banks and by floating bond issues, and then loans this money through IBRD and IDA to troubled countries."[21]

The BIS, as central bank to the other central banks, facilitates the movement of all of this money. "It is well-known for issuing "bridge loans" to central banks in countries where IMF or World Bank money is pledged, but has not yet been delivered," says Wood. "These bridge loans are then repaid by the respective governments when they receive the funds that have been promised by the IMF or World Bank."[22]

Notice the parallel lending roles of the World Bank, which loans money to governments for economic development projects, and the IMF, which loans money to governments in financial crisis. There's the catch: the IMF is the BIS' "ace in the hole" when monetary crisis hits.

For example, the 1998 Brazilian currency crisis was caused by that country's inability to pay inordinate accumulated interest on loans made over a protracted period of time. These loans were extended by banks like Citigroup, J.P. Morgan Chase and FleetBoston, which all stood to lose a huge amount of money. But the IMF, along with the World Bank and the U.S., bailed out Brazil with a $41.5 billion package that saved Brazil, its currency, and, not incidentally, those certain private banks.

Congressman Bernard Sanders (I-VT), the ranking member of the International Monetary Policy and Trade Subcommittee, blew the whistle on this money laundry operation, exposing the $30 million IMF bailout of Brazil to be a windfall to banks, but a disaster for the U.S. Sanders, who strongly opposed the bailout and considered it corporate welfare, wanted Congress to find out why U.S. taxpayers were being asked to provide billions of dollars to Brazil – and how much of that money would be funneled into U.S. banks such as Citigroup, FleetBoston and J.P. Morgan Chase. These banks had about $25.6 billion in outstanding loans to Brazilian borrowers. U.S. taxpayers funded the IMF through a $37 billion line of credit.[23]

Sanders said, "At a time when the U.S. has a $6 trillion national debt, a growing federal deficit, and an increasing number of unmet social needs for our veterans, seniors, and children, it is unacceptable that billions of U.S. taxpayer dollars are being sent to the IMF to bail out Brazil. This money is not going to significantly help the poor people of that country. The real winners in this situation are the large, profitable U.S. banks, such as Citigroup, that have made billions of dollars in risky investments in Brazil and now want to make sure their investments are repaid. This bailout represents an egregious form of corporate welfare that must be put to an end. Interestingly," the Congressman added, "these banks have made substantial campaign contributions to both political parties." [24]

Sanders noted that the neo-liberal policies of the IMF developed in the 1980s – that pushed politically and economically immature countries toward the noble causes of unfettered free trade, privatization, and slashing social safety nets – had been a disaster for Latin America and had contributed to increased global poverty throughout the world. At the same time that Latin American countries such as Brazil and Argentina followed these neo-liberal dictates imposed by the IMF, from 1980-2000 per capita income in Latin America grew at only one-tenth the rate of the previous two decades.[25]

Sanders continued, "The policies of the IMF over the past 20 years . . . have only helped corporations in their constant search for the cheapest labor and weakest environmental regulations. Congress must work on a new global policy that protects workers, increases living standards and improves the environment." [26]

From this example, Wood surmises "that a financial circle exists where the World Bank helps nations get into debt, then when these countries can't pay their massive loans, the IMF bails them out with taxpayer money – and in the middle stands the BIS, collecting fees as the money travels back and forth like the ocean tide, while assuring everyone that all is well." [27]

Because two of these three financial entities are the economic arms of the United Nations, this small but powerful circle ultimately oversees execution of the regional policies that affect the economic conditions and security of billions of people by working closely (behind the scenes, of course) with the office of the Secretary General of the United Nations.

Now come back to the logic being applied here as we explore each of these global areas of activity. We're assembling the pieces of a jigsaw puzzle that combine together to put a face on this beast rising out of the sea, this dangerous *system*, a rising system of global control.

This beast is a *global system of control* that is rising out of the sin of the world. It is being guided and directed by its seven heads, the authorities who blindly crave ultimate power. They understand that to achieve all power they must control all the wealth there is in the world. To control all the wealth in the world, they must control all of the currencies in the world. This rising global system is being constructed to completely manipulate currency – to track any currency being used, and to dictate the value of that currency being used at any given time.

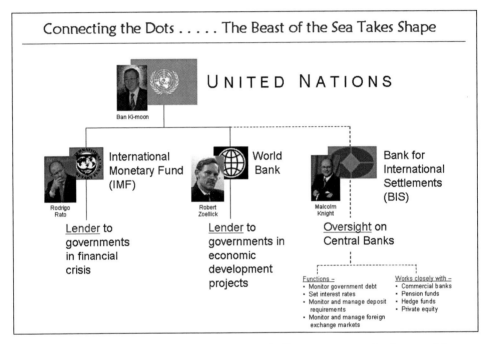

As these authorities rise into control of all the currency in the world, they are at the same time ultimately establishing regulatory and transactional control over all the commerce in the world. How?

Remember that the member nations of the G-8 constitute over two-thirds of the world's total economic output. Each of these nations is a pillar of economic influence within its own local region of trade. Over time, these influences have allowed the central bankers and politicians in the G-8 to work towards the formal alignment and coordination of economic interdependence – along with the consolidation of political power – through regional trade alliances.

Just as it is with the global banking system, when viewed as isolated regions of commerce, each of these trade alliances *just happens* to take the same shape, *coincidentally* with the same interdependent structure, but over entirely different economies across the globe.

For example, the North American Free Trade Agreement (NAFTA) is a regional trade alliance among Canada, the U.S., and Mexico that eliminates trade barriers and facilitates the cross-border movement of goods and services between the 430.5 million people in these countries to create a combined gross domestic product (GDP) of $12.9 trillion.[28]

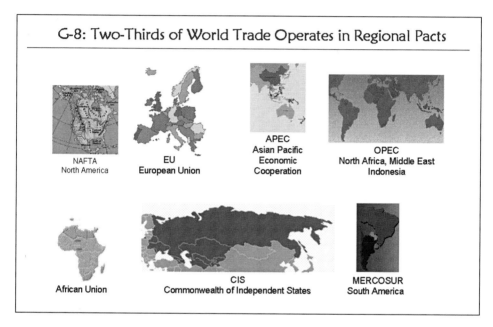

G-8: Two-Thirds of World Trade Operates in Regional Pacts

NAFTA
North America

EU
European Union

APEC
Asian Pacific
Economic
Cooperation

OPEC
North Africa, Middle East
Indonesia

African Union

CIS
Commonwealth of Independent States

MERCOSUR
South America

In the exact same manner, the European Union (EU) is a common market consisting of 25 countries, 460.1 million people, and a GDP of $11.7 trillion. The Asia-Pacific Economic Cooperation (APEC) is a regional trade alliance of 21 Pacific Rim countries with economic ties to another 10-nation regional alliance, the Association of Southeast Asian Nations (ASEAN), consisting of 553.9 million people with a combined GDP of almost $2.1 trillion. The African Union (AU), modeled after the EU, is a regional trade alliance of 53 nations, 853.5 million people, and a GDP of $2.05 trillion. The Mercosur alliance is a South American common market composed of Brazil, Argentina, Paraguay, and Uruguay that has a combined GDP of $1.9 trillion.[29]

Two other major international alliances have assembled in the midst of politically volatile environments that have limited their regional development in economics, security and foreign policy. One is the Commonwealth of Independent States (CIS), an alliance of 11 former

Soviet Republics that has been marred by revolutions and civil wars. Russia (the former Soviet Union), a member of the G-8, plays a vital role in the alignment, coordination, and promotion of this alliance.

The other is the Organization of the Petroleum Exporting Countries (OPEC), the well-known industrial alliance of eleven nations that accounts for about 40 percent of world oil production ands hold about two-thirds of the world's proven oil reserves.[30]

Viewed as isolated trade alliances, each of these regional channels of international commerce just happens to foster economic interdependence, between member states and even between the alliances themselves. Each coincidentally operates under the same financial template and basic regulatory principles, but over totally different and culturally diverse economies of the world.

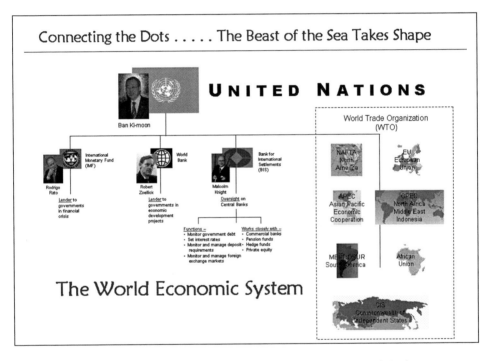

Connecting the Dots . . . . . The Beast of the Sea Takes Shape

But now consider these same regional alliances from a global perspective, specifically within the context of the seven heads of the beast rising from the sea in verse one. Remember again that the *heads* John describes in verse one denote *authority, direction, guidance*. They represent seven authorities (individuals or groups of individuals), seven *directions* (*regions* or *areas*), seven paths of guidance (cultural diversity), all working together under an evil system of rebellion against God, an unholy union that desires to replace the worship of God with an irreverent lust for power.

The seven heads here symbolize these seven commercial trade alliances, each being used by central banking authorities and G-8 politicians to direct the aggregation of all the world's currencies and guide economic and political interdependence through a larger commerce system: the World Trade Organization (WTO).

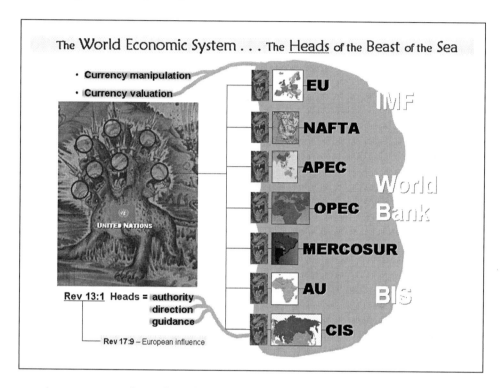

As an economic and social regulatory arm of the United Nations, the WTO is a powerful international, multilateral organization that sets the rules for the global trading system and resolves disputes between its member states, all of whom are signatories to its approximately 30 agreements. Headquartered in Geneva, Switzerland, the WTO consists of 150 members, most of whom are already members of one of the respective regional trade alliances.

All of the regulatory principles for world trade that are established by the WTO fall within the currency guidelines and commerce framework set forth by the central banks in the BIS, IMF, and World Bank.

As the pieces of this jigsaw puzzle start to come together, we begin to see that the beast rising out of the sea is taking the shape and form of the world economic system.

None of this is coming together by chance. Given the global scale of activity, the creation of this system is simply too complex, too large to be happening through coincidence. So who are the authorities that direct the assembly of these complex economic and political alliances? Who is actually guiding the development of the interdependent networks?

Let's inspect some of the organizations that are assembling this system behind the scenes.

CHAPTER 3

The Beast in Global Politics

The authorities driving the creation of this interdependent global system operate in a space largely hidden from the public eye, within the confines of international think tanks that are geared towards a one-world system of government.

These globalists, working in accordance with the United Nations Charter, reside in influential behind-the-scenes organizations – the Council on Foreign Relations (CFR), the Trilateral Commission (TC), the Bilderbergers, and the Club of Rome (COR) – that exert deep and broad counsel on a wide array of global policies. This hierarchy of private organizations wants to achieve world government in stages, starting with the creation of world administrative regions – a process that first began by conceptualizing and forming the regional trade alliances discussed earlier.

In his book *En Route to Global Occupation*, Gary Kah reminds us that the CFR Handbook of 1936 provides the details concerning the establishment of the Council on Foreign Relations: "On May 30, 1919, several leading members of the delegations to the Paris Peace Conference met at the Hotel Majestic in Paris to discuss setting up an international group which would advise their respective governments on international affairs . . . at a meeting on June 5, 1919, the planners decided it would be best to have separate organizations cooperating with each other. Consequently, they organized the Council on Foreign Relations, with headquarters in New York . . ." [31]

Most interesting, however, is the fact that the money for founding the CFR came from the same individuals who were involved in forming the central banking operations of the Federal Reserve banking system.[32]

This organization, credited with more or less creating the United Nations in 1945, is funded by numerous globalist institutions, including the Rockefeller and Ford Foundations. Over 3,000 current members of the CFR occupy key positions in government, mass media, financial institutions, multinational corporations, the military, and national security, where they develop and implement strategies for international integration and interdependence in the areas of finance, business, labor, military, education and mass communications media.[33]

Behind the Scenes . . . . . The Politics of Globalism

Council on Foreign Relations (CFR) – 1921

Alan Greenspan

- Created by the founders of the Federal Reserve central banking system

Dick Cheney

- 3000+ members – only from the US – occupy key positions in government, mass media, financial institutions, multinational corporations, the military, and the national security apparatus

David Rockefeller

- Develops – and implements – strategies for international integration and interdependence in areas of finance, business, labor, military, education and mass communications media

- Credited with creating the United Nations (UN) in 1945

Henry Kissinger

- Funded by Rockefeller and Ford Foundations, numerous globalist institutions

- Presidents come and go, but the CFR's power – and agenda – always remains
  ———————————— Rev 17:9 – European influence

Bill Clinton

The CFR has driven the formation of the NAFTA regional trade alliance among Canada, the U.S., and Mexico. Presidents come and go, but the influential power of the CFR – and its agenda of one-world government – always remains in place. Given that its high-profile membership includes most of our nation's top leaders in government, business, education, labor, the military, the media, and banking, how has the CFR stayed out of the public eye for so long? By formally ensuring that the important meetings of its membership remain secret.[34]

Another private organization, the Trilateral Commission, was founded by David Rockefeller (a prominent leader of the CFR) in 1973 to promote world government by encouraging economic interdependence among the superpower nations, all of which are members of the G-8 and their own respective regional trade alliance. This secretive group, headquartered in Washington, DC, is also funded by the Rockefeller and Ford Foundations and the other globalist institutions that fund the CFR.[35]

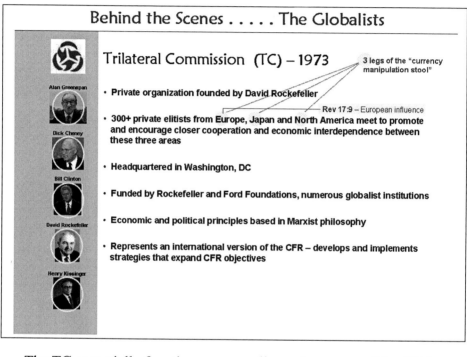

The TC essentially functions as a smaller carbon copy of the CFR, with over 300 private elitists from Europe, Japan and North America meeting periodically to promote and encourage closer cooperation and economic interdependence between these three regions through economic and political principles based in Marxist philosophy. Since many of the highest-profile members of the CFR are also members of the TC, the TC serves as the shadow international version of the CFR because it develops and implements the tactical planning that is used to expand the CFR's broader strategic objectives.[36]

An even smaller sister organization of the CFR, the Bilderberger Group (or Bilderbergers), is largely responsible for the global economic integration and regionalization of Europe into the common market of the European Union.

Funded by the Rockefeller and Ford Foundations and other globalist institutions that fund the CFR and TC, this private organization consists of over 100 elitists from the member nations of the North Atlantic Treaty Organization (NATO). The leadership between the CFR and the Bilderbergers is interlocked, and virtually every one of the American Bilderbergers is a current or former member of the CFR.[37]

Another small, secret sister organization that has drawn a high percentage of its members from the CFR, TC, and Bilderbergers is the Club of Rome (COR), an informal private group of scientists, economists, humanists, industrialists that has been charged with the regionalization and unification of the entire world.[38]

Behind the Scenes . . . . . The Globalists

Alan Greenspan

Henry Kissinger

Bill Clinton

The Bilderbergers – 1954

Rev 17:9 – European influence

- Private organization of 100+ elitists from member nations of the North Atlantic Treaty Organization (NATO)

- Sister organization of the CFR – leadership between the two is interlocked

- Funded by Rockefeller and Ford Foundations, numerous globalist institutions

- Expressed mission is the integration and regionalization of Europe

Etienne Davignon

James Wolfensohn

Club of Rome – 1968

Rev 17:9 – European influence

- Private organization of less than 100 international elitists – 25+% of members belong to the CFR, TC, Bilderbergers

- Strong European + Middle Eastern representation for closer international economic integration and interdependence

- Divided the world into ten political/economic regions

The COR's findings and recommendations are published in special, highly confidential reports that are sent to the power-elite of the other three organizations for implementation. On September 17, 1973, the COR released a report called *Regionalized and Adaptive Model of the Global World System*. In this document, the COR uses a computer model that divides and restructures the world into ten political/economic regions, which it literally refers to as "kingdoms" (a direct fulfillment of Revelation 13).[39]

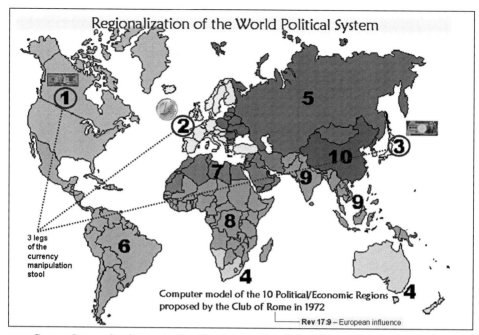

Source: *Regionalized and Adaptive Model of the Global World System, Club of Rome, 1973*

Notice that three anchors are used to maintain economy continuity and stability during this division into regions: the dollar (Region 1), the euro (Region 2), and the yen (Region 3), the three strongest currencies we have today.

Viewed as an isolated document, each of these proposed "kingdoms" *just happens* to take the same shape, *coincidentally* with the same structure, as the regional trade alliances that have been formed since this report was published over 30 years ago. But when the dots are connected to view the "kingdoms" in this report from a global perspective, you can see that this is the *exact* system that the globalists are following in establishing the one world economic/political system.[40]

In Revelation 17, John confirms the truth behind this globalist plan:

> **"And the ten horns which thou sawest are ten kings, which have received no kingdom as yet; but receive power as kings one hour with the beast. These have one mind, and shall give their power and strength unto the beast." – Revelation 17:12-13**

John relates "power" here to "kingdoms" ruled by "kings." A king exercises absolute authority – economic, political, and legal – over his kingdom and his servants. By relating the power structure of this system to

33

absolute authority, John reveals deeper insights into the absolute power of the *ten horns* on the heads of the beast and the *ten crowns* upon those horns that he first describes in Revelation 13:1. To better understand this, let's briefly recap what we've learned.

The seven heads of this beast symbolize seven regional trade alliances. They are being used by the globalists (the brains inside the heads) to aggregate the world's currencies, foster economic and political interdependence, and establish regulatory control over world commerce. By manipulating the controls established through these interdependent regional alliances, the globalists aim to expand their political and legal control into a one-world system that is divided into ten regions – the *ten horns* on the heads of the beast.

The fact that *ten* political regions are planned is significant, because in the Scriptures the number ten symbolizes a *testimony of law and responsibility*. *Ten* testifies here to the fact that economic interdependence ultimately translates into legal responsibility. In other words, those who rule all the commerce will eventually dictate all the rules of law. This is the final evolution of the economic system that European banking magnate Mayer Amschel Bauer Rothschild discovered at the turn of the 19th century: "Give me control of a nation's money, and I care not who makes the laws."

The Scriptures are telling us that the absolute power, influence and control being structured within this system cannot be understated.

In the ancient Greek, the *horns* here in verse one mean to *push out* or *project out* of the heads. By controlling the value of currency, and establishing the legal regulations that manipulate the use of that currency, the globalists use the seven regional alliances to consolidate the comprehensive economic and legal authority necessary to create an arsenal of "silent weapons" that can be used to *push* (establish or exercise, whether desired or not) their political authority over their member states.

By silently (behind the scenes) controlling the supply of printed currencies, and manipulating the value of those currencies, the globalists can literally fire (impose) the interdependent weapons of inflation, deflation, interest rates, debt, and exchange rates at one or more targeted economies to limit their respective production and labor capacities. The severity of the limitations imposed can be used to shock their standard of living and, if extended, alter their cultural lifestyle.[41]

These weapons are already being used today. As a simple and obvious example, consider how the manipulation of oil prices by the OPEC alliance

34

can quickly trickle down to shock an entire economy, impact a stock exchange, alter exchange rates, trigger inflation and limit the standard of living. Gasoline prices literally dictate how automobiles are designed, manufactured and priced. Vehicle prices alter personal transportation lifestyles. When enough personal lifestyles are altered to reach critical mass, a cultural shift occurs. The weapon hits its mark.

Ultimately, the degree and speed at which a cultural lifestyle is altered can be used to modify the belief system of that society . . . and that's the end game. The ability to modify a person's beliefs is the ability to control that person. Silent weapons are highly effective economic sanctions that can be used to control entire populations.

Silent weapons convert a regional trade alliance into a "kingdom," where the "kings" (central bankers, G-8 politicians) exercise absolute authority over their servants.

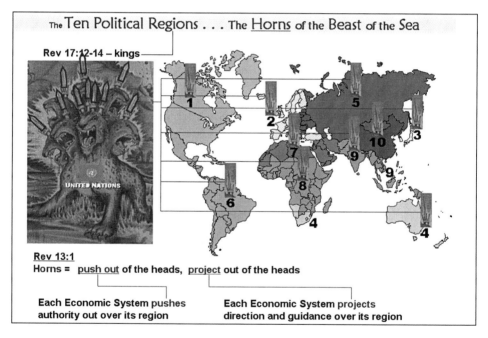

The Ten Political Regions . . . The Horns of the Beast of the Sea

Rev 17:12-14 – kings

Rev 13:1
Horns = push out of the heads, project out of the heads

Each Economic System pushes authority out over its region

Each Economic System projects direction and guidance over its region

These alliances are being silently converted through the regulatory controls of the WTO, the ruling political body (globalists) of economic interdependence that is financially manipulated by the IMF, World Bank and BIS (globalists). As it grows in power through the economic and political strength of the seven primary regions, the WTO can use those same silent weapons on a global scale to *project* (expand and enforce, whether desired or not) its political authority into the remaining regions of the world that have less political and economic acumen.

By duplicating the economic and political footprint of the seven primary regional alliances, the globalists running the WTO will silently convert the remaining planned political regions into "kingdoms" as well, placing ten "kings" (central bankers and politicians acting as regional authorities) in absolute authority over the regions and effectively converting the populations in those regions into servants.

The WTO will exercise absolute political authority over all ten regions, as symbolized by the *ten crowns* upon the horns of the heads of the beast. The number *ten* again symbolizes a *testimony of law and responsibility*. In the ancient Greek, *crowns* here have two meanings: *bound about the head* or the *channel of an act*.

Ten testifies here to the fact that each region will be legally *bound* (comply with) under the economic and political responsibility of its respective regional authority. This means all petitions and requests (all sorts of begging) must be *channeled* (processed or handled) through the legal system, which falls under the responsibility of the regional authority.

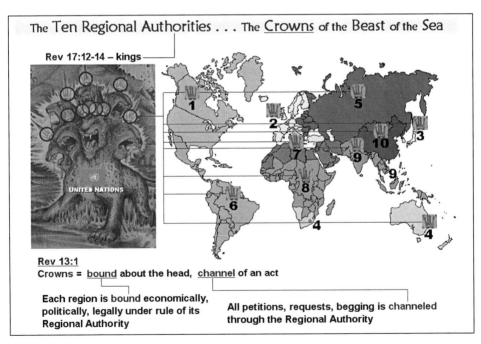

The Ten Regional Authorities . . . The <u>Crowns</u> of the Beast of the Sea

Rev 17:12-14 – kings

UNITED NATIONS

Rev 13:1
Crowns = <u>bound</u> about the head, <u>channel</u> of an act

Each region is bound economically, politically, legally under rule of its Regional Authority

All petitions, requests, begging is channeled through the Regional Authority

Since all of the regional economic and political footprints are duplicates of one another, all of these regional authorities, in turn, will be *bound* under the global economic and political responsibility of the WTO. This means all petitions and requests will be *channeled* through the global legal system, which falls under the responsibility of the WTO.

At this point it becomes obvious that all of these activities can no longer be viewed as isolated events, alliances, organizations, and systems. Assembled together, all of these pieces of the puzzle show that the beast of the sea is taking shape through the deliberate, diverse strategies of globalist organizations working behind the scenes. All of these strategies aim to hit the final target: the ultimate consolidation of power through the control structure of the United Nations – the "body" of the beast (the final "kingdom") that is described in Revelation 13:2.

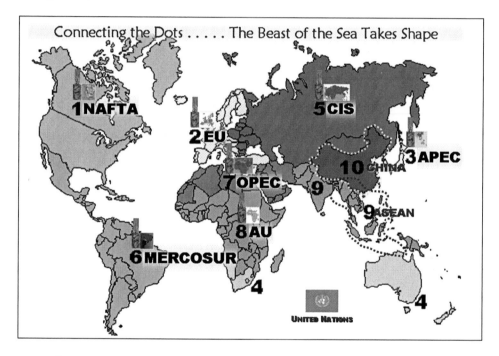

All of us who instinctively feel a conspiracy is going on behind the scenes are absolutely correct. The Holy Spirit reveals to us in verse two that this *is* a conspiracy, but not the kind we typically think about. Verse two explains that these behind-the-scenes activities are actually another stage of a much longer process, the continuation of an *ancient* conspiracy being carried out by a consuming force of evil that aspires to control the world. The beast of the sea is the final stage of Satan's conspiracy to rule all of mankind and this world.

Before going further, an important point must be emphasized here. God is the eternal Creator, which means *only God can create*. Satan is simply a creature that was created, meaning he cannot create. Satan can only copy or duplicate. Since our Lord uses different people in different places throughout time to spread the Gospel of His Kingdom, then Satan copies this blueprint to spread his counterfeit kingdom as well. Each stage of Satan's conspiracy basically repeats the previous stage's cycle of operation from an earlier time, using different people in different places to duplicate and expand upon it.

The Scriptures treat this conspiracy as a loathsome beast that grows and matures during each stage, under God's permission, just as a child grows and matures in stages. Just as children learn through *thinking* (Stage 1), learn to *rise* (2), *stand* on their feet (3), *walk* (4), and *speak* (5), this beast develops and matures in power through the same stages.

By describing these stages of growth, the Holy Spirit grants believers the ability to *see* (understand, perceive, recognize) this satanic empire *rising* around us by relating the progress of how this beast *thinks, stands, walks,* and *speaks* through previous world empires described in the Scriptures.

> **"And the beast which I saw was like unto a leopard, and his feet were as the feet of a bear, and his mouth as the mouth of a lion: and the dragon gave him his power, and his seat, and great authority." – Revelation 13:2**

John's vision of this beast began from the top down in verse one, starting with the crowns on the horns of its heads, to explain to us how the beast *thinks* (Stage 1): its motives, its character, its mission. Now John scans its body from the bottom up in verse two, describing how this beast has progressed by what it can do: the *risen beast* (2) *stands* like a *leopard* (3); further up, its feet *walk* like a *bear* (4); moving up higher, its mouth *speaks* like a *lion* (5). In other words, this beast has fully matured in all stages of strength and power.

Notice how John's vision here lines up (in the *exact* reverse order) with Daniel's Old Testament vision of the four great beasts which also come from the sea:

> **"And four great beasts came up from the sea, diverse one from another. The first was like a *lion* . . . and a man's heart was given to it. And behold another beast, a second, like to a *bear* . . . and they said thus unto it, Arise, devour much flesh. After this I beheld, and lo another, like a *leopard* . . . and dominion was given to it. And behold a fourth *beast*, dreadful and terrible, and strong exceedingly . . . and it had ten horns." – Daniel 7:3-8**

38

In these two visions, the Holy Spirit reveals how this satanic conspiracy has matured through each stage (empire) of its growth into the horrible beast that John sees. In 535 BC, Daniel sees the conspiracy from its infancy forward, beginning in its first empire (the *thinking* stage) and growing in stages of power through other empires in the future. Six centuries later, in 95 AD, John sees the fully mature conspiracy (the *risen* stage) openly exposed, flaunting the power it has accumulated through those same empires of the past.

The fourth beast (or fourth stage) having ten horns that Daniel saw has now matured into the beast that John sees as the one *rising* (the fifth and final stage) around us today. Both visions describe a system that is increasing in size and intensity, slowly assuming authority over everything else. The danger and destruction that John sees in the intellectual, economic and political power of the ten horns today is the dreadful terror that Daniel first saw growing out of the exceeding strength of those same ten horns from an earlier time.

In fact, the beast rising around us today is the matured composite of all four beasts in Daniel 7:3-8. Their characteristics – which symbolize the combined strength and brutality of historical Babylon, Medo-Persia, Greece, and Rome – are seen by Daniel in another vision, one where he sees a great image (or statue):

> "Thou, O king, sawest, and behold a great image . . . and the form there of was terrible. This image's head was of fine gold, his breast and his arms of silver, his belly and his thighs of brass, his legs of iron, his feet part of iron and part of clay . . . and wheresoever the children of men dwell, the beasts of the field and the fowls of the heaven hath he given into thine hand, and hath made thee ruler over them all. Thou art this head of gold.
>
> And after thee shall arise another kingdom . . . and another third kingdom of brass, which shall bear rule over all the earth. And the fourth kingdom shall be strong as iron . . . and whereas thou sawest the feet and toes, part of potters' clay, and part of iron, the kingdom shall be divided; but there shall be in it of the strength of iron . . ." – Daniel 2:31-41

In this vision, Daniel sees the satanic conspiracy in the form of a great statue, a man-made idol of worship. He begins describing it from the top down, with a head of gold symbolizing the ultimate authority of the Babylonian empire (612-539 BC) under King Nebuchadnezzar, a type of the future Antichrist. Like a lion, this "king of the jungle" appealed to the masses by articulating his thoughts, opinions and feelings, with actions that spoke louder than words. This points directly to the rising beast that John sees *speaking* with the same unquestioned authority of a lion, roaring the blasphemies of the antichrist spirit.

Moving down the great image, the breast and arms that Daniel sees symbolize the second kingdom, the Medo-Persian empire (539-331 BC) that advanced on others with ferocious military might. This points to the rising beast that John sees *walking* (advancing) like a *bear*, a term in the ancient Greek that means *ferocity*. The global system will ferociously advance its political course of action, its economic way of life, its *impure walk* upon everyone, trampling all that is good.

Further down the statue, the belly and thighs that Daniel sees represent the Greek empire (331-323 BC) under Alexander the Great, symbolized by the leopard for its ability to rapidly overpower, conquer and instill a new cultural heritage. This points to the risen beast that John sees *standing* (firmly occupying) in complete power, with a cultural heritage based upon government control that promises security to all – but control for the few.

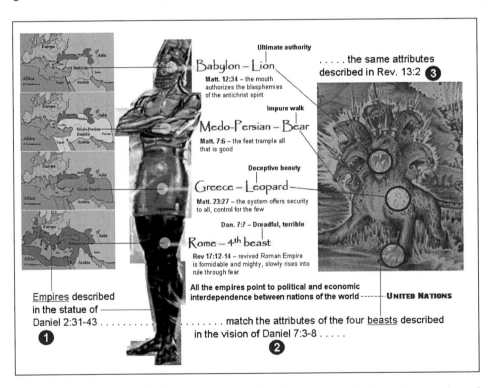

Ultimate authority

Babylon – Lion

Matt. 12:34 – the mouth authorizes the blasphemies of the antichrist spirit

. . . . . the same attributes described in Rev. 13:2 ❸

Impure walk

Medo-Persian – Bear

Matt. 7:6 – the feet trample all that is good

Deceptive beauty

Greece – Leopard

Matt. 23:27 – the system offers security to all, control for the few

Dan. 7:7 – Dreadful, terrible

Rome – 4ᵗʰ beast

Rev 17:12-14 – revived Roman Empire is formidable and mighty, slowly rises into rule through fear

All the empires point to political and economic interdependence between nations of the world ------ UNITED NATIONS

Empires described in the statue of Daniel 2:31-43 . . . . match the attributes of the four beasts described in the vision of Daniel 7:3-8 . . . . .

❶   ❷

At the bottom of the image, the legs Daniel sees symbolize the empire of ancient Rome, with its military agility, catlike vigilance and craft, and fierce cruelty. The feet and toes he sees represent the final stage, the last great empire: the restored and revived Roman Empire, formidable and mighty, slowly *rising* into rule through fear.

The empires of Babylon, Medo-Persia, Greece, and Rome were all world empires of political, economic and legal power. All of their characteristics point to the final stage of the satanic conspiracy that culminates in the global empire that John sees: a feared system that exalts humanity as a god; that imitates and mocks the power of Christ through determined opposition to God; that is brutal to anyone who refuses to serve it.

By recognizing that this evil beast, rising out of the sea (the culmination of sinful mankind), represents a sinister global system being installed – under God's permission – around us through the economic (heads), political (horns) and legal (crowns) arenas of the United Nations, we can better understand the series of events that occurs next in John's vision.

Each event that John describes is of epic proportions. Each one builds upon the previous event, creating enormous economic, political, cultural and religious trauma on a global scale. In fact, the impact of the first event that happens is of such magnitude that it literally changes the world as we know it.

CHAPTER 4

The Event That Changes the World

The first catastrophic event involving the beast rising out of the sea (the United Nations) occurs in verse three. John sees that one of the heads is wounded to death, but the wound miraculously heals and the entire world is amazed by this:

> "And I saw one of his heads as it were wounded to death; and his deadly wound was healed: and all the world wondered after the beast." – Revelation 13:3

In other words, the *condition* of the head fails, but its condition is miraculously revived back into energy and life. This single event is of such epic magnitude that it causes the *entire* world to adore the global system. Think about that. A single event causes every person in the world to either admire the United Nations as a body, or admire an individual within the UN as a person. What kind of monumental event could possibly trigger this sort of admiration?

To understand exactly what happens here, we must first ask the question: how is this head wounded?

John answers this later on, explaining that the head is wounded by a sword:

> ". . . that they should make an image to the beast, which had the wound by a sword, and did live." – Revelation 13:14

By merging John's description about the wound here into what we have already learned about the beast, it is possible to evaluate this event as an equation that has potentially different outcomes.

On one side of this equation, we know that the head here represents a regional trade alliance, a regional commerce system that is ultimately run by central banking authorities within the WTO of the UN. No doubt there will be an individual person, probably a politician, appointed as the formal leader of this alliance – perhaps a prime minister or a finance minister within a G-8 member country.

On the other side of the equation, the term *sword* here in the ancient Greek translates into dual meanings. *Sword* means *a knife*, but it also means *judicial punishment*, *controversy* and *strife*. These two meanings immediately identify two outcomes for consideration.

One scenario points to a regional commerce alliance (a head) that is crippled economically or politically, probably both, through judicial punishment of some sort. In other words, some type of legal enforcement is used to force an entire regional commerce alliance to collapse, thereby causing a global ripple of massive problems that economically and politically cripple many nations at the same time, impacting mass populations of people at once. Bottom line: economic and political chaos.

Could something like this first scenario actually happen today? Absolutely.

The bloodline of the global economy pumps through the digital veins of the Internet, a vulnerable worldwide network that is continually threatened by catastrophic shutdowns from electronic "bugs" created by anonymous software hackers in hidden places. As if these external attacks aren't scary enough, unknown internal code limitations can creep up to pose a software threat as well. Remember the global panic that the Y2K problem caused a few years ago?

The second scenario points to an individual leader of a regional commerce alliance being physically and mortally maimed, perhaps through some sort of assassination attempt. This would immediately create a huge leadership vacuum for that alliance, potentially triggering political revolts that could quickly evolve into economic and cultural anarchy on a wide scale, impacting mass populations of people at once. Bottom line: economic and political chaos.

Notice that in either outcome, the overall sequence of events remains the same:

- The beast has seven heads.
- One of these heads is violently maimed and disabled somehow, leaving a crippled system that must function with only six heads.
- The disability creates economic and political chaos on a global scale.
- Then, miraculously, the healing of this wound restores the system back to its original number of heads, and the system is stronger than it was before.

What we see here is the system advancing forward, similar to a military force that is conquering territory. It takes a direct hit (in the head) and sustains a casualty in fighting (it is *wounded to death*), just as soldiers sustain casualties in the midst of heavy fighting. But it recovers to advance again and resume taking more ground. John is really describing nothing less that warfare on a global scale. The economic, political and cultural turmoil happening in the visible (natural) world is the physical manifestation of spiritual warfare being fought in the invisible (supernatural) realm.

Warfare on any level, natural or supernatural, is orchestrated through the execution of strategy. Since this wound to the head occurs during the midst of spiritual warfare, then the wound is being orchestrated (visibly occurring in the natural world) through the execution of some sort of strategy (invisibly occurring in the supernatural realm). In other words, this wound is no accident. This catastrophic event is strategically arranged to achieve a desired maximum impact.

The beast is, in effect, wounding itself to grow stronger. Remember that the *number* of heads represents the character of the beast – and *seven* in this evil system points to its spiritual imperfection. The names of blasphemy upon each of those heads represent *self-rule* over and against the rule of God. They ultimately point to a satanic power that has leeched deeply into the evil thoughts of men in high places of authority, manifesting itself in anarchy against God.

These mortal authorities operate under the deceptive illusion that *they* are the ones directing the events that unfold. They incorrectly believe that *they* are the ones who develop the circumstances and achieve the results. But John reveals at the end of verse two that they are nothing more than mere pawns. Behind the scenes, Satan (the dragon) is actually the one controlling this complex system:

> "... and the dragon gave him his power, and his seat, and great
> authority." – Revelation 13:2

The Scriptures explain in detail how the enemy is advancing his *visible* political and economic global network through an *invisible* spiritual army that he has assembled:

> "For we wrestle not against flesh and blood, but against
> principalities, against powers, against the rulers of the darkness
> of this world, against spiritual wickedness in high places."
> – Ephesians 6:12

The Bible clearly states that this is not a wrestling match against a human opponent. We are not in a conflict with mere flesh and blood. This is combat against supernatural rulers, invisible authorities, demonic powers who govern this world of darkness (the sea), and spiritual forces that control evil in the supernatural realm. We are fighting the spiritual hosts of evil arrayed against us in heavenly warfare.

In the spirit realm, a demonic army is clashing with a heavenly army. Spiritual armies are assembled the same way that soldiers in the armed forces are organized by ranks, with each order subordinate to the one above it.

The highest ranking demons are the *principalities*, or princes, which are really archangels who fell with Lucifer when he was expelled from heaven in Isaiah 14:12 and Ezekiel 28:17. In spiritual warfare, a prince has the same political power as a lord, executing strategic authority over an entire region of areas to draw mankind into hell. In the Old Testament, the archangel Gabriel explains to the prophet Daniel how one of these satanic princes attempted to hinder Daniel's prayer:

> "Fear not, Daniel: for from the first day that thou didst set thine heart
> to understand, and to chasten thyself before thy God, thy words were
> heard, and I am come for thy words. But *the prince* of the kingdom of
> Persia withstood me one and twenty days: but, lo, Michael, one of the
> chief princes, came to help me ..." – Daniel 10:12-13

The princes delegate their political influence down to the next rank, the *powers*. These demons are the spiritual magistrates that convert the evil strategies handed down by their lords into tactical strategies of darkness aimed at establishing spiritual rule, or dominion, over those areas. These satanic tactics are carried out by the *rulers*, or spiritual generals, that organize and lead the lower legions of rank-and-file demons in executing *wickedness*, the spiritual attacks behind the depravity, malice, plots, sins, and iniquities that captivate, weaken and render mankind defenseless. These attacks of wickedness against humans are continually happening in *high places*, the spiritual realm.

Who Do We Wrestle?   Ephesians 6:12

Principalities – "arche" in Greek – **prince** or **lord** over a region of areas
» Develop evil strategies to draw mankind into hell

Powers – "exousia" in Greek – **rulers** over the areas
Convert evil strategies into tactical strategies

Rulers of Darkness of this World – "kosmokrator" in Greek – **generals**, head of the legions
» Organize and lead demons that carry out the tactics within an area

Wickedness – "poneria" in Greek – legions of demons, rank-and-file **soldiers**
» Carry out depravity, malice, plots, sins, and iniquities to captivate, weaken and render mankind defenseless ("to sift mankind as wheat" Luke 22:31)

High Places – "epouanios" (*high* in Greek) = above the sky, celestial, in heaven" "pantachou" (*places* in Greek) = universally, in all places, everywhere; spiritual realm in the air.

Psalm 139:15 explains that every human being is first created *in secret*, which translates from the ancient Hebrew as a "hidden" place, or spiritual realm. This means that because God first creates us as spirits with souls (and adds our physical bodies later during pregnancy), we are engaged in this spiritual warfare by default, whether we want to be or not. In fact, humans play a central role in spiritual conflict.

In his commentary *What I Believe About Conspiracy Theories*, John W. Ritenbaugh states that "our warfare, then, has all the trappings of a literal war, but it is something that we cannot see, yet it is happening nonetheless." [42]

Satan does not advance this global system with a large human army. Instead, he strategically places a few people in positions where they wield a great deal of authority – and can exercise that authority at just the right time, in just the right place.

Ritenbaugh points to the corruption of the American public education system as an example. He explains that the enemy has not used many people to destroy our public education, but he has used individuals in the right places at the right times, where they could wield a great deal of influence over others. He singles out authorities such as John Dewey, B.F. Skinner, and John Watson, who used their expertise to legally corrupt the very foundation of American education.[43]

"Satan's use of men compares with KGB operations that used spies in the United States," says Ritenbaugh, referring to the secret communist intelligence agency. "The only difference is the purpose. The KGB's purpose was not to draw us into a world government, but to weaken and destroy us as an enemy. The KGB operated a web of people rarely known to each other, occupying positions that influenced decisions and obtained information."

Likewise, Satan's sole objective is to weaken and destroy mankind, using a web of authorities rarely known to each other, who occupy positions that influence decisions and obtain information.

"There were never many KGB spies in the U.S., but these spies were induced through bribes, sex, and psychological manipulation," adds Ritenbaugh. "The spy may have had entirely different motivations for his disloyalty to his country: money, revenge, feelings of power, or misguided loyalties. But each spy had his own interest, and he allowed himself to be manipulated to fulfill them."[44]

Satan also induces his spies through bribes, sex, and psychological manipulation. Some of the authorities he uses are motivated by money, others by power. But each authority has his own selfish interest, and he allows himself to be manipulated by the army of the enemy to fulfill them. This is the selfish drive that Satan works on to snare a person to do his will, to manipulate a mind to the place where that person sees personal advantage in being disloyal to others. The enemy educates that person with things that they feel will enhance their position, then places the person into a role of power or prominence in the event that is coming.[45]

The enemy is not strategically manipulating just one group to advance his system. We have already seen several groups that have the same basic agenda and the same basic interests: the Counsel on Foreign Relations, the Trilateral Commission, the Bildebergers, the Club of Rome, and, of course, the United Nations.

"There are many others," adds Ritenbaugh. "The Catholic Church, the Jesuits, Opus Dei, the Masons, the Illuminati, and international communism are all moving in the same general direction. We must understand that these groups don't necessarily agree with one another perfectly, because Satan is the author of confusion. He's the most subtle and cunning of all the beasts of the field. They don't have to agree with each other perfectly or even cooperate with each other. In fact . . . their specific interests and their methodologies frequently clash.[46]

This explains why there is sometimes aggressive competition, conflict, and deceit among these people. They operate how the enemy operates. Their thinking reflects his mind. These people not only may not cooperate together, they'll even go against one another – as we shall see in a moment with the catastrophic wound. But they all share the ultimate goal of the enemy: to bring the entire world, all of mankind, under the control of a single, sovereign, global government.

This is the strategy of warfare being orchestrated by the enemy. When the conditions are right, the beast will be able to take over without firing a shot. The global system deceives humans into believing they are the ones that make things happen. But behind the scenes, invisible to the human eye, they are deluded slaves serving a satanic army that draws its energies from the spirit of antichrist in fallen man that covets wealth and power.

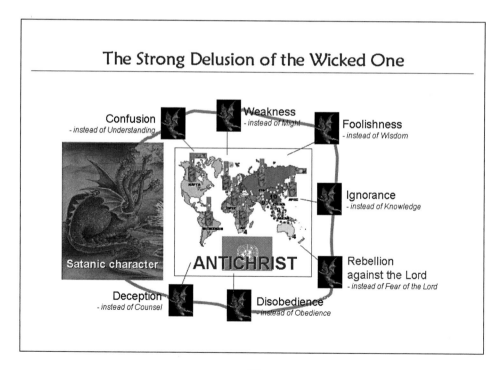

The Strong Delusion of the Wicked One

Confusion
- instead of Understanding

Weakness
- instead of Might

Foolishness
- instead of Wisdom

Ignorance
- instead of Knowledge

Satanic character

ANTICHRIST

Rebellion against the Lord
- instead of Fear of the Lord

Deception
- instead of Counsel

Disobedience
- instead of Obedience

Fallen man's insatiable desire for wealth and power in high places is satanically constructing an enormous political and economic global network that will one day control the entire world.

It's important to understand that the *spiritual* motivation behind the political and economic global network of the United Nations is rooted in a satanic desire for wealth and power. This same satanic desire is an insatiable force that both the Apostle Paul and Jesus Himself strictly warn us against:

> **"For the love of money is the root of all evil: which while some coveted after, they have erred . . ." – 1 Timothy 6:10 (Paul)**

> **"No servant can serve two masters: for either he will hate the one, and love the other; or else he will hold to the one, and despise the other. Ye cannot serve God and mammon." – Luke 16:13 (Jesus)**

Taken together, these Scriptures remind us of how the unbridled coveting of wealth is the spiritual equivalent of worshipping an idol – the exact worship John sees happening here in our text:

> **"And I saw one of his heads as it were wounded to death; and his deadly wound was healed: and all the world wondered after the beast. And they worshipped the dragon which gave power unto the beast: and they worshipped the beast . . . " – Revelation 13:3-4**

The Beast Rising Out of the Sea

In other words, *worship* and *coveting* are one in the same here. To understand this better, Jesus relates coveting to worship in a practical sense:

> **"For where your treasure is, there will your heart be also."**
> **– Matthew 6:21, Luke 12:34**

The *treasure* that our Master refers to is the thing most valued. The *heart* He refers to is the mind. Jesus says that people always invest the most time and energy they have toward the thing they value most. The thing they value most occupies their mind the most. The thing they value most occupies their lives the most.

Let's apply His insight to the circumstances here in Revelation 13. The motivation behind this global system is rooted in man's satanic desire for wealth and power. Since this global system reflects the most valued thing that occupies people's minds everywhere, then their *treasure* is the same desire for wealth and power – on a personal level.

In the last days, people will be consumed with accumulating wealth and power in their personal lives. Wealth and power defines who they are as people. Work becomes their reason for existing. The global system eagerly provides busy people everywhere with channels to invest their time and energy. It tempts them with what they value most – what they covet continuously – *an appearance* of wealth and a sense of power over their lives.

John explains here at the end of verse three that the entire world is drawn into this covetous lifestyle – it states that *all the world wondered.* Everybody admires this system and the way of life it appears to offer. The more people observe this lifestyle in others around them, the more they themselves are drawn into competing for its wealth and power – the worship described in verse four.

This is the essence of a world devoid of love and respect for one another, a world that totally ignores the Tenth Commandment:

> **"Thou shalt not covet thy neighbor's house, thou shalt not covet thy neighbor's wife, nor his manservant, nor his maidservant, nor his ox, nor his ass, nor any thing that is thy neighbor's." – Exodus 20:17**

Note the detail that God goes into here. Can you relate the progressive decline of our culture that we see happening around us to the breaking of sections of this Commandment down the line?

Notice that the entire world is engulfed in coveting only after some

51

sort of life-changing event occurs, a defining moment in time – the healing of the deadly wound here in verse three. The healing of the deadly wound is *the* critical act in history that deceives the entire world into coveting the lifestyle offered under the United Nations. Again, this implies that the healing of the deadly wound is being deceptively orchestrated.

What is this deadly wound? How does it happen? And how is this deadly wound miraculously healed? To answer these questions, let's start by considering points 1, 2, and 3 on the nearby chart titled *The Event That Changes the World.*

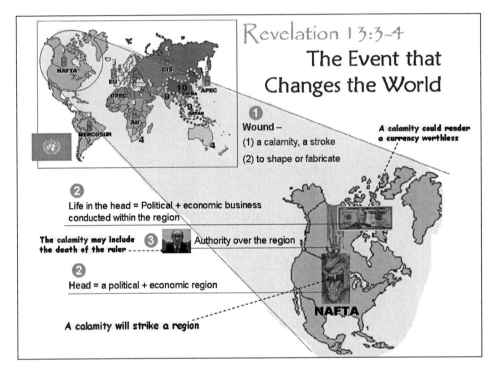

The ancient Greek term *wound* John that refers to has a dual meaning (see point 1). Wound here first means *a calamity, a stroke.* This wound will be a calamity of tremendous magnitude that eventually strikes the lives of everybody in the world. But wound also means *to shape* or *fabricate.* So this calamity is being shaped and fabricated to strike in such a way that it draws all the people in the world in for a closer look – a classic case of the ends justifying the means.

John explains that one of the heads of the beast is wounded *to death.* This head actually dies. Now we know that each head represents a political and economic region within the United Nations. This means the "life" of each region flows through its political and economic business activities (see point 2). So for a region to "die," its political authority must cease, its economic influence must expire. So this calamity is being shaped and fabricated to strike and kill the political authority and economic influence of one of these regions.

We also know that each head wears a crown on its horn, meaning each region has an authority ruling over its political and economic business (see point 3). This implies that this orchestrated calamity may also involve the person ruling over that region being struck "dead," either physically or politically.

Regardless of the scope or depth of its strike, this orchestrated political and economic catastrophe will immediately interrupt the covetous lifestyles of the people within that region – they will not be able to pursue their personal accumulation of wealth and power.

While this calamity will instantly disrupt everybody within the region it strikes, John also clearly explains at the end of verse three that the entire world *wonders*, or admires, the solution to this catastrophe. The only way the entire world would be interested in this is if the covetous lifestyles of everyone – *all* people – were impacted. What sort of catastrophe can possibly have such a significant impact on everybody in the entire world at the same time?

This catastrophe is being shaped and fabricated, implying that the authorities and the bankers driving the system from behind the scenes are the ones really shaping how this catastrophe will happen. This implies that the catastrophe will most likely occur through the currency channels they control.

Remember that the anchors of economic stability in this global system are Region 1 (the dollar), Region 2 (the euro) and Region 3 (the yen). These form the '3-legged stool of currency manipulation.' A catastrophic event that seizes the value of the dollar, the euro or the yen in one of these regions will immediately ripple through all political and economic channels across the world – impacting everybody, all at once.

What if one or more of these currencies were suddenly rendered worthless overnight? There would be instant chaos and mass panic across the globe. If, for example, the dollar was suddenly rendered worthless, the United States would immediately cease being the world's lone superpower. NAFTA (Region 1) would immediately collapse. Could this actually happen?

Yes, definitely. In fact, the problems that are currently weakening the dollar have already prepared the stage for this event to occur. As of October 2006, the gross domestic product (GDP) of the United States was $12.5 trillion. This is the total market value of our nation's output of goods and services. However, this enormous image of wealth is stained by taxes that consume 18 percent of this output from the outset.[47]

But there are much deeper structural problems in the dollar that are rooted behind the scenes. According to Michael Pento, a senior market strategist for Delta Global Advisors, Inc., the U.S. has developed a dependency and an addiction to foreigners who hold our dollar, and subsequently our economy, hostage.

"Our trade deficit mandates that we entice foreigners to commit at least $2 billion per day into our markets in order to maintain dollar stability," states Pento. "The total U.S. debt is now over $8.6 trillion. This debt has allowed China to hold $1 trillion in foreign reserves (or 70 percent of their reserves in U.S. dollars). Foreigners now hold nearly 50 percent of our publicly traded debt. The major holders of our debt are Japan, China and the U.K. They currently hold $639.2, $342.1 and $207.8 billion of our treasury debt, respectively. In all, foreigners hold about $9 trillion of U.S. financial assets."[48]

Former Treasury Secretary Robert Rubin agrees with Pento, claiming in November 2006 that "The U.S. is five years away from rapid acceleration of spending tied to Social Security and Medicare." At the same time, former Federal Reserve head Paul Volcker proclaimed, "It's incredible that people have gone on so long holding dollars." Volcker was unwilling to even extend a prediction of a dollar crisis in the next two and one half years.[49]

That's not all. "Trustees from the Medicare and Social Security trust funds estimate that 26.6 percent of Federal income taxes will be needed to fulfill obligations in 2020, up from 6.9 percent today," adds Pento. "By 2030 that number will increase to 49.7 percent. Bear in mind the U.S. has a negative savings rate, which further underscores our reliance on oversees borrowing."[50]

Pento points out that the Federal Reserve must appease foreign holders and prospective buyers of our treasuries by offering higher relative yields in interest rates, but this is becoming tougher to do as the central banks in Europe (Region 2) and Japan (Region 3) raise their rates. "With real rates of return after taxes in negative territory, bonds currently offer little investment value," he says. "This explains why Chinese officials recently expressed an interest to diversify their dollar holdings. It will not be an easy task to attract foreign buying, especially in light of our falling currency."[51]

Suppose the dollar was deliberately allowed to fully collapse by the globalists. Or suppose the collapse of the dollar was triggered by the rapture of the Church, which removes millions of true Christians from the planet in the blink of an eye. Or suppose nuclear war erupted in the Middle East and ceased the transfer of oil across the planet.

In all of these cases, all of the worldwide currency structure valued to the dollar would also collapse. With the U.S. economy in chaos, there would be no superpower to step in and resolve the situation. The world will scream for a solution to the problem – and the United Nations, emerging from behind the scenes, will be well equipped to answer the need. Revisit the end of verse 14 of our text again for a moment to continue this scenario:

> **". . . that they should make an image to the beast, which had the wound by a sword, and did live." – Revelation 13:14**

This wound, this catastrophe, is inflicted with a sword. The term *sword* here in the ancient Greek means *a knife*, but it also means *judicial punishment, controversy* and *strife*. Remember that this wound is being planned by the authorities behind the scenes in the United Nations, and the principle judicial organ of the UN is the International Court of Justice (ICJ), also known as the World Court.

Shaky Financial Legs

U.S. GDP $12.5 trillion
The October 2006 market value of the nation's output of goods and services

U.S. Debt $8.6 trillion
As of December 9, 2006

Our debt is 69% of our revenue!

Net U.S. Foreign Debt as % of GDP

At the end of 2006, foreigners owned almost 50% of publicly traded US debt.

• The U.S. economy now depends on cheap imported goods to sustain its economic growth and domestic consumption. Because of this dependence, the trade gap between what we export and import has reached an unsustainable level.

• To pay for our import habit, we must attract approximately $2 billion *per day* from foreign investors. This means foreign investors are increasingly essential to the functioning of the U.S. economy. But foreigners are now reluctant to invest in U.S. assets to due our debt.

• To cover the shortfall between what we must borrow and what private investors will lend, foreign central banks are filling the gap. Foreign governments now own almost 50% of our publicly traded debt, almost equal to that of our Federal Reserve. Their willingness to continue subsidizing our import habit is unclear due to our debt burden.

Located in the Peace Palace at The Hague, Netherlands, the World Court was established in 1945 as part of the Charter of the United Nations. It began work in 1946. The ICJ consists of 15 judges of various nationalities that are appointed by the UN General Assembly and the UN Security Council to serve nine-year terms. As such, these judges are independent magistrates who *do not* represent the domestic laws of their respective governments. Instead, they represent the *international* laws established through the global government of the United Nations. They may also be re-elected. In accordance with international law, the World Court settles any legal disputes between countries and advises on legal questions.

When the dollar collapses, what happens if several influential foreign nations – such as Japan, China, and the U.K. – join together to sue the U.S. government for repayment of our $1.2 trillion debt to them immediately? The scenario is easy to imagine. They take a global class action lawsuit into the World Court for trial, where our government is then found guilty of violating international law. Since we cannot possibly repay the debt, the ICJ decides to punish us by rendering the dollar insolvent and worthless. The head is immediately wounded, and the resulting economic controversy will cause instant strife across the world.

The World Court of the UN will now have to intercede with a solution to the problem. What if they choose to replace the dollar with a currency that is solvent, a currency that is stronger and favorably recognized throughout the world? What if they select the Euro?

This decision would essentially restructure and authorize all political and economic control of the world's systems to be channeled through Region 2, the European Union, which fulfills yet another prophecy about the beast:

> **"And here is the mind which hath wisdom. The seven heads are seven mountains, on which the woman sitteth." – Revelation 17:9**

Most scholars associate the seven mountains here with the Roman Empire, which was historically known as the "City of Seven Hills," referring to the seven hills of Rome, Italy. By relating the seven mountains to the seven heads, John explains that the power base of ultimate authority in the global system – the power that heals the wound – will reside in Europe.

The Beast of the Sea Takes Shape

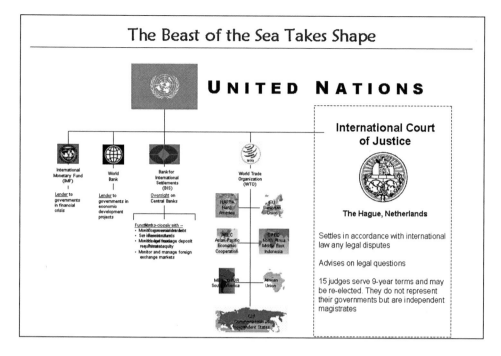

Before we scoff and say that all of this simply could not happen, we must remember what signs Jesus tells us to look for as signs of the end in the last days:

> "And as He sat upon the mount of Olives, the disciples came unto Him privately, saying, "Tell us . . . what shall be the sign of Thy coming, and of the end of the world? . . . There shall be famines, and pestilences, and earthquakes, in divers places . . . And when these things begin to come to pass, then look up, and lift up your heads; for your redemption draweth near." – Matthew 24:3, 7; Luke 21:28

Our Lord identifies three characteristics (famine, pestilence, and earthquakes) of this coming catastrophic event, along with the broad expanse of its impact (diverse places). And recently, as if to place an exclamation point on all of this, God gave us a working model of how the UN will come to the rescue.

I personally believe that the great tragedy of the massive tsunami that struck Indonesia and East Asia in December 2004 is a shadow of an even greater catastrophe to come. Between 275,000 and 290,000 people died in the regional disaster resulting from this magnitude 9.0 earthquake, leaving a literal "tsunami generation" of children orphaned. Hundreds of thousands more were injured in the devastation.

Almost immediately following the Asian tsunami, a concerted disaster relief effort essentially reorganized and changed the image of global economic leadership as it's perceived on the world stage. Though numerous religious and charitable organizations in America contributed a great deal of finances, gifts, efforts, manpower and time to rescuing these victims from turmoil, the UN quickly grabbed the mass media spotlight by formally coordinating pledges of $2.3 billion of relief from governments, business, celebrities and others across the globe.

During this effort, the U.S. government (which was still broadly heralded as the wealthiest on the planet prior to the tsunami) was apparently unable to fund enough money to lead these coordinated pledges for disaster relief, a problem the media propaganda claimed was largely due to the war against terrorism. Instead, the EU (Region 2) and Japan (Region 3) led the way, each contributing $500 million. The U.S. was next at $350 million, followed closely by the World Bank (in other words, the UN itself) at $250 million.

"I've never seen anything like this . . ."

Colin Powell

- Magnitude 9.0 earthquake – December 26, 2004

- Estimated 275,000 to 290,000 dead
  - estimated 50,000 children dead
  - estimated 10,000+ more children orphaned 'The Tsunami Generation'

- Estimated 500,000 injured across six nations

- Mass devastation across India, Sri Lanka, Sumatra and other nations

Illustration and photos courtesy of Associated Press

58

This struck a huge blow to the world's perception of America's financial ability to maintain the moral high ground and fill her traditional role as the faithful leader of nation building. Instead, through strong political and financial support from Europe, the UN publicly replaced the U.S. in that role. Almost matching the United States in pledges would, in itself, have established the United Nations as some sort of formidable economic power. But Europeans inside the UN moved much further than that, implementing a proactive response that aggressively captured the overall strategic role of global relief leadership.

The Tsunami – Catastrophe Changing the World

The Tragedy   Kofi Annan   Jan Egeland

UN coordinates $2.3 billion of relief pledged across the globe –

- EU $500 million

- Japan $500 million

- U.S. $350 million

- World Bank $250 million

* World leaders met in Jakarta to coordinate international relief efforts for the tsunami victims.

* Lack of warning system blamed as a major reason behind the huge death toll.

* Discussed creating global civil crisis management instruments + early tsunami warning system to minimize damage from major natural disasters in the future.

* Instruments = rapid response teams of doctors, firefighters, other experts.

* UN assumed coordination roles for the whole operation.

* Catastrophe cast new relevance on the UN Conference on Disaster Relief held in Kobe January 2005 to set plans in motion.

The UN assumed the coordination of international relief efforts for the tsunami victims through a meeting of world leaders in Jakarta immediately following the disaster. In Jakarta, the UN managed the tactical functions of the entire rescue operation, including the dispatch of rapid response teams of doctors, firefighters, and other experts (referred to as rescue "instruments").

The meeting also began to identify solutions that could prevent this sort of disaster from being repeated. For example, the lack of some sort of warning system was blamed as a major reason behind the huge death toll. Answers to this were planned around the creation of global civil crisis management "instruments" in some sort of early tsunami warning system to minimize damage from major natural disasters in the future. These answers cast new relevance on the UN Conference on Disaster Relief that was held in Kobe, Japan in January 2005 to set all of these plans into motion.

The beast had risen to center stage in the world theatre, not only to solve a global problem, but to prevent the problem from being repeated. That's an admirable goal, the mark of a star. The Asian tsunami disaster became a working model of the wound to come, a model that prepares the stage for the beast to become a star of the people.

CHAPTER 5

A Star Is Born

Without question, we now live in a world that covets wealth, a place that is reflected by the *wonder* and *worship* of all the people in John's vision:

> "... and all the world *wondered* after the beast. And they *worshipped* the dragon which gave power unto the beast, and they *worshipped* the beast . . ." – Revelation 13:3-4

These Scriptures expose mankind's unbridled coveting of wealth as the global system takes center stage. The people here are consumed with accumulating wealth and power in their personal lives. Work – more specifically, *being paid* for work – is their sole reason for existing. Materialism has become the purpose of their journey through life. Pleasure is the spiritual equivalent of an idol they worship.

This idol that they covet/worship manifests itself through an *appearance* of personal wealth (an illusion, for they actually finance their possessions through debt) and a *sense* of power over their lives (an illusion, for they are actually slaves to their financial debt). John is ultimately describing a time in the near future when these personal illusions – which represent spiritual bondage to idolatry – are being financially manipulated on a local level through the widespread, global economic distribution channels of the United Nations.

In other words, the lives of these people are entirely manipulated through the financial propaganda of the global system. Illusions of wealth and power define who they are as people. Wealth and power define who they consider to be their leaders, who they will imitate, who they will follow. In fact, their entire worldview is based solely upon the distribution of wealth and power – who has it, who doesn't – as it relates to individuals, companies, or organizations.

There was no coincidence when the world's media focused extensively on UN efforts to redistribute wealth (through global contributions) as a means of providing relief to the Asian tsunami disaster in December 2004. This attention served a covert purpose because now, whenever and wherever disaster relief is needed, many people across the world fawn over the UN as their savior.

We watch celebrity politicians, businessmen, actors and other popular figures pay highly publicized visits to various areas in need to "help" the UN coordinate global relief efforts. All of this celebrity "assistance" is deceptively manipulated through media propaganda that builds a profile of the UN as the servant solution to disasters, the healer of the wounded.

This servant profile is continuing to grow, subtly influencing the world's search for one source of global relief. When the wound to the head of the beast happens, those same celebrities will again point to the UN to coordinate the world's relief efforts at that drastic moment. Across the world, all voices will call upon the UN to solve this disaster, to heal the deadly wound:

> ". . . all the world wondered after the beast. And they worshipped the dragon which gave power unto the beast, and they worshipped the beast, saying, Who is like unto the beast? Who is able to make war with him?" – Revelation 13:3-4

Just as the UN *started* to reorder the world's global relief leadership by stepping up to manage the redistribution of wealth for relief to the Asian tsunami (a *natural* disaster), it will *finish* reordering its relief leadership through managing the redistribution of wealth to solve an *economic* disaster – the healing of the deadly wound.

Rendering the dollar worthless overnight will cause an economic tsunami unlike any before. Absolute chaos and mass panic will swarm over the globe. The United States will immediately cease being the world's lone superpower. The NAFTA economic region will totally collapse as all business there comes to a screeching halt. The economy of this region will die – and suddenly all of the worldwide currency structure valued to the dollar will collapse. As the world economy sinks toward destruction, there will be no superpower to politically step in and resolve the situation.

Enter the United Nations. The global scream for relief that sounded for the Asian tsunami disaster will echo through the media propaganda for a cure to this economic tragedy. People everywhere will publicly cry for the UN to be their servant savior. Celebrities will sacrifice their cause to the UN to coordinate the global economic relief effort.

The World Court of the UN, located in Europe, will respond with a legal solution that replaces the insolvent dollar with a strong Euro. The Europeans, established by this legal default as the world's financial leaders, will push through a massive and complex restructuring of the global economy. This restructuring will set the stage for a dynamic individual to appear who has all the answers, a person who has already risen to authority within the EU and is now prepared to assume ultimate control over the entire world system.

People will adore this brilliant politician, a man who can reconstruct cultural policies and revamp social systems around the world without riots and war. They will reverence this astute economist, a man who can pacify the chaos associated with global debt and sooth the poverty created from a worthless dollar. He will be a financial wizard, capable of restructuring all the debt incurred in the collapse into favorable contracts and payments for everyone using the Euro.

He'll be an effective manager, a man who rebuilds all of the damaged accounting and financial institutions and returns them to smooth functioning. He will restructure the entire global system and solve the catastrophe. This European leader will "heal" the deadly wound. People will be amazed at how well everything works. In Revelation 13:4, the people *worship* the dragon and the beast: in other words, they covet the character of the one they see operating the system, they covet his abilities, his competency, his influence, his charisma, his authority – his power.

In fact, the word *worship* here literally translates from the ancient Greek to mean *to kiss, like a dog licking his master's hand*. The global system that offers the people of the world the appearance of personal wealth and power that they crave has been damaged and stopped. These people are all teetering on the brink of disaster. But this man resurrects the system to life, in all its imperfection and incompletion – and this time, with total and complete control over the people.

Because this rebuilt system functions so efficiently and effectively, the people totally buy into this man's satanic character. They are completely deluded into believing all his lies. They wonder, at the end of verse four, who can compete with this system? Who can argue against the lifestyle it provides? Who is smart enough to engage a thoughtful fight against the worldly wisdom and direction of this man?

What we see here is the rise and positioning of *the* Antichrist, a single man who will be recognized as the supreme ruler over the entire world. In all honesty, making this statement sounds corny, doesn't it?

One man rules the entire planet? This thought almost seems ridiculous when you meditate upon it. We live in a world of 220 nations, widely diverse cultures spread across the globe, speaking over 7,000 languages. My mind simply treats this concept as fiction. 'One man ruling the world' is the plot of one of those old Superman or Batman comic books.

My rational mind argues that there is no way that this can possibly happen, not in the sophisticated, educated world we live in today. People are simply too intelligent for something like this to be allowed. And even if some evil guy did actually begin to gain this sort of power, we all would surely be able to recognize him and fight any attempt he makes to control our lives. Right?

Wrong. The Apostle Paul answers this rational logic by describing the supernatural delusion that actually happens when this wicked man rises to power:

> "... except there come a falling away first, and that man of sin be revealed, the son of perdition: Who opposeth and exalteth himself above all that is called God, or that is worshipped . . . then shall that Wicked be revealed . . . . . whose coming is after the working of Satan with all power and signs and lying wonders . . . with all deceivableness of unrighteousness in them that perish . . . for this cause God shall send them *strong delusion*, that they should believe a lie . . ." – 2 Thessalonians 2:3-4, 8-11

Paul is saying that the Antichrist will not rise to power by force – at least not at first. The people will *willingly give* him all power over their lives. Paul is sharing a deep insight into how people everywhere will be deluded into accepting the Antichrist. Notice that he says there will first be *a falling away*.

Revealing the Wicked One ... The People Fall Away

UNITED NATIONS

The beast rising from the sea =
a global economic and political system
rising into control.

Its control is ultimately rooted in
people's desire for personal wealth and
power. 1 Timothy 6:10

It operations channel the world's
unbridled coveting of the *appearance* of
wealth and *sense* of power. Luke 16:13

Wealth and power define who people are – and who they consider to be their leaders.
High-profile politicians, businessmen, celebrities

Their entire worldview is based upon distribution of wealth and power – who's got it, who doesn't – as individuals, organizations, companies.

In the last days, the masses are consumed by the desire for personal wealth and power. In 1 Timothy 6:10, the Scriptures emphasize that this love of money is the root of all evil. Because the people covet money, they errantly fall into the rampant worship of mammon (the spiritual idolatry of money), manifested through self-centered lifestyles that openly despise the goodness of God. Since the global system controls all of the money, the system becomes able to control the masses as well. By financially manipulating their base desires for materialism, the beast entices the people to fall away from their worship of God.

For this reason, Jesus specifically warns us against allowing money to become an idol:

> **"No servant can serve two masters: for either he will hate the one, and love the other; or else he will hold to the one, and despise the other. Ye cannot serve God and mammon." – Luke 16:13**

Our Savior is warning us here that, spiritually, this penetrates much deeper. By manipulating the base desires of the people, the beast is able to create a political, social and religious vacuum that allows man-made *reason* to replace spiritual *faith*. To fill this void, the beast creates a *climate of conviction* that dogmas, ideologies and traditions – whether religious, political or social – must all be weighed and tested by each individual, and not simply accepted on faith.

The manipulated masses are convicted to start using critical reason, factual evidence, and scientific methods of inquiry – all opposed to faith – in seeking solutions to human problems. Their lives become a constant search for *objective* truth in an environment where there is no *absolute* truth. They become enlightened to "understand" that any new knowledge and experience constantly alters their imperfect perception of it.

The manipulated masses become convicted to refocus their entire purpose for living: to better understand themselves, their history, their intellectual and artistic achievements, and tolerance for the outlooks – political, social and religious – of those who differ from them. Personal conviction evolves into an open marketplace of ideas, good will and tolerance that supposedly builds a better world for the people and their children.

This manipulation of the masses, living in a man-made climate of conviction, is the "falling away" that Paul refers to – and we already see this happening around us in the rise of secular humanism.

The Rise of Secular Humanism

What Is Secular Humanism?

• A conviction that dogmas, ideologies and traditions – whether religious, political or social, must be weighed and tested by each individual and <u>not simply accepted on faith</u>.

• Using critical reason, factual evidence, and scientific methods of inquiry, <u>rather than faith</u>, in seeking solutions to human problems.

• A constant search for objective truth – there is no absolute truth – understanding that new knowledge and experience constantly alter mankind's imperfect perception of it.

• The entire purpose of life is to better understand people, their history, their intellectual and artistic achievements, and tolerance for the outlooks of those who differ from them.

• An open marketplace of ideas, good will and tolerance builds a better world for people and our children.

All around us, personal lifestyles that were once crafted upon a Judeo-Christian worldview are now being manipulated to transition into a secular humanist worldview. Secular humanists only believe in *naturalism*, a belief that the physical laws of the universe are not superseded by non-material or supernatural entities such as demons, gods, or other "spiritual" beings outside the realm of the natural universe. Supernatural events such as miracles, where physical laws are defied, are not totally dismissed but viewed with high skepticism.

The Rise of Secular Humanism

How do Secular Humanists View Religious and Supernatural Claims?

• They only believe in naturalism – the physical laws of the universe are not superseded by non-material or supernatural entities such as demons, gods, or other "spiritual" beings outside the realm of the natural universe. There is no God.

• Supernatural events such as miracles (where physical laws are defied) are not totally dismissed, but viewed with high skepticism.

Are Secular Humanists Atheists?

• They typically describe themselves as atheist or agnostic. They do not rely upon gods or supernatural forces to solve their problems or provide guidance for their conduct.

• They rely upon the application of reason, the lessons of history, and personal experience to form their ethical/moral foundation and meaning in life. Science is their most reliable source for all information.

Secular humanists typically describe themselves as atheist or agnostic. To them, *there is no God.* They do not rely upon gods or supernatural forces to solve their problems or provide guidance for their conduct. Instead, they rely upon the application of reason, the lessons of history, and personal experience to form their ethical/moral foundation and meaning in life. Science is their most reliable source for all information.

In essence, the secular humanist views man as his own god. Rather than adhering to Judeo-Christian principles and looking to the church for God's guidance and leadership, secular humanists adhere to their own rationale and reason, and look for legal guidance and advice on living life. The bloodline of the beast and its secular humanist worldview is instant gratification, and everyone gets a blood transfusion. When disaster strikes, the manipulated masses need help – and they whine for it *now.*

For this reason, Paul goes on further to explain that at that crucial moment when people need him most, the Antichrist will have the *power to do signs and wonders.* In other words, he will possess amazing talents that can accomplish extraordinary, inexplicable, marvelous and unusual deeds. This high-profile secular humanist will not only politically and financially heal the wound of the beast, he will manage the social transition of the masses into the "climate of conviction."

Before the wound to the beast, the U.S. was the default superpower and its Judeo-Christian values were still acknowledged. But after the wound, when the Euro replaces the dollar and the secular EU takes over, the Antichrist will replace Judeo-Christian values with secular humanism – a stage that is already set today. In post-Christian Europe, for example, there are reports that less than 3 percent of people currently attend church on a regular basis. In England, that number drops to less than 1 percent. In France, only five percent attend church on a weekly basis, and most of them are the elderly. Only 10 percent think religion is "very important." In fact, for all Europeans, that figure is only 21 percent.[52]

The Antichrist will save these people from catastrophe, and he will relate to them because he speaks their language. Their idol is mammon, and he speaks mammon. As a secular humanist, he will rationally commit to free market enterprise and high-tech industry, and he uses secular rationale and reason to begin a subtle – but strong and extended – deception against righteousness:

> **"And there was given unto him a mouth speaking great things and blasphemies; and power was given unto him to continue forty and two months." – Revelation 13:5**

The secular talents of this European will enable him to totally delude the masses for 42 months, or three and one-half years. Here we have the satanic antichrist character of the people freely electing this man as *the* Antichrist. They are asking who can make war with him – in other words, who can debate his ideology? They raise him to power by their own free will.

Consider, for a moment, how the Antichrist will preach his strong delusion. There is only one system of economics in the history of mankind that truly works through common sense and leads people to prosperity and well-being. That system is *free-market, profit-motivated capitalism,* grounded in the nobility and responsibility of Christianity. Christianity is the anchor to personal success in capitalism, because if we believe what Jesus teaches, then we are His bond slaves, bought with a price. This means all of our money, possessions and capital belong to our Lord, not us. We are merely the life stewards of any wealth He places at our disposal through the mechanism of capitalism.

Now envision the Antichrist preaching a twisted version of capitalism, one without any Christian morals. The anchor to personal success is removed. Because of man's fallen nature, unbound capitalism inevitably morphs into terrible greed and corruption – a perfect delusion for people whose base nature is consumed with wealth and power. Drowning in the deluded "convictions" of secular humanism, these people will grow wicked to the core and create perilous times:

> "... in the last days perilous times shall come. For men shall be lovers of their own selves, covetous, boasters, proud, blasphemers, disobedient to parents, unthankful, unholy, without natural affection. . ." – 2 Timothy 3:1-3

In 2 Thessalonians 2:10, Paul describes the strength of the Antichrist's talent for lying and deception as *all deceivableness of unrighteousness*. Playing the global system like a harp, the Antichrist will deceptively "satisfy" the craving of the masses for wealth and power, and in return, they will covet his abilities, his competency, his influence, his authority – his power. Who can compete with his system?

The Antichrist preaches prosperity and well-being through free-market, profit-motivated capitalism without any Christian foundation. In doing so, he rationally chains the people to unbound greed and corruption. Who can argue against his lifestyle?

Only one system of government has ever existed in the history of mankind that truly works through common sense and leads people to truth and freedom. It is *democracy*, grounded in the nobility and responsibility of Christianity. Christianity is the anchor to personal freedom in democracy, because if we believe what Jesus teaches, then His Truth is absolute and His Word defines those limits that separate freedom from anarchy. This means God's Word is the absolute authority on our free pursuit of life, liberty and happiness. We are merely life stewards of the freedom God grants us through His Grace.

Now envision the Antichrist preaching a twisted version of democracy, one without any Christian principles. The anchor to personal freedom is removed. Unbound democracy inevitably evolves into the relative truth of circumstance. It declines into anarchy, chaos and rebellion that require some form of totalitarian control – a perfect delusion for the secular character of the people in the last days:

> "... trucebreakers, false accusers, incontinent, fierce, despisers of those that are good, traitors, heady, highminded, lovers of pleasures more than lovers of God; having a form of godliness, but denying the power thereof..." – 2 Timothy 3:3-5

The Antichrist preaches democracy without any Christian morals. He rationally couples it to the secular environment of conviction, where Truth becomes relative to the circumstance, and fear and insecurity arise from imperfect and corrupt values. He instills the need for totalitarian control so that he can provide security for all, and he implements this control by delegating power to a few elite globalists.

All Deceivableness
Revealing the Wicked One ... of Unrighteousness

The system satisfies their craving for wealth + power – they covet the European's abilities, his competency, his influence, his authority – his power.
Rev. 13:4-6 ... Who can compete with this system?

He preaches prosperity and well-being through free-market, profit-motivated capitalism – without any Christian foundation.   Unbound greed + corruption
Rev 13:4-6 ... Who can argue against this lifestyle?

He preaches democracy – without any Christian morals. Truth becomes relative to the circumstance
Rev 13:4-6 ... Who can engage in thoughtful debate?

Rise of the Antichrist in secular life

Fear + insecurity arise from imperfect + corrupt values
Need for totalitarian control to provide security for all
- power for the few

This evil man will ultimately represent everything Satan is: the rational composite of satanic substance being worked out through human beings. Man without God is nothing more than a brute beast in rebellion against

God. The Antichrist follows his own instincts rather than God's will. The Antichrist attempts to repair what is wrong with himself without God's help.

Christianity says that the only way to life is through death to self, through the Cross of Calvary. But the Antichrist teaches that you don't need the Cross, you don't need to die to self, and you certainly don't need to surrender anything to Jesus Christ. Why? Because you can have everything in this world, if you will follow his system. In other words, you can be as a god: the same lie that Satan fed to Eve through the fruit of the original sin:

> **"And the serpent said unto the woman, Ye shall not surely die: For God doth know that in the day ye eat thereof, then your eyes shall be opened, and *ye shall be as gods*, knowing good and evil." – Genesis 3: 4-5**

Just as his master did before him, the Antichrist offers his apple – the global system in all its material imperfection and wealthy corruption – to the Eves of the world, using "a mouth speaking great things and blasphemies; and power was given unto him to continue forty and two months."

Just as Eve succumbed to her own insecurity and fear of how the serpent thought of her, the Eves of the last days will succumb to their own world of fear and insecurity: of losing their appearance of personal wealth, of losing their sense of personal power. The Antichrist speaks in strong language (*great things*) to confuse the world. He utters fancy words of foolishness and ignorance (*blasphemies*) that deceive everyone into believing that he is the savior of the world.

But notice that in the middle of this description of the Antichrist's power, the Scriptures announce in Revelation 13:5 that he is *granted* the privilege of forcing his system onto the world, of abusing his abilities and influence for a period of 42 months. In other words, his power is being *allowed* by the One Who created all things.

The Holy Spirit reminds us here that our Lord, Jehovah Adonai, still reigns above the storms of this world. Our God is in complete control of everything going on here. In fact, the numeral *42* in the ancient Hebrew represents *preservation*. How comforting and encouraging it is to know that in the middle of our catastrophes, no matter how large our problems become, Jehovah God preserves us. The Scriptures are again emphasizing that no weapon formed against us can prosper.

This insight is inserted here to remind us that during these darkest hours there will be those who were "left behind" that will realize that they must place their trust, their faith, and their hope in Jesus Christ alone, never in the deeds of any man. Jesus is the Light of the world. His Word is a Lamp unto their feet. Jesus can always be trusted, because He alone is Unchanging, Faithful and True. Our Savior always preserves His own, no matter how dark the situation becomes.

In the last days, after the rapture of the true Church of Jesus Christ, as the Antichrist ascends to power he will spread a heavy cloak of darkness over the entire world. After institutionalizing the secular climate of conviction, the Antichrist will introduce an agenda of pure evil into the public domain:

> "And he opened his mouth in blasphemy against God, to blaspheme His Name, and His tabernacle, and them that dwell in heaven."
> – Revelation 13:6

Moral confusion reigns as this evil leader spiritually rebuilds all of society into a global Tower of Babel.

Here in Revelation 13:6, John describes an evil man leading a direct uprising against God. Throughout the Scriptures, the number six represents the spiritual *weakness of man*, the *evils of Satan*, and the *manifestation of sin*. This is exactly what we see happening here as the Antichrist ascends to global power.

The Antichrist blasphemes *against* God. *Against* here in the ancient Greek means *to place in priority above, to direct in front of*. As the Antichrist publicly defames the authority and character of Jehovah, His irreverence serves to ratchet himself up to a higher priority over God in the eyes of the people.

In other words, this evil man positions himself to be a god of higher authority than Jehovah, just as Nimrod (the original prophetic version of the Antichrist) did in an earlier time:

> "And Cush begat Nimrod: he began to be a mighty one in the earth. He was a mighty hunter before the Lord: wherefore it is said, Even as Nimrod the mighty hunter before the Lord. And the beginning of his kingdom was Babel . . ." – Genesis 10:8-10

Just as Nimrod rose to become the key player in the grand scheme of the pagan system, so will the Antichrist. Scripturally speaking, this means that the story of Nimrod reveals prophetic insights into the workings of the Antichrist.

For example, Jewish legend has it that there were no physical walls around the city of Babel where the people lived to protect themselves from wild beasts. Many people were killed by these animals. Nimrod was a mighty hunter that killed those beasts, and people began to exalt him as their leader because of his physical prowess. When the Bible says he was a mighty hunter *before* the Lord, it doesn't mean Nimrod was literally standing face-to-face in front of God. Instead, it means he was a leader *opposed* to God, against Him, exalting himself to be mighty over Him.

In the same way, there will be no economic walls around the global system that the people work in to shield themselves from financial disaster. Many people will be killed (bankrupted) by the epic wound to the head. Antichrist will be a mighty savior that removes their financial disaster, and the people will exalt him as their leader because of his economic and political prowess. He, too, will be a mighty hunter before the Lord: a leader *opposed* to God, against Him, exalting himself to be mighty over Him.

Or consider this. After Nimrod rose to power, he spiritually and emotionally corrupted the people who followed him, guiding them toward destruction through pagan worship and satanic rituals:

> **"And they said, Go to, let us build us a city and a tower, whose top may *reach unto heaven*; and let us make us a name, lest we be scattered abroad upon the face of the whole earth." – Genesis 11:4**

Jewish legend has it that Nimrod built this tower and called it *baal-ed*, which means *gateway to God*. The name *Baal*, which broadly refers to pagan worship throughout the Scriptures, originates from this term. Scholars agree that this tower was actually a ziggurat, an ancient temple used for deeply satanic rituals. Jewish sages explain that Nimrod, the prophetic shadow of the coming Antichrist, reintroduced the satanic rituals which had been practiced prior to The Flood in Genesis 7.

In other words, Nimrod revived all of the occultism and witchcraft that brought on Noah's flood in the first place – the same occultism and witchcraft that prophetically points to the evil practices of the last days. Nimrod treated the rituals surrounding these practices as mysteries, so that he alone became known as the wise one. As Nimrod was maneuvering himself into this position, the people still knew who God was – but they didn't pay much attention to Him, no different than today.

We see these same maneuvers happening now in the form of New Age mysticism and oriental enlightenment, with various pagan priests rising up and proclaiming to have the mysterious wisdom of the bygone ways. As people search through those same mysteries today, they lose sight of the true God. The coming Antichrist will utilize these same maneuvers to position himself as the wise one, and his global system will reap economic profits from occultism and witchcraft.

That's not all. The Jewish sages claim that Nimrod's reign institutionalized sexual perversion and prostitution. When a young girl came of age, she began worshipping in the temple of Baal-ed. How did she worship? A man came to her and selected her. He gave her a piece of money, then they committed fornication. Sexual perversion was instituted as virgin girls were paid and used for rituals of temple prostitution and fertility worship in the tower. The money was given to the priesthood. Eventually, not one young woman was clean anywhere.

This is exactly what we see happening around us right now. Our public school system educates our children to go ahead and practice sexual perversion. Government-sponsored education teaches our kids that virginity, purity and holiness are nonsense. It replaces these traits with sexual immorality and even proclaims that homosexuality is normal. Because parents cannot legally spank or discipline their children, they must helplessly sit and watch the government create future monsters out of the gifts that God gave them. All of the sexual perversion and prostitution that seethes throughout our society today started with Nimrod. It points to the coming culture that will be governed by the Antichrist and promoted through his global system, which will reap economic profits from sexual lewdness.

Jewish sages also teach that Nimrod restarted the ritual of human sacrifice. He began killing the first-born of the girls conceived in the tower, because they were considered illegitimate anyway. Since the child was conceived in the temple, Nimrod said the child was divine and a god, so they offered the child as a blood sacrifice to the fertility god of the temple. Today, we perform daily child sacrifices in temples called abortion clinics. Over 40 million children have been sacrificed in them over the past 34 years. Their blood is offered as a sacrifice to the god of mammon. All the abortions happening in the world today – ultimately driven by the profit motive – started with Nimrod, and they point to the coming culture of death directed by the Antichrist.

Just as it was in the days of Nimrod, the evil practices we see rising up around us point toward the days of the Antichrist in Revelation 13:6, a time when he will publicly revile the *tabernacle* of Jehovah God, which represents the faiths of Christianity and Judaism. The Antichrist will rail against Christian churches, speak evil of Jewish synagogues, and denounce those once-respected Christians and Jews (the saints) who were heralded as *dwelling* in heaven. *Dwell* here in the ancient Greek means *to occupy (as a mansion)* or *to reside (as the shekinah glory of God did in the Tabernacle of the Old Testament)*.

Strong Delusion, They
Revealing the Wicked One . . . Should Believe a Lie

Positioning of the Antichrist in spiritual life

The Antichrist invokes the practical merits of secular humanism over any tenets of religious faith

Rev. 13:6-8 . . . He blasphemes against God and His Name

against – *to place in priority above, to direct in front of.* The Antichrist grows arrogant + *irreverent. He ratchets himself up higher in priority over God. He loudly defames the authority and character of Jehovah.*

He specifically mocks the tenets of Judeo-Christian faith

Rev. 13:6-8 . . . He blasphemes against His tabernacle + them that dwell in Heaven

dwell – *to occupy (as a mansion), or to reside (as the shekinah glory of God did in the Tabernacle of the Old Testament).*

In other words, the satanic ideology of the Antichrist, molded through the brainwashing of secular humanism, will breed deep contempt of all Christian and Jewish heritages that points toward protection and communion with Jehovah God. The purely evil nature of the wicked one will be revealed as he verbally fuels a hatred that eventually boils into physical persecution of Christians and Jews:

> **"And it was given unto him to make war with the saints, and to overcome them: and power was given him over all kindreds, and tongues, and nations." – Revelation 13:7**

The Antichrist will formally authorize a global reign of terror against anyone claiming to have Christian or Jewish faith in Jehovah God. These are the saints that have been left behind at the time of the end, and they are under tremendous persecution. These that were left behind are martyred during this period because they are unwilling to worship the Antichrist.

He has all the tools, money and technology of the global system at his disposal. He is looked upon as a man with the wisdom of a god. He can do no wrong. Everything he speaks is truth. This means all of the "myths" about Christianity and the Jewish faith must be wrong – and they must be dealt with before they can corrupt the lives of others.

The growing anti-Semitism and antagonism of Christian beliefs that we see today are ultimately heading toward a time when the Antichrist will commission military forces to destroy all the sacred artifacts of Judeo-Christianity, destroy anything consecrated as pure and blameless. He will use police, spies, and military force to persecute Christians and Jews everywhere across the globe. The sinister power of the United Nations reaches its apex here, and the true purpose of the one-world system is revealed in all its evil glory:

> **"And all that dwell upon the earth shall worship him, whose names are not written in the book of life of the Lamb slain from the foundation of the world." – Revelation 13:8**

For 42 months, the secular lifestyle of the masses under the Antichrist thrives as it never has before. Who needs spiritual values when the pocketbook is full? Big house and vacation home, a garage full of nice cars, the best clothes money can buy, exotic foods on the table . . . everyone who follows the system of the Antichrist – all who *worship* the covetous lifestyle he provides – appear to possess heaven right here on earth.

This guy has got it right. He has all the answers. Sure, people see crime rising because there are no morals anymore. But lawlessness is not a problem, because the people will let the guy with all the answers take that over too. He solved all their other problems, so he can solve that as well. Give him *control* over everything – *I put my trust in him.*

The Bible specifically warns us against this deception:

> **"For when they shall say, Peace and safety; then sudden destruction cometh upon them, as travail upon a woman with child; and they shall not escape." – 1 Thessalonians 5:3**

The lifestyle of prosperity that the secular world worships will subtly transform into a life of bondage when the masses turn over complete control to the Antichrist. As his agenda shifts from security to control, his leadership style will harden – and so will the climate of conviction. The global system that once promised everyone their own personal wealth and a sense of power and security now *enforces* submission to the sole authority of the Antichrist, through fear, insecurity, and brute force. The people must worship him alone or face the consequences.

All of the remaining people that dwell upon the earth, those that are not martyred for their faith, will reject the Truth in return for "protection" from persecution. All of these people, trapped under the covetous weight of their own insecurity, will reject the Gospel and be doomed, for their names are not written in the Book of Life.

Everyone who rejects the Good News of the death and resurrection of Jesus Christ, those who flippantly scoff at God's Grace for mankind through His Son, will become slaves in fear of the Antichrist. The masses will be in utter bondage to his United Nations, to his elite group of globalist authorities . . . and they will lick the hands of their masters like dogs.

CHAPTER 6

New World Disorder

"If any man have an ear, let him hear. He that leadeth into captivity shall go into captivity: he that killeth with the sword must be killed with the sword. Here is the patience and the faith of the saints."
– Revelation 13:9-10

In these verses, the Holy Spirit pauses to profoundly explain the seriousness of what is actually happening here. Notice how God interrupts John's vision with this passage to speak directly to us. This emphasizes how important it is that we truly understand and broaden our knowledge of this situation from His perspective.

Our Lord is warning us to pay attention. He wants us to open our hearts (our spiritual ear) to His Word so that we can perceive (hear) the Truth being revealed here in these prophetic Scriptures. He wants to open our minds so that we can recognize the spiritual complexity of an enemy who seeks to devour us like a roaring lion. As Paul explains to us in Ephesians 6:17, our Savior really wants us to use the sword of the Spirit (His Word) to spiritually carve through the rising deception that threatens to seduce us with lustful desire, chain us to wickedness, and lead us to destruction.

Think through what John has shown us thus far. The verses up to this point in Revelation 13 have described the subtle creation of – or more appropriately, the transformation into – an entirely new culture of social disorder, where people and things are no longer in their proper place in relation to each other.

All moral guidelines of conduct have been replaced with irreverent behavior that is founded upon personal vanity. Lifestyles are constructed around and consumed with covetous insecurity, fear and humiliation. This is a time of deep moral, ethical and spiritual confusion that the prophet Isaiah warned us of:

> "Woe unto them that draw iniquity with cords of vanity . . . Woe unto them that call evil good, and good evil; and put darkness for light, and light for darkness, that put bitter for sweet, and sweet for bitter! Woe unto them that are wise in their own eyes, and prudent in their own sight!" – Isaiah 5:18, 20-21

In this new world of disorder, mankind has been mentally and emotionally reduced into a semi-civilized culture of animals that live off raw materialism. The Antichrist has become their owner and master. The United Nations has become their dog pound. This is literally hell on earth.

Strong terms are used here in Revelation 13:9-10 to warn us of the seriousness of the times, and the threat they pose. *Leadeth* means to *lead, collect, convene* or *entertain together, as in a pack.* The Antichrist will institute and impose social immorality onto the masses, leading mankind into destruction like a pack of stray dogs. Any lingering moral ethics will be collectively trashed by lifestyles that are distracted by and seduced into lewd entertainment. Shallow vanity will reduce the purpose of life to simply assembling (convene) for the next big party, the next big game, the next big social event. Sounds familiar, doesn't it?

These are the exact trends we see happening around us today. Naughty is nice, so sin is in. Society is now permeated by hypersexual marketing and entertainment that lustfully dumbs everything down into useless "infotainment." This continual lewd stimulation has essentially brainwashed masses of people into becoming irreverent creatures who can no longer maintain more than a moment's interest in anything that is truly important.

Jesus explicitly warns us to defy these evil trends and not follow the masses. He teaches us to be *in* this world of lustful desires, but not *of* this world:

> "If the world hate you, ye know that it hated me before it hated you. If ye were of the world, the world would love his own: but because ye are not of the world, but I have chosen you out of the world, therefore the world hateth you." – John 15:18-19

Like an enormous pack of stray animals, we see the masses being led into *captivity*. In the ancient Greek, *captivity* means *prisoners of war, lifted up and carried away*. Our Lord is explaining that this is all about complex spiritual warfare.

God wants us to prayerfully view the masses in pity, as spiritual prisoners of war that have succumbed to their own vain deception and are being lifted up and carried away to eternal destruction. They are bound by the lustful vanity of covetous competition that is manifested through adultery and premarital sex – all of which our culture lewdly markets through "infotainment." They are consumed with the spirit of rebellion that is manifested through alcohol and drug abuse, violence and murder – all of which our culture lewdly markets through "infotainment."

Our Lord reminds us here that destruction will fall upon the masses that have forgotten the difference between evil and good. The Apostle Paul specifically warns us not to succumb to these works of the flesh:

> **"Now the works of the flesh are manifest, which are these; adultery, fornication, uncleanness, lasciviousness, idolatry, witchcraft, hatred, variance, emulations, wrath, strife, seditions, heresies, envyings, murders, drunkenness, revellings . . . they which do such things shall not inherit the kingdom of God." – Galatians 5:19-21**

God is warning us that these fleshly desires, all of which we see rising in public around us today, herald the perverted new world of disorder that will eventually be instituted by the Antichrist. Fleshly desires are the weapons the enemy uses to kill the collective conscience of our Judeo-Christian heritage, destroy our civilized conduct and emotionally separate us from one another.

These controversial leeches of wickedness cause man to subtly depart from the protective common sense of tradition and reverse his course, sliding down instead into the seedy strife of destructive perversion that is manifested in homosexuality, lesbianism, incest and bestiality – a living hell where man is completely out of order. In this place, man ceases to have any dominion that God granted him in Genesis 1:28, for he has become nothing more than an animal himself.

Here in Revelation 13:9-10, God wants us to truly understand and broaden our knowledge of the destructive disorder we see rising all around us – and patiently pray for those who are being led captive to break free through Christ Jesus. Notice that our Lord concludes this passage by reminding us that, in the midst of this spiritual warfare, those who are captive can supernaturally break free from their bondage and persevere against it by placing their trust (faith) in Jesus Christ.

In this war, the Apostle Paul explains that the undefeatable power of Jesus' love transforms us into more than conquerors over the weapons of the enemy:

> "Who shall separate us from the love of Christ? Shall tribulation, or distress, or persecution, or famine, or nakedness, or peril, or sword? As it is written, for Thy sake we are killed all the day long; we are accounted as sheep for the slaughter. Nay, in all these things we are more than conquerors through Him that loved us. For I am persuaded, that neither death, nor life, nor angels, nor principalities, nor powers, nor things present, not things to come, nor height, nor depth, nor any other creature, shall be able to separate us from the love of God, which is in Christ Jesus our Lord." – Romans 8:35-39

Through the saving love of Jesus Christ, we are spiritually remade into new creatures in the image of God. Our Savior is reminding us that our fortitude and endurance – purchased by Jesus shedding His blood on the Cross for us – should, in turn, model His blameless life: a life completely and humbly consecrated to Jehovah God, a pure and sacred life, totally separated from the masses of this world.

This is the life we are called to lead, especially in the last days. A walk that peacefully treads against the grain of a culture in decline. A voice that boldly speaks a living testimony of Jesus Christ. A heart that humbly proclaims His love to the masses. Our Savior first chose us to lead this life, before we chose Him. Jesus summarizes this life as a walk that contradicts everything the world teaches:

> "So the last shall be first, and the first last: for many be called, but few chosen." – Matthew 20:16

That's not all, however, for God is speaking here to a variety of hearts (ears) that operate (understand) at three different degrees of hearing (perception).

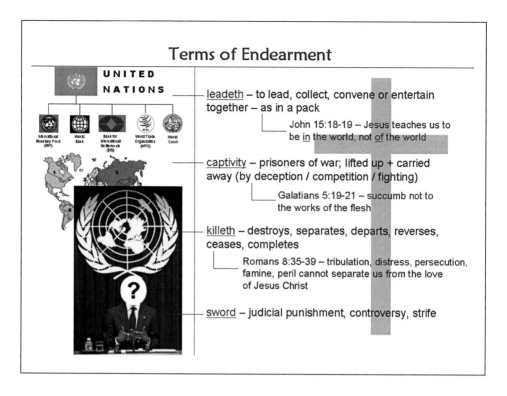

Terms of Endearment

UNITED NATIONS

International Monetary Fund (IMF) · World Bank · Bank for International Settlements (BIS) · World Trade Organization (WTO) · World Court

leadeth – to lead, collect, convene or entertain together – as in a pack

    John 15:18-19 – Jesus teaches us to be in the world, not of the world

captivity – prisoners of war; lifted up + carried away (by deception / competition / fighting)

    Galatians 5:19-21 – succumb not to the works of the flesh

killeth – destroys, separates, departs, reverses, ceases, completes

    Romans 8:35-39 – tribulation, distress, persecution, famine, peril cannot separate us from the love of Jesus Christ

sword – judicial punishment, controversy, strife

First, we hear our Savior strongly urging those of us who are already attentive and aware to remain patiently faithful for His glorious coming and return. We saints are to be living testimonies of His love to those around us. Next, we can hear our Lord threatening the wicked to depart from their evil ways and turn their hearts to Him before the coming judgment. We saints are to boldly warn those around us.

Finally, we hear God comforting all of those who have been left behind, whose hearts (their spiritual ears) have now been opened so that they can perceive (hear) the Truth being revealed here. The Lord wants them to understand that they, as saints, must now patiently endure trials and persecution so that *they* can be living testimonies of His love to those around them. Their ability to suffer persecution for their testimony will bring many to a saving knowledge in the last days.

God will allow this persecution because it is only temporary and – most importantly – this trial by fire will expose those who dwell on the earth for who they truly are. The Lord promises to not only resurrect these martyred saints following this short period of suffering, He also promises them a special role in His kingdom that awaits them:

> **"And I saw thrones, and they sat upon them, and judgment was given unto them: and I saw the souls of them that were beheaded for the witness of Jesus, and for the Word of God, and which had not worshipped the beast, neither his image, neither had received his mark upon their foreheads, or in their hands; and they lived and reigned with Christ a thousand years." – Revelation 20:4**

Hallelujah! These suffering saints of the last days should recognize that they are *called* – specially chosen and trusted by God for such a time as this – to endure. Their loyal endurance will win through the coming persecution, but they must realize that even those whose names are written in the Lamb's book of life must endure martyrdom. By recognizing that the pain of martyrdom is the will of God for their lives, these saints will show their patience, prove their faith – and testify to everyone of the one true, living God whose Name is Jehovah.

In the new world of disorder, God is reminding all of us as saints that we have been called to warn others about the dangers that lie ahead. The Lord strategically inserts His reminder at this stage of John's vision to prepare us for another great danger that is coming, an enemy that is more spiritually complex than anything man has ever seen.

Our discernment is about to be tested. God is telling us to kick it up a notch, for another beast is rising – a horrible, sinister, complex system that is bred directly from the same bloodline of the first beast.

The Beast
of the Earth

FALSE PROPHET

The Rise of the
False Prophet

CHAPTER 7

The Beast Coming
Up Out of the Earth

Down through the years, man has desired to create his own utopian vision of peace and happiness. The formation of a new world order has been a common theme shared over time by different leaders to display a heaven here on earth created by man himself, with no help from God.

Desiring the New World Order – a World Utopia

 "The *world order* which we seek is the cooperation of free countries, working together in a friendly, civilized society . . ." Franklin D. Roosevelt – State of the Union address, January 6, 1941

 "National Socialism will use its own revolution for the establishing of a *new world order*." Adolf Hitler – speech in Munich, World War II

 "Our nation is uniquely endowed to play a creative and decisive role in the *new world order* which is taking form around us" Henry Kissinger Seattle – Post Intelligencer 1975

 "We must establish a *new world order* based on justice, on equity, and on peace" Fidel Castro – speech to the United Nations, 1979

 "We are moving toward a *new world order*, the world of communism. We shall never turn off that road." Mikhail Gorbachev – speech to Politburo in Moscow, 1987

 "What is at stake is more than one small country; it is a big idea: a *new world order*, where diverse nations are drawn together in common cause to achieve the universal aspirations of mankind . . ." George H.W. Bush – State of the Union address, January 6, 1991

 "Now we can see a new world coming into view. A world in which there is the very real prospect of a *new world order* . . . " George H.W. Bush – after defeating Iraq in Gulf War I, March 1991

At this stage in Revelation 13, their desires have now become reality. However, this is no utopia.

Their New World Order is a secular place of disorder, dominated by a godless one-world political and economic system where man worships his own greed. As the first beast rises out of the sea, John explains that the Antichrist will assume world leadership by rising in stature and influence over the *secular lives* of people, and by positioning himself to influence the *spiritual lives* of people. His rise into leadership doesn't simply happen overnight. His ascendancy into leadership over mankind follows a satanic process of *spiritual* conditioning through *secular* humanism.

Think through this for a moment. For mankind to fully accept the Antichrist and give him the leadership he craves, the world must be conditioned in a *secular* way that creates a *spiritual* void, a *spiritual* emptiness, in people's lives.

God created people in such a way that all of us inherently know that there is more to life than material things. God created man to intrinsically recognize that fulfillment doesn't come from the things we possess, but rather by the relationship we have with Him. In fact, Jesus warns us against allowing our possessions to take possession of us:

> **"Take heed, and beware of covetousness: for a man's life consisteth not in the abundance of the things which he possesseth." – Luke 12:15**

Without relationship with God, man is an empty being. This is the truth of who we are as beings created in God's image. Satan knows this. As the power behind the Antichrist, he conditions the secular man to be spiritually empty through his craving for worldly wealth and power. The New Testament explains that this spiritual emptiness is manifested in the secular world through three different forms of lust:

> **"For all that is in the world, the lust of the flesh, and the lust of the eyes, and the pride of life, is not of the Father, but is of the world." – 1 John 2:16**

The secular one-world political and economic system of the Antichrist operates and thrives off these three lusts, which open a deep spiritual void in the masses that are being manipulated. As John opens the second half of his vision, we see the Antichrist filling this lustful spiritual void with a series of false religions that all *promise* relationship with God, but actually *collaborate* together as one religious system that push man further into the empty abyss of his own worldly cravings. The spiritual source of this demonic collaboration of false religions is found in the secular humanism that we see rising around us today.

John describes this collaboration of false religions coming up as another beast:

> **"And I beheld another beast coming up out of the earth; and he had two horns like a lamb, and he spake as a dragon."** – Revelation 13:11

Look at what John is saying closely, because there is a lot of meat to digest here. Notice that he says, "I *beheld* . . ." *Beheld* here in the ancient Greek means *to discern*, to *stare*, to *know*. The Holy Spirit is using some powerful expressions here to explain to us that we must use discernment to see this second beast, to know it and recognize it.

John not only discerns and recognizes that this beast is another type of system, he is staring at it – *studying* it – so that he can know and understand exactly what it is and specifically how it works. As Christians, we too must carefully study the current events going on today such that we can understand exactly what is really happening around us and specifically how it is working.

Notice that John immediately recognizes that this is *another beast* – a *different* one. He makes it clear that this system is something totally different than the political and economic system he saw rising out of the sea earlier. But his Greek term *beast* here has the same exact two meanings it did in verse one – *a dangerous animal* and *destruction*. This system represents an entirely different danger that also leads to destruction.

And whereas the first beast – the dangerous and destructive global political and economic system – *rose* out of the *sea*, which represents sinful mankind, this second form of danger and destruction is *coming up* out of the *earth*. *Coming up* here means to *grow, ascend, climb up*. *Earth* here means the soil, as in *regions*.

Whereas the first system rises out of the people, this second system grows out of the political and economic operations of the ten regions of the first system. This is an important fact to remember. John tells us here that we must discern and recognize a different type of danger and destruction from another system that grows and ascends out of the political and economic behaviors of the antichrist system. In other words, *the source of the second beast is the first beast*.

In his study *Revelation 13: Closer Home Than We Think*, David A. DePra explains that "the *coming up out of the earth* here shows that this *coming up* denotes a *progression*. There is a *coming up*, as opposed to being there all of a sudden. So everything this beast represents is *progressive in nature* – this beast is progressing toward maturity, just as the first beast is progressing toward maturity." [54]

This helps us understand a lot about this second beast. Follow through the logic here. The Antichrist has established a shallow world of spiritual disorder, a secular global system of politics and economics where everyone is covetously judged by their own outward appearance of wealth and power. Recall also that in verses six and seven, John explains how this secular culture will trash any remaining Judeo-Christian values, creating a dark place where all morality is relative, nothing is absolute truth.

This will be a time when evil is called good, and good evil – a confusing time that God specifically warns us about:

> "Therefore My people are gone into captivity, because they have no knowledge, and their honorable men are famished, and their multitude dried up with thirst. Therefore hell hath enlarged herself, and opened her mouth without measure: and their glory, and their multitude, and their pomp, and he that rejoiceth, shall descend into it . . . Woe unto them that draw iniquity with cords of vanity, and sin as it were with a cart rope . . . Woe unto them *that call evil good, and good evil*; that put darkness for light, and light for darkness, that put bitter for sweet, and sweet for bitter! Woe unto them that are wise in their own eyes, and prudent in their own sight!" – Isaiah 5:13, 14, 18, 20, 21

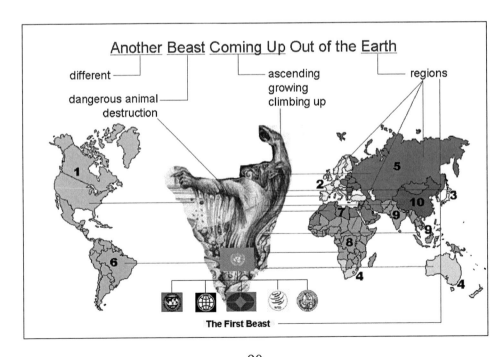

Another Beast Coming Up Out of the Earth

different — dangerous animal — destruction — ascending, growing, climbing up — regions

The First Beast

90

By overlaying the secular template of Revelation 13 across these passages in Isaiah 5, we see that both sets of Scripture describe a global political and economic system (the first beast) constructed upon a secular worldview that is spiritually empty.

Under the Antichrist, all politics and economics are driven entirely by secular rationale and reason – the *cords of vanity* that are corrupted by the three forms of lust used to fill spiritual voids. Although secular humanists claim no religious ties, humanism is actually a very strong religion because in his core beliefs, vanity leads the humanist to view *man as his own god*.

Rather than adhering to Judeo-Christian principles and spiritually seeking God's guidance, vanity drives the humanist held captive by the global system to trust only in himself. Vanity breeds his unbridled coveting of wealth and power. Vanity draws out his personal pride and public pomp. Vanity creates his craving for materialism through greedy consumerism. Vanity ultimately breeds his destructively competitive lifestyle, filled with stress and anxiety.

Bound by the vanity of the secular global system, the humanist captives no longer have knowledge of their true purpose in life. Their insatiable worship of materialism and pleasure drives them to become irreverent, rebellious, and uncivilized. Their public esteem (honor) suffers (famished) because their private self-respect has disappeared (dried up). Woe to them held captive by the first beast!

For the Christian, faith is our spiritual bloodline that flows from God's guidance. Faith is the substance of things hoped for, the evidence of things not seen, the essence of peace reflected through patience. As our faith enlarges, our trust in God deepens – and the love of Jesus Christ shapes our lives.

But for the humanist captives of the global system, vanity is their secular bloodline, and it flows from the guidance of the Antichrist. The further they fall away from God, the more they are deceived into *viewing themselves as gods*. As their vanity enlarges, their trust in the Antichrist deepens – and the spiritual void within their lives grows deeper too.

Why? Because the material prosperity and pleasures reaped from the science and technology of the global system cannot gratify man's intrinsic need for relationship with God. Materialism simply cannot answer the nagging questions about man's existence. People continue to search for the truth to life's deeper questions: Who am I? Why am I here? Where is my life going?

In this secular world of spiritual disorder and judgment, people still need an inner solution that offers true peace and fulfillment. Since Judeo-

Christian values no longer exist in this new secular world of disorder, where will they turn?

The second beast coming out of the earth is their answer. For the spiritually empty man, this dangerous religious system lies within the political and economic destruction rendered by the first system. Because the masses will need something to fill the spiritual void within their lives, this second beast represents some sort of spiritual system, some new form of religion that they can turn to – a corrupt one created out of the secular politics and economics of the Antichrist.

What does this spiritual system look like? Notice how John points out that, unlike the first beast that had ten horns, this beast has only *two horns*. In Scripture, the number *two* always represents *unity*, *division* and *witnessing*. The *horns* here denote the *projection of power*. In other words, this spiritual system projects the power to unify, divide and witness.

In a secular world of disorder, this system will appear to *unify* everyone. People will turn to this new form of religion because it tolerates everyone, regardless of their physical appearance, the clothes they wear, what or how they eat, their personal lifestyle, or how much money they have. This new spirituality will collaborate with all other faiths, regardless of doctrine, because in the new secular world of disorder there is no absolute truth, so everyone worships the same god – which is, ultimately, themselves!

People will run to this new form of religion that is created from global politics and economics because it is a progressive system that upholds sin in the name of *freedom* and *rights*, a progressive spirituality that frowns upon righteousness by calling it *ignorance*. It represents a "feel-good" form of love that rejoices in values such as gay marriage – which it interprets as freedom and open-mindedness. This form of religion will permit the world to cast off any morale restraints. This new spirituality will allow man to finally *do as he pleases* – and give him freedom!

In other words, this deceptive outward appearance of "unity" will inwardly construct a spiritual anarchy within the souls of each person. This new form of spirituality will *accept* and *promote* the rebellious behavior of the carnal man, driven by the secular behaviors of the global system, to the point that:

> "... every man did that which was right in his own eyes."
> – Judges 17:6

Sound familiar? We can already see these "unifying" characteristics of the two horns of the second beast rising up in liberal circles around us today, can't we?

We already hear the ecumenical voices of both liberal religious and secular organizations across the world working to unite different religious beliefs, different doctrines, different morals, different truths. These attempts at unity represent the exact form of religion that Paul warns us will rise in the perilous times of the last days:

> "Traitors, heady, highminded, lovers of pleasures more than lovers of God; having a form of godliness, but denying the power thereof: from such turn away." – 2 Timothy 3:4-5

Paul's warning here reminds us that this liberal religious system has *two* horns. This is significant, because lurking just beneath its surface of ecumenical unity, this system also projects the power to *divide* those people who don't "fit in."

This new form of spirituality is a compromised soup of beliefs, doctrines, morals and truths that grow out of the secular behaviors (those worldly vanities of lust of the flesh, lust of the eyes, and pride of life) of the global system driven by the Antichrist. This means that the compromising beliefs, doctrines, morals and truths of this new liberal religion are based in the vanities of secular behavior.

Since everyone in the secular global system is covetously judged by their own outward appearance of wealth and power, then believers in this new liberal religion will also be covetously judged by their own outward appearance of wealth and power. Both systems grow out of the same seeds of vanity, so this new form of religion judges others by the same template as its secular counterpart.

When its liberal believers gather to unite for various ecumenical causes, their social behaviors and mannerisms will subtly separate those gathering into informal classes, dividing those who are perceived to be economically and politically poor from those who appear to be economically and politically wealthy. People who present themselves as physically or emotionally weak will be subtly separated from those who are seen as mentally and physically disciplined.

Through all of its deceptive outward appearances of unity, this new form of religion will be a spiritual *witness* to everyone of the inner peace that supposedly comes from the material blessings found in the political power and economic wealth gained only through covetous competition in the global system. This liberal religion will testify of the spiritual wellness that is supposedly reaped from the mental and physical discipline required to compete in the global system.

In other words, this new form of religion promises to fill the spiritual emptiness of people by teaching them an "enlightened" way to pursue the secular behaviors of the global system of the Antichrist – the same behaviors that caused their emptiness in the first place. The second beast is a witness for the first beast.

But that's not all. The deception behind this destructive new spirituality is highly complex, because John describes the horns of this second beast as being *like those of a lamb. Lamb* here in the Greek means *to take up or away, to raise the voice, to keep the mind in suspense, to expiate sin.*

A lamb implies a gentle nature, a character of innocence that inherently points people to the office of Christ, our Savior, the true Messiah. This liberal religious system projects a deceptively gentle nature, an innocence and goodness that attracts and raises a person's spiritual well-being. It appears to point to the office of a savior that can cleanse man of sin, a messiah that can take man's spirit up and away from the anxiety and stress of this world.

However, this appearance of innocent goodness is a deception, because the true Church – all the devout Christians who followed Jesus Christ as their Savior – is already gone, taken earlier by the Lord in the Rapture

94

before the appearance of the Antichrist:

> "For the Lord Himself shall descend from heaven with a shout, with the voice of the archangel, and with the trump of God: and the dead in Christ shall rise first: Then we which are alive and remain shall be caught up together with them in the clouds, to meet the Lord in the air: and so shall we ever be with the Lord . . . behold, a door was opened in heaven: and the first voice which I heard was as it were of a trumpet talking with me; which said, Come up hither, and I will shew thee things which must be hereafter." – 1 Thessalonians 4:16-17, Revelation 4:1-2

From this perspective, let's follow through the religious deception that is going on here. All Judeo-Christian values and the Christian worldview have been trashed and removed by the secular vanity of the global system. All relationships in this new world of disorder are rooted and built upon the coveting of wealth and power. Man is left spiritually empty, and all that is left for him to turn to are secular behaviors deceptively repackaged as religious rituals.

In the midst of all this, John says that this beast *speaks as a dragon*. This means that Satan speaks through this dangerous spiritual system. How do we know this? The Scriptures explain that this dragon is Satan himself:

> "And the great dragon was cast out, that old serpent, called the Devil, and Satan, which deceiveth the whole world: he was cast out into the earth, and his angels were cast out with him . . . And he laid hold on the dragon, that old serpent, which is the Devil, and Satan . . ." – Revelation 12:9, 20:2

Why is it so important to recognize this? Because Jesus identifies Satan as the father of lies:

> "Ye are of your father the devil . . . When he speaketh a lie, he speaketh of his own: for he is a liar, and the father of it." – John 8:44

In other words, this new form of religion looks loving, kind, tolerant and innocent, but its teachings are corrupt and its doctrine is rotten from the inside out. All of its spiritual answers are lies. This second beast is a satanic spiritual system that lies to people about their questions of life, their meaning and purpose for living. And these satanic lies are deceptively filtered through the vanity of the global political and economic system – which is also satanic, because John explained to us in Revelation 13:2 how that system draws its power and authority from Satan as well.

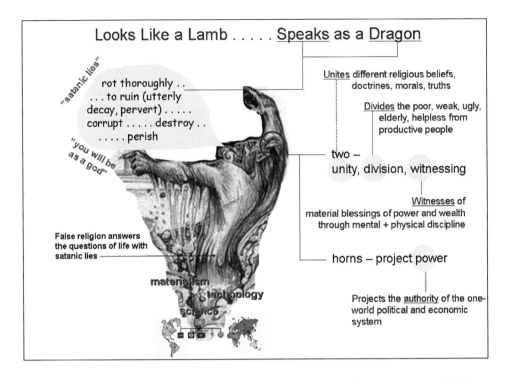

Looks Like a Lamb . . . . . Speaks as a Dragon

"satanic lies"

rot thoroughly . .
. . . to ruin (utterly
decay, pervert) . . . . .
corrupt . . . . . destroy . .
. . . . . perish

"you will be as a god"

False religion answers
the questions of life with
satanic lies

materialism
technology
science

Unites different religious beliefs,
doctrines, morals, truths

Divides the poor, weak, ugly,
elderly, helpless from
productive people

two —
unity, division, witnessing

Witnesses of
material blessings of power and wealth
through mental + physical discipline

horns – project power

Projects the authority of the one-
world political and economic
system

What we see happening here is the global stage being set to recycle the original temptation that first occurred with Eve:

> "And the woman said unto the serpent, We may eat of the fruit of the trees of the garden: But of the fruit of the tree which is in the midst of the garden, God hath said, Ye shall not eat of it, neither shall ye touch it, lest ye die. And the serpent said unto the woman, Ye shall not surely die: For God doth know that in the day ye eat thereof, then your eyes shall be opened, and *ye shall be as gods*, knowing good and evil." Genesis 3:2-5

Man is a spiritually hungry being, and these secular teachings and doctrines are the fruits that Satan wants to feed him. They *look* good to eat, they *appear* to be good for a person. But, in fact, they represent a false spirituality that is man-based – a spiritual disorder that *tempts man to be his own god*.

To Eve, it is "eat the fruit, it looks good, it will open your eyes and you shall be as gods." To the secular man, it is "practice these (false) beliefs, they will open your eyes, you will achieve enlightenment and you shall be as gods."

It's all the same satanic fruit that has been seductively offered to man by the enemy, repeatedly down through the ages. Though the fruit comes in various colors, flavors, teachings, beliefs, doctrines and practices, the source of all of it is the same – it is all a satanic lie.

The two horns on this second beast also reflect how Satan markets his corrupt fruit through two different sets of religious ceremonies. The horns are on top of the head. As this beast climbs up out of the first system, the first thing being exposed to John's eyes are its two horns. The two horns are the first things that are seen, meaning they have been seen longer than any other portion of this beast, i.e. they have been around (existed) longer than any other portion of this system.

So these two horns represent ancient dual religious ceremonies that have been, and still are, performed throughout the world in rituals that date back to antiquity. One ceremony involves the occult and mysticism, while the other is found in organized religion.

At first glance, these two sets of ritualistic ceremonies would appear to be diametrically opposed to one another. The practice of the occult and mysticism is always connected with the dark side: witches, covens, sorcery, demons and sinister powers, the path to evil. But organized religion, on the other hand, is typically connected to respect and dignity: ministers, priests, congregations, enlightenment toward God, the path to goodness.

However, deeper inspection of both sets of ceremonies through the lens of the Scriptures reveals that, in the spiritual realm, they all worship at the same altar. Jesus says to us:

> **"I am the Way, the Truth, and the Life: no man cometh unto the Father, but by me." – John 14:6**

Our Savior explains that there is *only one way* to get to Jehovah, the One True and Almighty God, and that is through Him alone. The Lord is telling us that *any* occult, mystical or religious practice that promises to get to God by another route is nothing more than a lie. Since Jesus identifies Satan as the father of lies, that means any occult, mystical or religious ceremony that tries to get to God by another means is actually an instrument of Satan, its father.

Now test the two horns against this Scriptural truth.

Obviously, the darkness associated with the occult and mysticism does not represent truth. The Bible strictly warns us against these pagan practices:

> **"A man also or woman that hath a familiar spirit, or that is a wizard, shall surely be put to death: they shall stone them with stones: their blood shall be upon them . . . There shall not be found among you . . . a charmer, or a consulter with familiar spirits, or a wizard . . . for all that do these things are an abomination unto the Lord . . ." – Leviticus 20:27, Deuteronomy 18:11**

Sin literally entered our world through the first practice of the occult, when Adam and Eve fell in the Garden of Eden in Genesis 3:1-7. They succumbed to the mystical lie that they could *be as gods* and allowed demon spirits into their lives. Because they were no longer pure, God physically drove them out of His Garden for their failure (see the "Two Horns Down Through Time" chart).

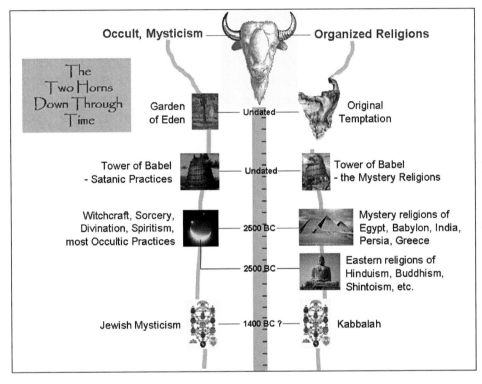

The human lifeline became tainted and demonic activity reappeared in their oldest son Cain, who committed the first murder in Genesis 4:8. From there, man's wickedness sank into satanic worship rituals that were so perverted that demons literally left their first estate (Jude 6) and mated with human women in Genesis 6:2-4. Their offspring were the *giants*, enormous and wicked partial-human/partial-demon creatures that began to dominate the world. Mankind was so saturated with evil (Genesis 6:5) that these horrific perversions led to the destruction of the entire planet in the great Flood of Noah's day in Genesis 7.

All human and animal life that existed in the natural world was wiped out in the Flood, except for Noah and his family. In the supernatural realm, this left the remaining demon spirits without hosts to inhabit, so they began searching for humans they could leech to (Matthew 12:43-45). They found one in Noah's son Ham in Genesis 9:22-24. The human lifeline was again tainted as demonic activity reappeared through his son Canaan and his grandson Nimrod, who built the Tower of Babel in Genesis 11.

As we discussed earlier in Chapter 5, Nimrod was the first prophetic shadow-in-type of the Antichrist that eventually rises to power in Revelation 13. Genesis 11:1-4 explains how he established a political and economic system over all the people. Jewish sages explain that in Genesis 11:4-6, Nimrod revived all of the satanic perversions that brought on Noah's flood in the first place, constructing the Tower of Babel as a satanic temple to introduce the occult, mystical practices and witchcraft.

Through the operations of the Tower, Nimrod organized satanic mystery religions based upon the occult and witchcraft to institute sexual perversion, prostitution, and human sacrifices (see the "Two Horns Down Through Time" chart).

When God scattered mankind across the earth in Genesis 11:8-9, they took with them the witchcraft, sorcery, divination, spiritism, and other occult practices they had learned through the organized mystery religions in Babel. These practices became the roots of all the mystery religions that were passed down through time, starting as far back as 4,500 years ago in Egypt, then Babylon, India, Persia, and Greece. This explains why the design of the pyramids in Egypt matches the basic configuration of the ziggurats found in the Middle East, Asia, Central America and South America.

Widely disparate peoples, in distant lands, speaking different languages, yet they all constructed pagan temples based upon the original design of the Tower of Babel. They all instituted religious ceremonies based upon the same practices of witchcraft, sorcery, divination, and spiritism.

Practicing the same sexual perversions as their mystical ancestors before the Flood, the ancient pagans gave birth to the evil Anakim and other tribes of giants that Moses, Joshua, and David defeated in the Old Testament. Using the same witchcraft as their mystical ancestors before the Flood, the ancient pagans reintroduced the sacrifice of humans that was later practiced by the giants, the Canaanites, Sodom and Gomorrah, the Incas, Aztecs, and Mayans.

Just as their mystical ancestors before them were destroyed in the Flood because of their perversion, all of these tribes were eventually erased by God because of their perversion. In the spiritual realm, each removal of a tribe launched the same search that happened after the Flood, as the demons that inhabited those ancient pagans roamed the planet until they could find other human hosts.

This cycle has been repeated over and over down through the ages of time, as the same satanic ceremonies reappear in common rituals found in both the occult and organized religions across the world. Over time, these ancient satanic ceremonies evolved into the origins of all the widely respected Eastern religions of Hinduism, Buddhism, Shintoism, etc. (see the "Two Horns Down Through Time" chart).

The names of the rituals may change, the faces that participate and the formats they follow may differ, but their core beliefs and fundamental practices remain unchanged. They planted the ancient origins of Jewish mysticism found in the practice of Kabbalah. They were the roots of Gnosticism that Paul fought against in the New Testament over 1,900 years ago. They form the heritage upon which the Illuminati, Freemasonry, Skull & Bones, the Thule Society, Theosophy and all other secret societies are organized. They are the deeper source of the political principles of Marxism, Darwinism, and secular humanism.

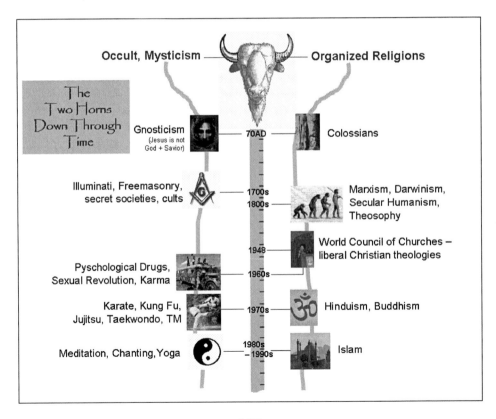

It is ultimately from these political principles that we are witnessing the two horns of the second beast coming up all around us today. The false fruits of these political principles are being used to blend a *secular* worldview into liberal *spiritual* beliefs.

This liberal secular/spiritual worldview has been the source of the cultural explosions of psychological drug use, the sexual revolution and the acceptance of karma, karate, kung fu, jujitsu, taekwondo, transcendental mediation, yoga and the other Eastern practices now influencing our society.

This same secular/spiritual worldview feeds the ecumenical theology found in liberal Christian doctrines, such as those of the apostate Episcopal and Presbyterian denominations and the World Council of Churches (see the "Two Horns Down Through Time" chart). It blasphemes the Scriptures with a feminist edge and ordains homosexuality from the pulpit.

All of the cultural practices and religious theologies that we see following this liberal secular/spiritual worldview promise to connect man to God by another route other than Jesus Christ. They are all lies. They are all instruments of Satan. These satanic fruits all paint portraits of morality that is relative, that nothing is absolute truth.

The great spiritual irony in all of this is that the man who eats from these satanic fruits, in search of the knowledge of good and evil, can no longer discern between good and evil. He becomes a blind and *spiritually disordered* religious person that can fall prey to the warning of Isaiah 5: he calls evil good and good evil.

We already see this state of spiritual disorder rising in people all around us. We must recognize this condition for what it really is: each stage of decline into further spiritual disorder exposes more of the two horns of the second beast. The deeper that spiritual disorder occurs on a mass scale, the more of the two horns of the second beast we see coming up out of the earth.

CHAPTER 8

A Spiritual Blur Occurs

Spiritual disorder blurs the lines between good and evil. This means that religious and secular lines blur as well, because *spiritual disorder applies a secular worldview to religious ritual.* For this reason, spiritual disorder is primarily manifested in religious activities as a sense of spiritual impatience – the exact opposite of the peace that surpasses all understanding that is found only in true spiritual order with God.

Patience is no longer a virtue for a spiritually disordered person that practices religion, because the drive for instant gratification, fed from their secular worldview, bleeds over into their spiritual ceremonies. On the outside, they appear to practice a form of godliness. But on the inside, they remain bound to the insecurities rooted in their secular worldview.

This impatient and stressful nature is exactly the opposite of God's divine nature for us, described in the New Testament:

> **"Whereby are given unto us exceeding great and precious promises: that by these ye might be partakers of *the divine nature*, having escaped the corruption that is in the world through lust. And beside this, giving all diligence, add to your faith virtue; and to virtue knowledge; And to knowledge temperance; and to temperance patience; and to patience godliness; And to godliness brotherly kindness; and to brotherly kindness charity. For if these things be in you, and abound, they make you that ye shall neither be barren nor unfruitful in the knowledge of our Lord Jesus Christ." – 2 Peter 1:4-8**

Because spiritual disorder calls evil good and good evil, it creates a fleshly nature in people that is exactly the opposite of God's divine nature for them. Our Savior's divine nature of spiritual order represents His spiritual governance over a person, His spiritual management of their personal character, His spiritual Truth in their personal beliefs, His spiritual purity in their personal activities, His spiritual control over their personal life.

In contrast, spiritual disorder represents imperfect worldly governance over someone's personal character, where fleshly lies blur their personal beliefs, carnal dishonesty blurs their personal activities, inner rebellion and anarchy blur their personal life.

As humans living in a fallen world, we all fight a complex personal battle for spiritual order over inner chaos, the war for personal governance over fleshly rebellion. The Apostle Paul details the personal complexity we all face in the battle for spiritual order:

> "But sin, that it might appear sin, working death in me by that which is good; that sin by the commandment might become exceeding sinful. For we know that the law is spiritual: but I am carnal, sold under sin. For that which I do I allow not: for what I would, that do I not; but what I hate, that do I. If then I do that which I would not, I consent unto the law that it is good. Now then it is no more I that do it, but sin that dwelleth in me. For I know that in me (that is, in my flesh) dwelleth no good thing: for to will is present with me; but how to perform that which is good I find not.
>
> "For the good that I would I do not: but the evil which I would not, that I do. Now if I do that I would not, it is no more I that do it, but sin that dwelleth in me. I find then a law, that, when I would do good, evil is present with me. For I delight in the law of God after the inward man: but I see another law in my members, warring against the law of my mind, and bringing me into captivity to the law of sin which is in my members. O wretched man that I am! Who shall deliver me from the body of this death?" – Romans 7:13-24

Imperfect governance is no different than imperfect government – it *always* leads to rebellion and anarchy. Because spiritually disordered people allow imperfect governance over their personal lives, they become rebellious to the Truth of the Scriptures.

This is why the walk of spiritually disordered people does not match their talk. On the outside they may practice religious rituals, but on the inside they continue to judge everyone else on their looks, their possessions and their wealth. Most importantly, rather than turning to the Bible that they profess for guidance, they actually turn to cultural influences for their role models, their leadership, the way they live their lives.

The Divine Nature of Spiritual Order	The Fleshly Nature Spiritual Disorder
• Spiritual management – of personal character	• Imperfect governance – over personal character
• Spiritual Truth – in their personal beliefs	• Spiritual lies – in their personal beliefs
• Spiritual purity – in their personal activities	• Spiritual dishonesty – in their personal activities
• Control – over their personal life	• Rebellion and anarchy – in their personal life
• Spiritual governance – over a person	

What are the cultural influences of our day teaching them?

Cultural influences have become the "sources of significant influence" according to George Barna, the founder of a market research firm specializing in studying the religious beliefs and behavior of Americans, and the intersection of faith and culture.[55]

He conducted a survey in 2004 on the institutions having the heaviest influence on our culture. In a positive message from his survey, Barna discovered that morals are typically instilled in a person before the age of 9, and their religious view of the Church is typically established before the age of 12. This confirms the reason why the Bible teaches:

"Train up a child in the way he should go: and when he is old, he will not depart from it." – Proverbs 22:6

But another message that the survey revealed was very disturbing. Of the actual institutions that had the most profound impact in establishing those morals and religious views, the Church *wasn't even listed in the top 10.* The survey revealed that the top cultural influences that are feeding our society's view of morality and the church are:

105

1. Movies	5. Sports	9. Food/Cuisine
2. Television	6. Entertainment	10. Financial management
3. Music	7. Fashion	
4. News	8. Fitness	

This reveals that our society is already drowning in spiritual disorder. How do we know this? In his study *Media and Worldviews*, Kerby Anderson of Probe Ministries explains how these cultural influences are staining our moral and religious views as a society.[56]

"These media present an unreal view of our world, an oversimplified view of life that desensitizes its viewers," says Anderson. "The worldview of the media is 1) *Liberal*: 80% of news and television employees always vote for a Democratic candidate; 2) *Secular*: 86% of news and 93% of television employees seldom or never attend religious services, while 50% of news and 45% of television employees have no religious affiliation; and 3) *Humanistic*: 90% of news employees percent support a woman's right to choose." [57]

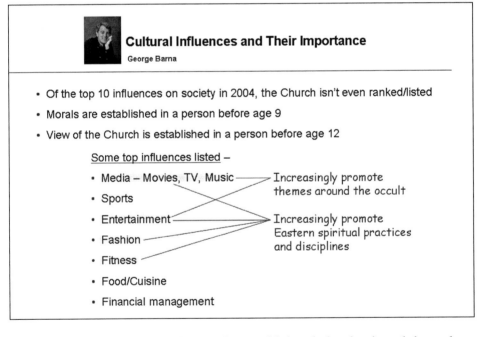

Cultural Influences and Their Importance

George Barna

- Of the top 10 influences on society in 2004, the Church isn't even ranked/listed
- Morals are established in a person before age 9
- View of the Church is established in a person before age 12

Some top influences listed –

- Media – Movies, TV, Music
- Sports
- Entertainment
- Fashion
- Fitness
- Food/Cuisine
- Financial management

Increasingly promote themes around the occult

Increasingly promote Eastern spiritual practices and disciplines

Anderson believes that the secular worldview being instituted through movies, television, music, etc. is built upon "naturalism ("The cosmos is all there is, ever was, and ever will be," said Carl Sagan), hedonism (pleasure is the ultimate good), syncretism (all religions are basically the same), pragmatism (whatever works is good), existentialism (existence precedes essence/there is no meaning), and postmodernism (there is no truth)."[58]

Consider this for a moment. What are some rebellious notions that were once considered inappropriate that are now accepted or becoming publicly accepted in our culture because of these sources of significant influence?

Through television and movie entertainment, some *secular* things that are immediately obvious are sexual promiscuity, homosexuality, offensive language, tattoos, continual partying and drug usage. But *spiritual* practices are becoming accepted too, including astrology, witchcraft and the occult (*Charmed*, the *Harry Potter* series, the *Lord of the Rings* trilogy), meditation (yoga), and eastern beliefs (feng shei). The same themes permeate sports entertainment, as seen in gambling (World Series of Poker), drug usage (steroids), offensive language, and decadent lifestyles (rebellious hip-hop and thugs).

How much of this is anti-Christian behavior that was once rejected and unacceptable in our society?

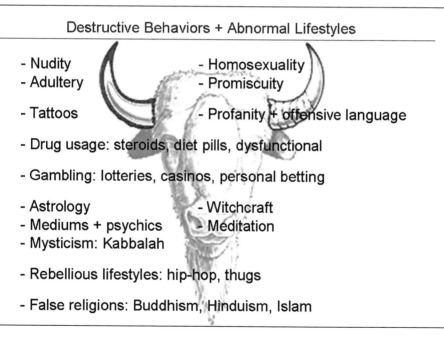

Destructive Behaviors + Abnormal Lifestyles

- Nudity
- Adultery
- Homosexuality
- Promiscuity
- Tattoos
- Profanity + offensive language
- Drug usage: steroids, diet pills, dysfunctional
- Gambling: lotteries, casinos, personal betting
- Astrology
- Mediums + psychics
- Mysticism: Kabbalah
- Witchcraft
- Meditation
- Rebellious lifestyles: hip-hop, thugs
- False religions: Buddhism, Hinduism, Islam

As a society, we are living proof that cultural influences have power – tremendous power . . . over personal lives, over the masses. These sources of significant influence possess the literal power to change the way people perceive things, the way they live their lives, the way they think and feel about themselves. We see it happening all around us, in the destructive behaviors and abnormal lifestyles that are now becoming publicly acceptable to our society. Discerning eyes can see quite plainly that all of these deviant behaviors have their roots in the two horns of the second beast.

Discerning eyes can also begin to connect the dots here. *All* of these sources of significant influence are driven by the marketing technologies of the secular powers behind the global political and economic system. These sources of significant influence are the secular tools used by the global system to control what people buy and sell in every dimension of daily life.

They influence what we buy and sell in *physical* transactions tied to money, property and assets. They influence what we buy and sell in *emotional* transactions tied to fitness, diet and fashion. They influence what we buy and sell in *ideology* tied to our laws, personal rights, and freedoms. And they influence what we buy and sell in *spiritual* transactions tied to our purpose, well-being and worldview.

These sources of significant influence exercise secular power over the political views, the economic prosperity and the spiritual well-being of the people. In other words, these tools of cultural influence are the secular powers of the first beast that will be exercised by the second beast:

> **"And he exerciseth all the power of the first beast before him, and causeth the earth and them which dwell therein to worship the first beast, whose deadly wound was healed." – Revelation 13:12**

Notice that the second beast "exerciseth *all the power* of the first beast before him . . ." Let's digest this for a moment by considering how cultural influence guides spiritual disorder.

Spiritual disorder searches for solutions that offer *true* peace and fulfillment, freedom from the stress and anxiety of the world. Driven by the instant gratification that these cultural influences teach them, spiritually disordered people will attend religious rituals in search of immediate healing of everything, from their health problems to their financial difficulties.

And if they can't get their "fix" at church, these cultural influences quickly bleed them into other secular venues with answers, such as gambling for financial problems, or spiritual venues, such as mystical healing for health problems.

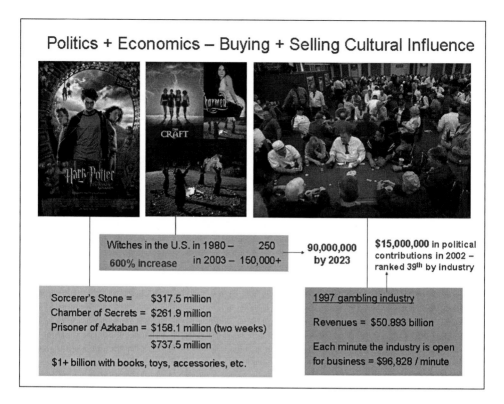

Politics + Economics – Buying + Selling Cultural Influence

Witches in the U.S. in 1980 – 250	
600% increase in 2003 – 150,000+	90,000,000 by 2023

$15,000,000 in political contributions in 2002 – ranked 39th by industry

Sorcerer's Stone = $317.5 million
Chamber of Secrets = $261.9 million
Prisoner of Azkaban = $158.1 million (two weeks)

$737.5 million
$1+ billion with books, toys, accessories, etc.

1997 gambling industry

Revenues = $50.893 billion

Each minute the industry is open for business = $96,828 / minute

Now fast forward to the Brave New World under the Antichrist. With the true Church raptured from its position of influence, this search for answers will create an inner confusion where the secular and the spiritual blur. In many respects, we can already see this blur happening around us.

We already see this blur in the search for secular and spiritual venues that tolerate everything regardless of moral values, because everything is treated as relative. We see this blur when inner confusion turns to liberal religious practices that collaborate with secular and spiritual venues regardless of doctrine, because everyone "worships the same god."

The blur of spiritual disorder flocks to *progressive* theologies that collaborate with secular and spiritual venues to uphold sin in the name of *freedom* and *rights*. The blur searches for liberal spirituality that is filtered through secular and spiritual venues, one that frowns upon righteousness by calling it *ignorance.*

The blur of inner confusion misapplies love by rejoicing in values such as gay marriage, seeing it as freedom and open-mindedness. The blur of spiritual disorder allows man to finally cast off any restraint of morality and allows him to do as he pleases. It gives him freedom! Freedom from the stress and anxiety of this world. Freedom that defines his purpose for living, his reason for being.

In other words, *spiritual disorder frees man from his true purpose for living, his real reason for being.* The spiritual irony here is that spiritually-disordered freedom actually binds man to the spiritual stress and anxiety he is trying to overcome. The Bible explains this inner state of confusion in greater detail:

> **"While they promise them liberty, they themselves are the servants of corruption: for of whom a man is overcome, of the same is he brought in bondage. For if after they have escaped the pollutions of the world through the knowledge of the Lord and Savior Jesus Christ, they are again entangled therein, and overcome, the latter end is worse with them than the beginning." – 2 Peter 2:19-20**

Now place this bondage of spiritual disorder in the context of Revelation 13:12, where John says this second beast causes the people to worship the first beast and immediately references the event that changes the world – "the deadly wound was healed." This significant point reminds us that the spiritual disorder of the masses – their mass desire to answer the personal questions of life, their mass desire to be free from the stress and anxiety of the secular pressures under the global system – all of this will reach a crescendo when the deadly wound occurs.

Before the spiritual earthquake of the deadly wound erupts, the masses must be conditioned in a *secular* way that creates a *spiritual* void of emptiness. They must be stained by the blur of spiritual disorder. We already see this conditioning stain taking place around us. We can already discern the two horns of the second beast coming up out of the earth as some sort of religious "one-stop shop" that promises to answer all of the problems of spiritual disorder.

Spiritual disorder will reach a crescendo on a global scale when the deadly wound of the first beast occurs. A personal spiritual earthquake will erupt inside every person when the orchestrated financial calamity explodes within the global system. You can already see it coming. Our entire world has become spiritually disordered, consumed with accumulating wealth and power. Work is the entire reason for existing. The masses, by and large, have lost real governance over their personal lives.

When the world's financial system collapses, their entire reason for existing will be challenged. They will abruptly lose everything that gives meaning to their lives: their jobs, their wealth, their sense of power over their personal sphere of influence. On the outside, the deadly wound will create financial and political calamity on a global scale. On the inside, it will wreak spiritual havoc on a personal inner level.

All of this devastation will leave the world at risk for total anarchy, unless all of the masses can somehow become united *internally* – somehow finding inner peace from their spiritual disorder.

But who has the power to do this? To whom will they turn? Enter the False Prophet.

CHAPTER 9

The Beast in Global Religion

Spiritual disorder will go into a mass meltdown when the global financial calamity happens.

Because of spiritual disorder, the masses are consumed with accumulating wealth and power, so work evolves into their entire reason for existing. Achieving material success through work – at any and all costs – replaces any real governance over personal life. When the world's financial system collapses during the deadly wound, their entire reason for existing will be challenged. They will lose everything that gives them meaning to their life – their job, their wealth, their sense of power over their personal sphere of influence.

When the Antichrist takes center stage to publicly reconstruct all of the social, political and economic arenas in the global system, the world will still be at risk for anarchy because of all this spiritual chaos – unless the people can be *spiritually* united to find inner peace from their rampant spiritual disorder.

The timing will be ideal for another individual to take center stage in the pulpit of religion, to publicly reconstruct the spirituality of the world. He will be the consummate priest of every religious ritual across the world, regardless of the disparate beliefs and ceremonial protocols, regardless of the culture. He will master the unending care of a pastor, to heal all the hurting people of every society and every nation. His voice will teach a doctrine that unites all the spiritual beliefs:

> **"And he exerciseth all the power of the first beast before him, and causeth the earth and them which dwell therein to worship the first beast, whose deadly wound was healed." – Revelation 13:12**

Enter the False Prophet. Because he shares the same source of satanic power as the Antichrist, he will bond with the son of perdition at the very core of his being. In fact, they will bond together so closely that the Scriptures here tell us that this False Prophet "exerciseth *all the power* of the first beast" . . . in other words, he possesses the same charisma, the same talents as the Antichrist. And because of these abilities, he is granted every privilege that the Antichrist enjoys, every freedom to do whatever he wishes.

In this balance of power, all of the Antichrist's social, political and economic influence is being delegated here to the False Prophet – a man who is so competent in manipulating *secular* politics and *secular* economics that he can *spiritually* influence and *spiritually* control the masses. His secular abilities and spiritual competence will give the False Prophet opportunities to bond with the masses in capacities that no one else can master. In return, the people will give him freedom to do as he pleases because of the trust he builds with them and between them.

Understand what is happening here in Revelation 13:12. The New World of Disorder is witnessing the global merger of Church and State, a formal delegation of social, political and economic powers handed down from the Antichrist to the religious system of the False Prophet. The False Prophet, in turn, will praise the spiritual importance of the Antichrist's social, political and economic solutions in people's lives. But most importantly, his Church will now possess State authority to invoke military might as needed upon the masses, to *enforce* those spiritual beliefs that support the world politics and world economics of the Antichrist.

Government and religious authorities will unite on a scale not seen since the ancient Roman Empire, as powerful social, political, economical and spiritual forces all converge together for one purpose: control. They will control people's money and finances, how much they earn, how much they save, how much they spend. They will control where they live their lives, how they live their lives, whether or not they marry, how many children they have, what they own, what they don't own.

And now they will control their spiritual beliefs, what they belief, where they worship, how they worship, who they worship with – absolute totalitarian control that has never been seen on a global scale before. This depth of power can only be accomplished when the second beast rises to center stage to implement the one-world religious system.

To our rational minds, this sounds pretty far-fetched, right? Surely something like this just can't happen. Nothing like this is really going on around us . . . or is it?

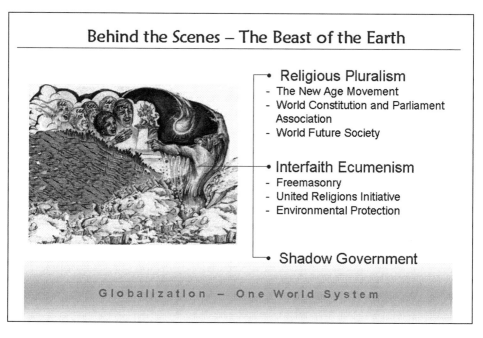

Behind the Scenes – The Beast of the Earth

Religious Pluralism
- The New Age Movement
- World Constitution and Parliament Association
- World Future Society

Interfaith Ecumenism
- Freemasonry
- United Religions Initiative
- Environmental Protection

Shadow Government

Globalization – One World System

We saw in the last chapter how this second beast coming up out of the earth is literally rising out of the unfulfilled spiritual emptiness of the people, an emptiness created and deepened by the secular worldview of the global system of the Antichrist that consumes their lives. The second beast is a destructive spiritual system created to fill that spiritual void in the masses – and Jesus warns us that it is worse than the first system:

> "When the unclean spirit is gone out of a man, he walketh through dry places, seeking rest, and finding none, he saith, I will return unto my house whence I came out. And when he cometh, he findeth it swept and garnished. Then goeth he, and taketh to him seven other spirits more wicked than himself; and they enter in, and dwell there: and *the last state of that man is worse than the first.*"
> – Luke 11:24-26

Our Lord emphasizes how the secular state of the first beast – operating with no belief in God, no reliance upon God – creates a deep spiritual disorder within people that leaves their souls empty. He also warns us that the false religion of this second beast, rising to fill that emptiness, is more devastating than the first beast.

115

We saw earlier that this second beast resembles the Lamb of God, Christ our Lord, but it speaks the lies of Satan, our Accuser. This satanic spirituality appears to be loving, kind, tolerant and innocent on the outside, but its teachings are corrupt and its doctrine is rotten from the inside out. It deceptively wreaks the souls of spiritually empty people, to the point they can no longer discern between good and evil.

The lies of this sinister form of religion leave people in a worse state of spiritual disorder than they were before, totally vulnerable to cultural influence. And in a world where there is no absolute truth, cultural influence will exercise its power over spirituality. In fact, the subliminal marketing power of the first beast is being deliberately *exercised* by the second beast in Revelation 13:12, where ". . . he *exerciseth all the power of the first beast before him . . .*" In other words, the False Prophet will actually market *the acceptance of spiritual disorder* through his satanic religious system.

With the true Church and the Holy Spirit gone, the False Prophet will become the default beacon of misguidance, the oracle of misdirection that all people follow. He will use cultural influence as a religious instrument to manipulate *everyone* into accepting spiritual disorder, as explained in Revelation 13:12, where "he . . . *causeth the earth and them which dwell therein to worship the first beast . . .*"

John is describing exactly how this deception will work. The False Prophet will use the social, political and economic cultural influences of the secular global system to *cause* the people to specifically worship the Antichrist. *Cause* in the ancient Greek means *makes.*

In other words, this sinister religious leader will *make* (manipulate) people to worship (as idols) secular lifestyles by endorsing liberal politics and economics that tolerate everything, because everything is relative. His social prosperity agenda will preach the free use of credit cards and plastic debt to instantly gratify material desires. His spiritual message will promote astrology, psychics, massage therapy, acupuncture and holistic medicine for healing everything from health to finances.

Sound familiar? We already see all sorts of secular and religious leaders following these themes, sounding off a public union of secular life with spiritual beliefs – a union that will eventually form the ecumenical body of the second beast, a global interfaith religion that will come up out of many disjointed secular and spiritual beliefs.

Behind the scenes, the organization that will create this interfaith religious system is already rising up out of the first beast. The UN Religious

Summit on World Peace (also known as the Millennium World Peace Summit of Religious and Spiritual Leaders) was held at the United Nations General Assembly Hall in New York on August 28-31, 2000.[59]

"This summit was attended by about 800 religious leaders and 1,000 observers from nearly 100 countries to focus on conflict resolution and reconciliation, as well as poverty and the environment," reports Tom Strode of the Baptist Press. "Leaders of the summit, however, agreed to establish a steering committee to find ways to collaborate with the United Nations." This is the second beast literally rising up out of the first beast. [60]

That's not all. Remember how this second beast will appear to be loving, kind, tolerant and innocent on the outside, but its teachings are corrupt and its doctrine is rotten from the inside out? Strode reports that "pronouncements were voiced by speakers from different religious traditions against attempts to convert people to other religions, and they met with strong affirmation . . . evangelicals especially would be targets for such sentiments, since they have sent missionaries throughout the world to proclaim the message of salvation exclusively by grace through faith in Jesus Christ." [61]

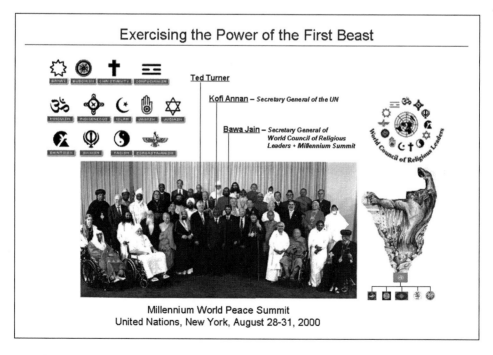

On numerous occasions, Strode reports that "there were very negative comments regarding proselytization . . . such declarations were met by

117

vigorous applause . . . that view was held by most of those at the conference . . . *representatives of Christianity* were joining that same call to denounce proselytizing, in particular Joan Brown Campbell. She came out with a strong statement that proselytizing must be renounced . . . the irony is that the UN charter documents affirm the right of people to change their religious beliefs." [62]

The bigger irony here is that these so-called "Christian representatives" are actually denying the teachings of Jesus Christ, the very One they are supposed to represent:

> **"Go ye unto all the world, and preach the gospel to every creature."**
> **– Mark 16:15**

Campbell is the former general secretary of the National Council of Churches, a coalition primarily made up of liberal Protestant denominations. Strode also reports that "some of the most rousing applause during the summit came when CNN founder Ted Turner denied the need for a blood sacrifice . . ." [63]

This applauded denial goes directly against the Scriptures, which teach that Jesus was the Perfect Sacrifice:

> **"Neither by the blood of goat and calves, but by His own blood He entered in once into the holy place, having obtained eternal redemption for us. For if the blood of bulls and of goats, and the ashes of an heifer sprinkling the unclean, sanctifieth to the purifying of the flesh: How much more shall the blood of Christ, Who through the eternal Spirit offered Himself without spot to God, purge your conscience from dead works to serve the living God?" – Hebrews 9:12-14**

Strode points out that "the weakest representation at the summit was from conservative Christianity . . . the focus was mostly on Eastern religions . . ." The week after this meeting, the Vatican released a 36-page directive targeting religious pluralism and pronouncing that salvation from sin is available *only through the Roman Catholic Church*. The statement said that not only other religions, but also Protestant churches, have weaknesses that endanger the eternal destiny of their members. [64]

This statement – again, proclaimed by a "Christian" body of authority – directly contradicts the teaching of Jesus, Who explains that *He* is the only way to salvation, not a church nor any other man-made religious organization:

"I am the Way, the Truth, and the Life: no man cometh unto the Father, but by me." – John 14:6

Behind the Scenes . . . . . Assembling the Pieces

- The Millennium World Peace Summit of Religious and Spiritual Leaders: held partly at the U.N. General Assembly Hall; attended by 800 religious leaders and 1,000 observers from 100 countries; focused on conflict resolution and reconciliation, poverty and the environment.

- The weakest representation was conservative Christianity. The heaviest focus was on Eastern religions.

- Different religious speakers denounced converting people to other religions. Missionaries were targeted that proclaimed salvation exclusively by grace through faith in Jesus Christ. ◄────**Mark 16:15**

- Joan Brown Campbell and the formal representatives of Christianity also renounced proselytizing. ◄────**Mark 16:15**

- The most rousing applause came when Ted Turner denied the "need for a blood sacrifice." ◄────**Hebrews 9:12-14**

- The only evangelical representative to speak was Anne Graham Lotz, who gave a Gospel presentation.

In addition to Christianity, other religious movements represented at the summit included Judaism, Islam, Buddhism, Hinduism, Ba'hai, Confucianism, Shinto, Taoism and Zoroastrianism. This sort of religious pluralism reminds us of our Savior's warning:

> **"Take heed that no man deceive you. For many shall come in My Name, saying, I am Christ; and shall deceive many." – Matthew 24:5**

In his speech at the UN General Assembly Hall, Turner, who helped fund the summit, called for cooperation among cultures and religions in order to achieve peace. [65]

But Turner didn't stop there. He explained to the audience that at one time he was going to be a Christian missionary, but changed his mind about the faith of his childhood after studying other religions. "What disturbed me is that my religious Christian sect was very intolerant – not intolerant of religious freedom for other people, but we thought that we were the only ones going to heaven," he said, according to his prepared remarks. "It just confused the devil out of me, because I said heaven is going to be a mighty empty place with nobody else there. So I was pretty confused and turned off by it. I said it just can't be right." [66]

After studying other cultures, Turner adopted a view outside biblical teaching. "Instead of all these different gods, I thought maybe there's one God who manifests himself and reveals himself in different ways to different people," he said.[67]

From these comments, we can discern how the voice of the second beast will eventually sound, twisting the Scriptures where Jesus speaks to Philip and to us:

> **"Have I been so long time with you, and yet hast thou not known me, Philip? He that hath seen Me hath seen the Father; and how sayest thou then, Shew us the Father?" – John 14:9**

This is the second beast, coming to life behind the scenes. The document on peace that was circulated among the religious leaders at the summit included a commitment to pursue peace in collaboration with the United Nations, as well as:

- The promotion of "the equitable distribution of wealth within nations and among nations"
- A call for the "universal abolition of nuclear weapons and other weapons of mass destruction"
- The development of a "global reforestation campaign" [68]

This summit, immediately followed by the UN Millennium Summit of leaders from more than 150 countries on September 6, 2000, raised public concerns about progress toward a one-world government because proposals being considered were a worldwide tax system, establishment of an international court and a full-time international security force.[69]

In his article *Interfaithism: The Religion of the New World Order*, Eddie Sax reveals that the seeds of this UN Religious Summit on World Peace were planted a few years before by globalists who concluded that world political unity could not be achieved without bringing an end to religious conflict.[70]

Robert Muller, the former Assistant Secretary General of the UN, wanted an institutional arrangement in the UN for a dialogue and cooperation between religions. His vision became reality in 1996 when he signed the United Religions Initiative with director William Swing, an Episcopalian bishop. The United Religions (UR) is an ecumenical organization that seeks to make peace among religions so they might work together for the good of all life and the healing of the earth.[71]

Sax explains that although the UR claims to be a bridge-building organization and not a religion, it does have a theology that concerns the relationship of human beings with their spiritual Origin. The UR believes in the universality and eternity of the Spirit, and that all religions derive their wisdom from that ultimate Source. "While there is some measure of comfort that the words 'Origin' and 'Source' are capitalized," remarks Sax, "it is difficult for a Bible-believer to agree that Wicca, Zoroastrians and Luciferians (a few of the UR member religions) derive their wisdom from God. Isaiah 14:12 states that Lucifer is not God." [72]

Sax continues, "The UR promotes . . . a theology of acceptance that will help the world's people explore common ground . . . awareness of unity within religious diversity promotes ever-increasing kinship." Whatever theology UR members adhere to, it must include *acceptance*, which means they accept Lucifer, Allah, Brahma, and Buddha. UR members must learn from these religions and embrace them. This is Interfaithism. [73]

"The God described in the Bible does not embrace diversity when it crosses the line to pagan worship," Sax reminds us. "His people are to be a separated people. The UR, however, "embraces all our diversity . . . sharing a profound respect for the sacred source and wisdom of each religion." [74]

Sax identifies the direct connections between the UR and UN. "The UR endorses the UN's International Criminal Court," he says. "Other 'non-religious' items on the UR agenda include open support of the UN's Universal Declaration of Human Rights and the Universal Declaration of Human Responsibilities. They parrot UN policy on 'Sustainable and Just Economics.' The UR intends to lead the way in addressing the issue of global climate changes by modeling the use of new, renewable energy sources and energy-efficient technologies, and creating pressure for lower-cost sources of renewable energy." [75]

Most importantly, Sax describes how the UN *needs* the UR: "There is a dire need to revisit the global economic system from a religious/spiritual perspective in order to make some fundamental changes. Efforts by the UN in this direction are often frustrated by the domination of national interests in that body . . . the corporate sector's dominance of world economic practice lacks a moral, socially responsible foundation. Without religious unity, world government has no chance. Hence, the United Religions. The UN is behind the UR. They call themselves sister organizations, but the fact is *one gave birth to the other.*" [76]

The second beast is literally coming out of the first beast. From the UN Religious Summit on World Peace arose the World Council of Religious Leaders, an organization formed in 2002 at the UN Economic and Social Commission for Asia and the Pacific. Its stated purpose is to serve the UN as a "resource of collective wisdom of the faith traditions" to resolve critical global problems.[77]

What is this collective wisdom? The World Council of Religious Leaders guides the creation of "a community of world religions by inspiring women and men of all faiths to pursue peace and mutual understanding." It provides spiritual resources to the UN to "prevent, resolve and heal conflicts, and address global social and environmental problems."[78]

The World Council promotes "the *universal human values* shared by all religious traditions and unites the human community for times of world prayer and meditation." It develops "the *inner qualities and external conditions* needed for the creation of a more peaceful, just and sustainable world society."[79]

The World Council believes religious leaders are more important than ever in setting direction for the human community. It closely cooperates with the UN in building a community of world religions for the benefit of the global family. It unites through further dialogue to build trust so that religious leaders are effective and powerful vehicles for peace.[80]

Wrapped inside all of this ecumenical mumbo-jumbo is the sinister deception of the role of world religious leadership in the search for spiritual guidance, something that Jesus warns us against in the last days:

> **"For many shall come in My Name, saying, I am Christ; and shall deceive many . . . For there shall arise false Christs, and false prophets, and shall shew great signs and wonders; insomuch that, if it were possible, they shall deceive the very elect . . . Wherefore, if they shall say unto you, Behold, he is in the desert; go not forth: behold, he is in the secret chambers; believe it not." – Matthew 24:5, 24, 26**

Our Savior is warning us that the satanic force behind the World Council lies in the *thirteen* different religious faiths that have joined together for its creation – eleven pagan beliefs combined with secular Judaism and apostate Christianity. It's no coincidence that the numeral 13 in the ancient Hebrew represents spiritual *depravity* and *rebellion*. Behind the scenes, the World Council is a depraved pagan organization that is leading a spiritual rebellion against the one true God, Jehovah, by twisting the teachings of His Son, Jesus Christ.

Behind the Scenes . . . . . Rise of the Second Beast

- The World Council of Religious Leaders was formed for the U.N. as a resource of collective wisdom of the faith traditions toward resolving critical global problems. **Rev 13:12**

- Launched in Bangkok, Thailand on June 12-14, 2002, at the U.N. Economic and Social Commission for Asia and the Pacific.

- It guides creation of a community of world religions by inspiring women and men of all faiths to pursue peace and mutual understanding. ◄─────── **Matt. 24:5**
──────────────────────────**Rev 13:12**
- It provides spiritual resources to the U.N. to prevent, resolve and heal conflicts, and address global social and environmental problems.

- It promotes the universal human values shared by all religious traditions and unites the human community for times of world prayer and meditation. ➣ **Matt. 24:26**

- It develops the inner qualities and external conditions needed for the creation of a more peaceful, just and sustainable world society.

The clever, deceptive twisting of the Scriptures by the World Council originates from the pagan beliefs of each of its member religions.

Behind the Scenes . . . . . Rise of the Second Beast

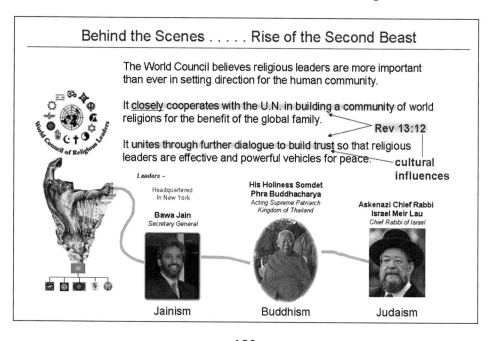

The World Council believes religious leaders are more important than ever in setting direction for the human community.

It closely cooperates with the U.N. in building a community of world religions for the benefit of the global family. **Rev 13:12**

It unites through further dialogue to build trust so that religious leaders are effective and powerful vehicles for peace. ─── cultural influences

Leaders –

Headquartered
In New York

Bawa Jain
Secretary General

His Holiness Somdet
Phra Buddhacharya
Acting Supreme Patriarch
Kingdom of Thailand

Askenazi Chief Rabbi
Israel Meir Lau
Chief Rabbi of Israel

Jainism   Buddhism   Judaism

123

For example, Buddhism teaches people how to achieve Nirvana, a place or state of oblivion to care, pain, or external reality. Nirvana is treated as a form of salvation that represents the end of all suffering. By entering into Nirvana, a person supposedly enters into knowledge about the true nature of reality. All of this directly parallels the abundant life of eternal salvation that Jesus promises each of His followers:

> "I am come that they might have life, and that they might have it *more abundantly* . . . In my Father's house are many mansions: if it were not so, I would have told you. I go to prepare a place for you. And if I go and prepare a place for you, I will come again, and receive you unto myself; that where I am, there ye may be also." – John 10:10, 14:2-3

However, Buddhists teach that Nirvana can only be achieved through a moral life and meditation. In other words, man can only achieve salvation *on his own*. He can only discover the true nature of all things *through his own behaviors – he can be like a god*. This directly contradicts the teachings of Jesus, who clearly states there is nothing a person can do by himself to attain salvation:

> "I am the Way, the Truth, and the Life: *no man cometh unto the Father, but by me*." – John 14:6

Buddhists also believe that a person is reincarnated. This means that after they physically die, their soul is born again in a new human body (if they are morally rewarded) or other physical form of life (such as an animal, if they are morally punished). This sequence of being physically reborn in new bodies or other forms of life repeats over and over until the person is morally good enough to reach the state of Nirvana.

Being "born again" directly parallels the teaching of the Scriptures on being reborn spiritually in Christ:

> "Verily, verily, I say unto thee, Except a man be *born again*, he cannot see the kingdom of God . . . Therefore if any man be in Christ, he is a new creature: old things are passed away; behold all things are become new . . . be renewed in the spirit of your mind; and that ye put on the new man, which after God is created in righteousness and true holiness" – John 3:3; 2 Corinthians 5:17; Ephesians 4:23-24

However, being *physically* reborn over and over in new human bodies

124

or other forms of life directly contradicts the Bible, which clearly states that after a person physically dies, their spirit can only enter into the spiritual realm, not another physical body:

"But God giveth it a body as it hath pleased Him . . . it is sown a natural body; it is raised a spiritual body . . . it is appointed unto men once to die, but after this the judgment . . . . . . he that goeth down to the grave shall come up no more . . . to be absent from the body, and to be present with the Lord." – 1 Corinthians 15:38, 44; Hebrews 9:27; Job 7:9; 2 Corinthians 5:8

Bahá'u'lláh, the Prophet-Founder, proclaims the oneness of humankind as the central principle and goal of His Faith, implies spiritual unity of the whole body of nations and signals the coming of age of the entire human race. Expressed purpose is to usher in the next stage in humanity's development – world unity and the Great Peace foretold in the sacred scriptures of the world's religions.

John 14:2-3

Buddhism was founded in India by Siddhartha Gautama, the Buddha or "Enlightened One." He teaches the way to Nirvana, the end of all suffering, through moral life and meditation, leading to knowledge of the true nature of reality. Buddhism is based on this and on compassion for all living beings. It believes in reincarnation and karma, the results of good and evil actions.

Hebrews 9:27   Ephesians 2:4-5

Confucianism is named from K'ung Fu-tzu, who lived in China. Following the Way of Heaven, Confucius teaches that a good society could be created through love for our fellow human beings, devotion to parents and elders, and study of the proper forms of life. His teachings became the central philosophy of traditional China.

John 14:6

Hinduism means simply 'the religion of the people of India', and is called the Sanatana Dharma or "eternal Dharma." Dharma means "righteousness," "law" and "duty" and refers to the right order of the world. Hinduism has no single founder. Its origins go back into the earliest history of South Asia. Its first known scriptures are the Vedas or "knowledge." Hindus worship God in many forms and believe in reincarnation and karma, the results of good and evil actions.

Notice how these Scriptures also explain that all judgment is issued by our Lord only, which directly opposes the Buddhist teaching on karma, a force of reward or punishment generated by a *person's own actions* that determine the nature of that person's next existence. Again, Buddhism emphasizes that man is his own god and directs his own way to salvation. But the Bible clearly says that only by God's grace can we be saved through Jesus Christ:

"But God, Who is rich in mercy, for His great love wherewith He loved us, even when we were dead in sins, hath quickened us together with Christ, (by grace ye are saved). – Ephesians 2:4-5

125

Indigenous religions are traditions of the native, aboriginal or indigenous peoples of all parts of the world. (The term "indigenous' is used by the U.N.) They have diverse cultures and religions but share a long-standing and profound connection to their land, a sense of the kinship of all life, and an intimate relation with ancestors, the spiritual world and the Creator or source of life.

Matthew 24:24

Islam is based on the revelation of the Qur'an, God's direct word given to the Prophet Muhammad in Arabia, succeeding earlier revelations given in Judaism and Christianity. It professes "There is no God but God and Muhammad is his Prophet." God Allah in Arabic is absolutely one, sovereign, just and merciful.

Jainism along with Hinduism is the most ancient religion of India. Mahavir, taught "those who make a river-crossing" or a way to liberation from suffering. The central principle of Jainism is ahimsa or nonviolence towards all living beings. Jainism accepts belief in reincarnation and karma, the results of good and evil actions.

Hebrews 9:27   **Ephesians 2:5**

Judaism is based on the covenant or mutual promise between God and the Jewish people. The covenant began with Abraham and was completed when God gave the Torah or Law to the Jewish people through Moses at Mt. Sinai. The Torah, or first five books of the Hebrew scriptures in the Bible, contains commandments for achieving holiness and righteousness in all aspects of life.

Hebrews 3:3

Other pagan members of the World Council mimic beliefs that are similar to Buddhism. For example, Jainism also believes in reincarnation and karma, and Confucius teaches that the way to heaven is created not through a relationship with Jesus Christ, but by leading a good life of love for fellow human beings, and devotion to parents and elders.

Some member religions directly challenge the authority of Jesus. For example, Islam believes that God's direct word was given to the prophet Muhammad, which means he supersedes the authority and position of Jesus. But the Scriptures clearly say:

> **"Wherefore God also hath highly exalted Him, and given Him a Name which is above every other name: that at the Name of Jesus every knee should bow . . . and that every tongue should confess that Jesus Christ is Lord, to the glory of God the Father . . . neither is there salvation in any other: for there is none other Name under heaven given among men, whereby we must be saved." Philippians 2:9-11; Acts 4:12**

Judaism believes God's covenant began with Abraham (which is true) and was completed in full when God gave the Torah, or Law, to the Jewish people through Moses at Mt. Sinai (which is incorrect). The Scriptures clarify that Jesus, not Moses, fulfills God's covenant with man:

> "Think not that I (Jesus) am come to destroy the Law, or the prophets:
> I am not come to destroy, but *to fulfill* . . . For this man (Jesus) was
> counted *worthy of more glory than Moses*, inasmuch as he who hath
> builded the house hath more honour than the house . . . For every house
> is builded by some man; but He that built all things is God. For Moses
> verily was faithful in all his house, as a servant, for a testimony of those
> things which were to be spoken after; but Christ as a Son over His own
> house, whose house are we . . ." – Matthew 5:17; Hebrews 3:3-6

Still other pagan members proclaim there are many gods, rather than one
God. For example, Shintoism worships all the deities of heaven and earth,
the same sort of pagan worship the Apostle Paul encountered in the ancient
Greek culture:

> "Now while Paul waited for them at Athens, his spirit was stirred in
> him, when he saw the city wholly given to idolatry . . . then Paul stood in
> the midst of Mars hill, and said, Ye men of Athens, I perceive that in all
> things ye are too superstitious." – Acts 17:16, 22

The priests of Taoism serve people through their knowledge of deities,
rituals, and divination, which the Old Testament clearly warns against:

> "There shall not be found among you any one that maketh his son
> or daughter to pass through the fire, or that useth divination . . ."
> – Deuteronomy 18:10

The spiritual irony here is that all of these pagan beliefs profess different
ways to God that are actually barriers that prevent access to God. Their practices
permit the enemy to block the only true path to God: through Jesus Christ. This
is the voice of the second beast, looking like a Christian lamb, but speaking as an
interfaith dragon blended from many disjointed religious and secular beliefs.

The second beast is now coming up out of the first beast in a sinister
balance of power that represents nothing less than an unholy trinity – a satanic
impersonation of the Holy Trinity.

The Holy Trinity is God the Father, Jesus Christ His Son, and Their Holy
Spirit. The unholy trinity is Satan the Dragon, the Antichrist his son of perdition,
and their False Prophet. In the New Testament, John explains how Almighty
God is One in Three Persons, the perfect balance of eternal power found only in
the Holy Trinity:

> "For there are Three that bear record in heaven, the Father, the
> Word (Jesus Christ), and the Holy Ghost: and these Three are
> One." – 1 John 5:7

Shinto is a general term for the activities of the Japanese people to worship all the deities of Heaven and Earth, and it was spontaneously developed through the lifestyle of ancient Japanese. It is based on a communal worship, being closely connected to each locality of the Japanese land and its nature.

pantheism
Acts 17:16,22

Sikhism was founded in north India by Guru Nanak. Sikhs worship the one God without form through devotion and service, and venerate as their scripture the Guru Granth Sahib, a collection of songs, poems and other writings by the ten Sikh Gurus and other saints, including Hindus and Muslims.

The earliest known figure of Taoism in ancient China is Lao Tzu, the legendary author of the Tao Te Ching or "Classic of the Way [Tao] and Its Power." The Tao is the formless and infinite origin of all things. Taoism became both a philosophical school and an organized religion, with orders of priests serving the people of China through their knowledge of deities, rituals, and divination.

Deuteronomy 18:10

Zoroastrianism was founded by the prophet Zarathustra in ancient Persia and is found today mainly in western India. Zarathustra in his Gathas or verses declared the sovereignty of the one God, Ahura Mazda or "Lord of all Wisdom," and the opposition of good and evil spiritual forces. Zoroastrian worship centers on a continually burning sacred fire. **mimics sacrificial fires of Leviticus**

John reminds us here that God is the eternal Creator, which means *only God can create.* As such, Satan is simply a creature who was created, meaning he cannot create. Satan can only imitate the balance of power in the Holy Trinity by assembling this unholy trinity. Now consider the comparisons.

Jesus Christ is the Son of Jehovah God, filled with the Holy Spirit of God. The Antichrist is the son of perdition, possessed by the spirit of Satan. Jesus is God in the flesh, come to save mankind. The Antichrist is Satan possessing the flesh, come to destroy mankind. Jesus saves mankind through the power of the Holy Spirit of God. The Antichrist deceives mankind through the power of the False Prophet of Satan. Through Jesus and the Holy Spirit, mankind worships Jehovah God. Through the Antichrist and the False Prophet, mankind worships Satan.

The second beast, an interfaith system coming up out of the first beast, will complete the unholy trinity. This balance of power is necessary to calm the religious conflicts that currently ignite dangerous wars on earth. This unholy trinity is the only means of ending religious conflict so that world political unity can be fully realized.

The False Prophet will mold and shape interfaithism into a religious image of the political and economic system of the Antichrist. Interfaithism will eventually reflect all of the goals, beliefs and purpose of the Antichrist, such that the second beast "causeth the earth and them which dwell therein to worship the first beast." Interfaithism will eventually enforce the same powers of control as the Antichrist, such that the second beast "exerciseth all the power of the first beast before him."

To accomplish these things, the False Prophet must first create harmony among the world's religions, such that they become tolerant and respectful of each other's beliefs. How will he do this?

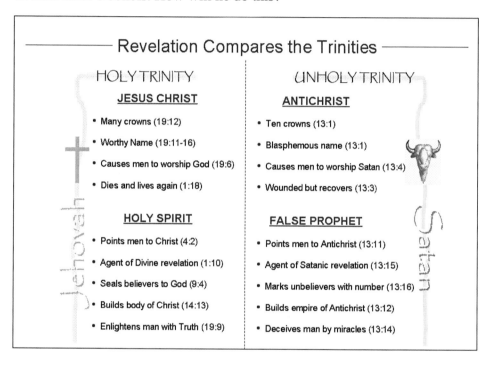

Revelation Compares the Trinities

HOLY TRINITY

JESUS CHRIST

- Many crowns (19:12)
- Worthy Name (19:11-16)
- Causes men to worship God (19:6)
- Dies and lives again (1:18)

HOLY SPIRIT

- Points men to Christ (4:2)
- Agent of Divine revelation (1:10)
- Seals believers to God (9:4)
- Builds body of Christ (14:13)
- Enlightens man with Truth (19:9)

UNHOLY TRINITY

ANTICHRIST

- Ten crowns (13:1)
- Blasphemous name (13:1)
- Causes men to worship Satan (13:4)
- Wounded but recovers (13:3)

FALSE PROPHET

- Points men to Antichrist (13:11)
- Agent of Satanic revelation (13:15)
- Marks unbelievers with number (13:16)
- Builds empire of Antichrist (13:12)
- Deceives man by miracles (13:14)

CHAPTER 10

Harmony in Motion

"The new world religion, now in the world's birth canal, will not be Christian, Buddhist, Hindu, Jewish, Wicca, or Muslim," explains Eddie Sax in his report on the religion of the New World Order. "It will be Interfaithism – the belief that all religions, while different on the surface, are each valid pathways to God." [81]

How in the world will it be possible to convince multitudes of diverse religious leaders to compromise their doctrines of religious exclusivity for the greater good that the globalists say will come to humanity?

The only way is to create a movement of harmony among all the various religions, an atmosphere of tolerance and mutual respect brought into existence through a global forum, by an acknowledged leader of one of the largest and most influential religions. This leader will become the icon of a sort of "harmony in motion" that *spiritually* understands, *politically* tolerates and *socially* respects the meanings behind all of the religious rituals of the world, regardless of their cultures.

This religious icon will teach about the morality and goodness that unites all spiritual beliefs. He will put those teachings into action, with tireless care for the hurting people of every society and every nation. All of this religious harmony will seemingly serve the greater good of humanity, but it will actually be a strong delusion that is spiritually legislated, politically authorized, and socially executed.

Who is the icon behind this spiritual delusion? He is the False Prophet. His harmony will appear to be as innocent as a lamb, but his doctrine of corruption will speak directly from a dragon. The Apostle Paul specifically warns us about this deception:

131

> "And for this cause God shall send them *a strong delusion*, that they should believe a lie: That they all might be damned who believed not the truth, but had pleasure in unrighteousness."
> – 2 Thessalonians 2:11-12

Who is this False Prophet? Can we identify his seat of authority, the religion he will use to assemble the second beast – the global interfaith system? The potential seats of authority available to him can be quickly narrowed down by answering a few questions.

First, is there any highly visible global position of leadership that presides over an extremely large and influential religion to such an extent that it is a virtual icon of that faith? Yes; there are two.

The five largest religions in the world are Christianity (2.1 billion followers), Islam (1.4 billion), Hinduism (1 billion), Chinese folk religion (850 million), and Buddhism (350 million). Only two of these recognize their leader as being synonymous with that faith: the Pope of the Roman Catholic Church (1.1 billion members, the largest religious body in the world) essentially speaks for all Christians in the global arena; and the Dalai Lama represents all Buddhists.[82]

Of these two seats of authority, does either counsel the various faiths of the world on tolerance and mutual respect? Both do to varying degrees, but without question, the seat of the Pope carries more spiritual "weight" than any other religious leader on the planet. His words alone are frequently broadcast across the globe by the mass media, scrutinized and interpreted by world leaders in diverse religious, political, and social settings.

For example, in September 2006, CNN Rome Bureau Chief Alessio Vinci reported that Pope Benedict XVI expressed "total and profound respect for all Muslims" at a meeting with 20 ambassadors from Muslim nations and other Islamic leaders that was called at his summer residence in an effort to repair relations following controversial comments he had made two weeks earlier during a speech to professors.[83]

Global reaction from Muslims to that earlier speech had been so strong that it prompted Italian police to raise the alert level around the Vatican and the Pope's summer residence. Protests were staged worldwide. The Pope expressed that he was "deeply sorry" for the reaction to the comments he had made, saying his remarks were intended to call for a dialogue on the role of religions in modern life. He told the envoys that he would "continue to consolidate the strong ties of friendship with the faithful of all religions, particularly with respect to the dialogue between Muslims and Christians." [84]

Only the Pope commands this sort of global audience regarding religious-political-social issues.

Finally, does either seat of authority play an influential role in political and social forums across the world? Only the seat of the Pope has unprecedented political influence. The headquarters of his Roman Catholic Church is the State of the Vatican City, a landlocked *sovereign city-state* whose territory consists of a walled enclave within the city of Rome. At approximately 108.7 acres, the Vatican is the *smallest independent nation* in the world.[85]

That's not all. In an age where so many official efforts attempt to separate church and state, Vatican City is a non-hereditary, elected monarchy that is ruled by the Pope. The highest state functionaries are all clergymen of the Catholic Church. It is the sovereign territory of the Pope and the location of the Apostolic Palace – his official residence – and the Roman Curia. In other words, while the principal ecclesiastical seat (Cathedral) of the Pope as Bishop of Rome (the Basilica of St. John Lateran) is located outside of its walls, in Rome, Vatican City is recognized as the *governmental capital* of the Catholic Church.[86]

There is only one highly visible seat of religious authority with the power to execute spiritual, political, and social initiatives across the globe: the Pope. The Pope is, in essence, the unquestioned supreme legislative, executive, and judicial authority of the largest religious body in the world – there are no "checks and balances" such as those found in secular governments.[87]

This seat of absolute authority is exactly what the False Prophet needs to assemble the global interfaith system. The Scriptures verify this in several passages, starting with a specific identification of the exact location of his seat of authority:

"And here is the mind which hath wisdom. The seven heads are seven mountains, on which the woman sitteth." – Revelation 17:9

John says wisdom must be applied here to discern and understand what he is describing. In other words, just as the politics and economics of the first beast are *married* to the religion of the second beast, his geographic history lesson here is married to a deeper spiritual reality.

Meditate on this for a moment.

Geographically, the "seven mountains" represent the city of Rome, which literally sits on seven hills: the Capitoline, Palatine, Viminal, Quirinal, Esquiline, Caelian, and the Aventine.[88]

Historically, these mountains symbolize Rome as the hub of the ancient Roman Empire, the prophetic European shadow-in-type of the beast having seven heads. From this perspective, the seven mountains (heads) represent the seven peaks (political authorities) in the global economic system of the Antichrist, which are situated (carry out operations) around the hub (headquarters) of Rome (a European base).

Notice "the woman" that sits on top of these seven political authorities. In the ancient Greek, the term *woman* here means *wife*, implying *marriage*. A religious authority typically presides over marriage, which implies that these seven political authorities are symbolically *married* to each other – intimately united (loyal) in their political and economic operations – by mutual consent and legal contracts presided over by a religious body that is centrally headquartered in Rome.

In the Scriptures, the number seven represents *spiritual perfection*. But these seven seats, ruled by the Antichrist, represent the exact opposite of the kingdom ruled by Jesus Christ. They symbolize *spiritual imperfection* – they do what is right in their own eyes – mutually consented to and legally contracted under an apostate religious authority that presides in Rome: the religious system of the False Prophet.

Now connect the dots here. Today, the Vatican and government of the Roman Catholic Church lie within this same city of Rome, and the Pope currently rules it with absolute authority, speaking on behalf of all Christianity. Tomorrow, the Vatican and government of the interfaith system will lie within Rome, and the False Prophet will rule it with absolute power, speaking on behalf of the Antichrist.

Along with identifying where this seat of authority is located, John also identifies the False Prophet as the religious leader who will occupy the seat:

> "...... even now there are many antichrists; whereby we know that it is the last time. *They went out from us, but they were not of us*: for if they had been of us, they would no doubt have continued with us: but they went out, that they might be made manifest that they were not all of us." – 1 John 2:18-19

The Apostle John was a Jew who literally followed Jesus during His earthly ministry. Here, his use of the terms "us" refers to Jews and Christians who are followers of Jesus Christ, and "they" refers to apostate or false Jews and Christians who really follow the Antichrist.

From this perspective, his phrase "*they* went out from *us*, but *they* were not of *us*" implies that the False Prophet will initially appear to be a Christian that follows Jesus Christ, but he will really be an apostate deceiver that follows the Antichrist. He may even have a Jewish heritage. But ultimately, this religious leader will possess an antichrist spirit that rises from the apostate church of false Christianity – looking like a lamb, but speaking as a dragon.

Finally, John reveals that this apostate Christianity will be the mantle of the interfaith religious component (the second beast) in the global system (the first beast) ruled by the Antichrist, as seen in the number of the beast:

> **"Here is wisdom. Let him that hath understanding count the number of the beast: for it is the number of a man; and his number is Six hundred threescore and six." – Revelation 13:18**

A snapshot of the ancient Greek numerals in the number of the global system shows that *six hundred* is represented by the symbol *chi* and threescore, or *sixty*, is represented by *xi*. But look closely at the numeral *six*, represented by the symbol *stigma*.

In the Scriptures, the number *six* represents the *weakness of man*, the *evils of Satan*, and the *manifestation of sin*. In the ancient Greek, the *stigma* is a mark incised or punched for recognition of ownership; a scar or *mark* of service. The *chi* appears as an obsolete character representing a *cross*.[89]

So the stigma is the mark of the spiritually weak man who is scarred by the manifestation of sin inside, an evil person who serves and is owned by Satan himself. And by simply rotating the chi 90 degrees clockwise, that symbol bears resemblance to the Cross currently representing the Episcopal Church today – a Protestant denomination that has become virtually synonymous with apostate Christianity.

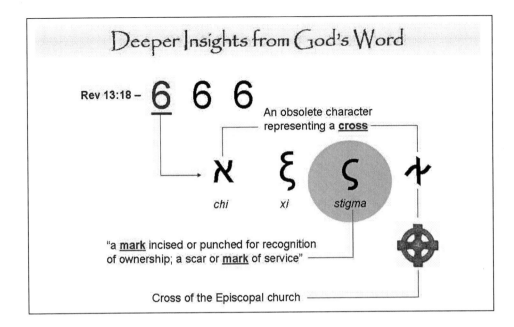

Deeper Insights from God's Word

Rev 13:18 – **6 6 6**

An obsolete character representing a **cross**

ϗ   ξ   ϛ   ϯ

chi   *xi*   *stigma*

"a **mark** incised or punched for recognition of ownership; a scar or **mark** of service"

Cross of the Episcopal church

The Episcopal Church is a textbook case of spiritual disorder. Episcopal leaders have formally ordained a homosexual bishop, promoted radical feminism along with gay and lesbian initiatives, disclaimed the authority of the Scriptures, and greatly divided their own denomination. These apostate leaders are spiritually weak men and women who are scarred by the stigma of sin that has manifested inside them. Without question, they are serving the evil mission of Satan himself.

The Episcopal Church represents the *via media* or "middle way" between Protestant and strictly *Roman Catholic* practices. In many ways, Episcopal liturgy *closely resembles that of the Roman Catholic Church*. Episcopalians ascribe to the Anglican Branch theory which posits three branches of *Catholic Christianity*: the Eastern Orthodox Church, the *Roman Catholic Church*, and the Anglican Communion.[90]

From this perspective, the stigma that scars the apostate Episcopal Church also points to the expanding *middle way* – religious compromise that will eventually tolerate and mutually respect *all* diverse religious practices under a Roman Catholic framework governed by the False Prophet.

The chi reveals that apostate Christianity – having "two horns like a lamb" – will be the "melting pot" of the interfaith religion used by the global system of the Antichrist. Already representing one of the 13 religions that serve the U.N. under the World Council of Religious

Leaders, apostate Christianity claims that all people "should seek the way of peace and finally come to peace with God." There is no mention that Jesus is the *only Way* of truly finding peace with God. [91]

Under the auspices of the World Council, the cross represents the life, death and resurrection of Jesus Christ, in whom Christians find an "ideal model and guide for right living" and a Savior who can transform their lives. That is certainly true, but there is no mention that Jesus is God Himself, the *only* model of guidance for *holy* living. Jesus, the Son of God who came in the flesh, lived a *perfect* life for us to study, not an ideal life. Also, remember that Joan Brown Campbell and the other World Council representatives of apostate Christianity denounced converting people to other religions – and officially renounced proselytizing anyone to salvation exclusively by grace through faith in Jesus Christ. [92]

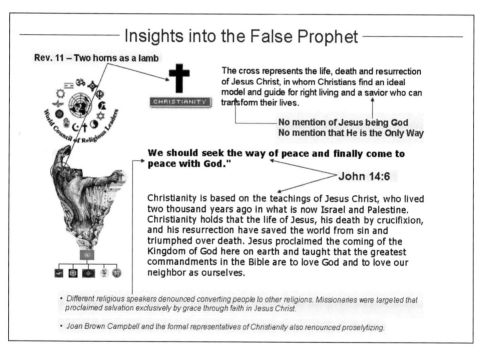

Insights into the False Prophet

Rev. 11 – Two horns as a lamb

CHRISTIANITY

The cross represents the life, death and resurrection of Jesus Christ, in whom Christians find an ideal model and guide for right living and a savior who can transform their lives.

No mention of Jesus being God
No mention that He is the Only Way

We should seek the way of peace and finally come to peace with God."

John 14:6

Christianity is based on the teachings of Jesus Christ, who lived two thousand years ago in what is now Israel and Palestine. Christianity holds that the life of Jesus, his death by crucifixion, and his resurrection have saved the world from sin and triumphed over death. Jesus proclaimed the coming of the Kingdom of God here on earth and taught that the greatest commandments in the Bible are to love God and to love our neighbor as ourselves.

• Different religious speakers denounced converting people to other religions. Missionaries were targeted that proclaimed salvation exclusively by grace through faith in Jesus Christ.

• Joan Brown Campbell and the formal representatives of Christianity also renounced proselytizing.

Under the guidance of the Antichrist, the False Prophet will formally merge the liturgical practices of apostate Christianity with various forms of occult mysticism, so that everyone can worship "God" in many forms, whether it be through Hindu beliefs of reincarnation and karma, or centering on the continually burning sacred fire of Zoroastrianism, or communal worship of all the deities of heaven and earth of Shintoism.

Catherine Millard, B.A., M.A., the founder and president of Christian Heritage Tours, explains how we saw the roots of this merger immediately following the 9/11 tragedy: "The National Prayer Service of The National Day of Prayer, proclaimed by President George W. Bush as September 14, 2001, was held at the National Cathedral, Washington, D.C. It commenced with Rev. Jane Holmes Dixon (Episcopal Bishop of Washington, pro tempore) presiding. She opened the service by welcoming the President of the United States and government leaders to the National Cathedral, which she described as "a house of prayer for people of all faiths, according to our National Cathedral Charter – Muslims, Buddhists, Jews, Christians." In doing so, Rev. Dixon rewrote America's history by misquoting the National Cathedral's Charter." [93]

Millard explains that the original Charter identifies the National Cathedral as "a House of Prayer for all people, forever free and open . . . It shall stand in the Capital of our country *as a witness for Jesus Christ,* the same yesterday, today and forever, and for the faith once for all delivered to the saints; and for the *ministration of Christ's Holy Word* and sacraments, which according to His own ordinance is to continue always to the end of the world." [94]

She continues, "Among those speaking from the pulpit during this National Prayer Service were 1) the Roman Catholic Archbishop of Washington; 2) a leader of the Muslim religion; 3) Nathan Baxter, Dean of the National Cathedral, and finally, Rev. Billy Graham. Dean Nathan Baxter prefaced his sermon with, "The God of Abraham, Isaac and Jacob, the god of Mohammed and the God of Jesus Christ." The god of Mohammed, founder of the Muslim religion, however, is Allah, who is not the God of the Bible, Almighty God, the One True God, whose Son is our Lord and Savior, Jesus Christ, the latter being extolled by the National Cathedral's Charter, as well as within and without her gothic walls." [95]

Millard explains the audacity of what took place: "Jehovah and Elohiym are God's Names in the Old Testament. Allah was one of numerous false gods worshiped by the Arabs, when Mohammed forced them to worship one of the many, whose name is Allah. In the Muslim religion, Allah has no son. Their "Holy War" is *against Christianity.* How amazing that, for the first time in America's history, the National Cathedral has violated its own Charter at a National Day of Prayer Service attended by the President of the United States and proclaimed by him as such." [96]

Millard was further surprised that, at the singing of the Star-Spangled

Banner, the National Anthem, the God of the Bible and of our forefathers was omitted from the Anthem and not glorified as Author and Protector of America's remarkable liberties and freedoms.[97]

All of this deceptive "harmony in motion" represents the "grievous wolves" that the Scriptures specifically warn us against:

> **"For I know this, that after my departure shall grievous wolves enter in among you, not sparing the flock. Also of your own selves shall men arise, speaking perverse things, to draw away disciples after them." – Acts 20:29-30**

We already see these perverse wolves wandering through various Catholic teachings.

For example, the Catholic Church officially confuses the role of Mary, the mother of Jesus, by recognizing her as Deity. In "The Deity of the Mother of God," Fr. Malcolm L. Broussard, Jr. explains that "Our Lady (Mary) is not God. She is a pure human creature who is absolutely singular and unique in creation. However, we . . . think the word "Deity" is proper for Our Lady to use, as it is clear from the context of Her words that She is referring to Her "Deity by participation" – i.e., Her absolutely singular and unique sharing in the Divine Nature by Grace (2 Peter 1:4); and because She is the Spouse of the Holy Ghost – Her union with God is immeasurably great and "Divine" by virtue of her participation in the inner life of the Most Holy Trinity."[98]

This Catholic priest continues, "There is no standard of measurement known to angels or men capable of measuring the height, breath and depth of Her union with the Triune God!! Even though She is a creature, She is the Immaculate Conception. Furthermore, Her Royalty and Dignity as Queen and Mother of God make Her Higher than all creation and thus able to intercede for all God's children. Remember too, that She is the Mediatrix of All Grace and the Co-Redemptrix. No other creature, angelic or human, has these privileges. She is closer to God than any being whatsoever! This is why we can refer to Her 'Deity.'"[99]

This belief that Mary is *higher than all creation* and *able to intercede for all God's children* is the reason why Catholics *pray to her* in Jesus' Name, not Jesus Himself. Notice how they recognize Mary as the *Queen*, as in the queen of heaven. Treating Mary as some sort of divine royalty reveals the paganism behind the interfaith movement, an idolatory that once plagued the ancient people of Judah in the Old Testament:

> "But we will certainly do whatsoever thing goeth forth out of our own mouth, to burn incense unto the *queen of heaven*, and to pour out drink offerings unto her, as we have done, we, and our fathers, our kings, and our princes, in the cities of Judah, and in the streets of Jerusalem: for then had we plenty of victuals, and were well, and saw no evil." – Jeremiah 44:17

These Jewish people had merged all of their proper worship of Jehovah God with the pagan practices of false religions – just as the Catholic Church does today. In fact, many prominent Catholic leaders have emphasized that the Catholic Church, not Jesus, is the only way to heaven.

Saint Augustine (died AD 430) taught that "No man can find salvation except in the Catholic Church. Outside the Catholic Church one can have everything except salvation. One can have honor, one can have the sacraments, one can sing alleluia, one can answer amen . . . but never can one find salvation except in the Catholic Church." [100]

Saint Thomas Aquinas (died AD 1274) stated that "There is no entering into salvation outside the Church, just as in the time of the deluge there was none outside the ark, which denotes the Church." Saint Robert Bellarmine (died AD 1621) said, "Outside the Church there is no salvation . . . 'I believe in the Holy Catholic Church, the communion of Saints, the forgiveness of sins' . . . For this reason the Church is compared with the ark of Noah, because just as during the deluge, everyone perished who was not in the ark, so now those perish who are not in the Church." [101]

All of these teachings – that Mary intercedes for people and that the Catholic Church is the only way to heaven – clearly contradict the teachings of Jesus in John 14:6. Even the recognition given to priests in the Catholic Church directly opposes the Scriptures, as the Pope is commonly acknowledged as the "Holy Father" over the entire Catholic body of believers and priests are referred to as "fathers." Yet Jesus clearly commands us not to acknowledge mere men in this way:

> "And call no man your father upon the earth: for One is your Father, which is in heaven." – Matthew 23:9

A critical mass of spiritual disorder is peeking over the horizon. The time is coming soon when all interfaith religions will officially recognize the queen of heaven, either as Mary or under other names. This ecumenical belief system will teach that to get into heaven, people must be members in the interfaith movement. They must tolerate, respect and, in some cases, even practice diverse faiths and behaviors. And eventually, they must all recognize the False Prophet as their "Holy Father" and his religious leaders as "fathers."

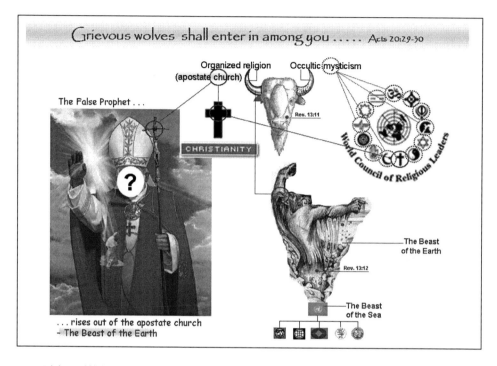

Grievous wolves shall enter in among you ..... Acts 20:29-30

Organized religion (apostate church)

Occultic mysticism

The False Prophet . . .

CHRISTIANITY

Rev. 13:11

World Council of Religious Leaders

The Beast of the Earth

Rev. 13:12

The Beast of the Sea

. . . rises out of the apostate church - The Beast of the Earth

This will be a time when the False Prophet possesses the privilege to work with the masses in capacities that no one else can imagine. We get a glimpse of this privilege today when the Pope has counsel with foreign heads of state in virtually every nation.

Although rogue nations openly detest democracy and use force to crack down on spiritual freedom, they still allow the leader of the Catholic Church special immunity within their cities and towns that would otherwise be restricted by the authorities. For example, the underground church of Jesus Christ is being physically persecuted in Sudan and in Marxist-Leninist Benin, yet the Pope was welcomed with pomp, grandeur and open arms by the politicians of these countries.[102]

Just as they do today with the Pope, the masses will give the False Prophet freedom to do as he pleases because of the trust he builds *with* the people and *between* the people. We can already see threads of this trust weaving through the Catholic Church and nations that support

141

militant Islam – a blatant enemy of true Christianity – as the Vatican declares that Muslims are saved because they all believe in the "same God" as Christians.

Catechism 841 of the Roman Catholic Church states "The Church's relationship with the Muslims. The plan of salvation also includes those who acknowledge the Creator, in the first place amongst whom are the Muslims; these profess to hold the faith of Abraham, and together with us they adore the one, merciful God, mankind's judge on the last day." [103]

The Catholic agenda behind this declaration on Islam clearly creates opportunities for other religions to enter the "family to God" and achieve salvation without Jesus. They can, for instance, enter through an ecumenical path that is morally linked to Abraham and Mary, because the Pope has noted that although Islam does not recognize Jesus as their Savior, they will *still attain salvation* because of their *link to Abraham*, their *recognition of Mary*, and their *moral values*:

"The Church regards with esteem also the Moslems. They adore the one God, living and subsisting in Himself; merciful and all-powerful, the Creator of heaven and earth, who has spoken to men; they take pains to submit wholeheartedly to even His inscrutable decrees, just as Abraham, with whom the faith of Islam takes pleasure in linking itself, submitted to God. Though they do not acknowledge Jesus as God, they revere Him as a prophet. They also honor Mary, His virgin Mother; at times they even call on her with devotion. In addition, they await the day of judgment when God will render their deserts to all those who have been raised up from the dead. Finally, they value the moral life and worship God especially through prayer, almsgiving and fasting." [104]

In other words, the Vatican has essentially declared that other religions have no need for the atoning sacrifice of Jesus. This allows the Pope today – and the False Prophet tomorrow – to bridge any spiritual division of the masses by avoiding the true purpose of the Cross and replacing it with an ecumenical "harmony" cloaked under humanitarian efforts.

The Apostle Paul warns us about the confusion of those who teach salvation by any means other than Jesus Christ. He exposes how any "trust" developed outside the truth of the Scriptures has no depth and will collapse under the prideful weight of intellectual arguments:

> **"If any man teach otherwise, and consent not to wholesome words, even the words of our Lord Jesus Christ, and to the doctrine which is according to godliness; he is proud, knowing**

> nothing, but doting about questions and strifes of words,
> whereof cometh envy, strife, railings, evil surmisings, perverse
> disputings of men of corrupt minds, and destitute of the truth,
> supposing that gain is godliness; from such withdraw thyself."
> – 1 Timothy 6:3-5

Here, Paul details how false teaching breeds competitive pride, envy, arguments, disputes and strife among people because it perverts the truth of Jesus by attempting to *learn about* God without *learning from* God. He is, in effect, exposing the internal corruption that occurs when a church declines into apostasy – a spiritual slide toward destruction that is characterized by five of the seven churches that Jesus Himself judges in Revelation 2-3.

In fact, the five spiritual characteristics of the apostate church that belongs to the False Prophet in the last days are typed through these five churches in Revelation 2-3 so that we can recognize them coming up around us. Meditate on these for a moment:

(1) Consider a church that devoutly searches for eternal salvation, but follows unbalanced teaching about godliness. Using Jesus as their model, they are taught to busily pursue spreading the Good News of the Gospel by living a moral life and doing good works. In fact, they are taught more about the works of Jesus than about Jesus Himself, to the point that His works are seemingly emphasized over His position.

Because some of their good works do indeed draw others to the Lord, they naturally begin to associate with and focus more on moral living and good works as their witness, rather than on relationship with Jesus. The busier they become, actively doing works and deeds for others, the less time they spend actively meditating with the Lord – until they inevitably *forsake their relationship with Him*. This is the busyness in churches that we see throughout communities so often today, the busyness of the Ephesus church that *loses their first love*:

> "I know thy works, and thy labour . . . and for my Name's
> sake has laboured, and has not fainted. Nevertheless, I
> have somewhat against thee, because thou hast left thy first
> love. Remember therefore from whence thou art fallen, and
> repent . . ." – Revelation 2:2-5

(2) A church that is too busy trying to act moral and perform good works, rather than building a strong relationship with Jesus through the Word of God, risks falling into the *spiritual compromise* that ruins the church at Pergamos:

> **"I know thy works, and where thou dwellest . . . but I have a few things against thee, because thou hast there them that hold the doctrine of Balaam, who taught Balac to cast a stumblingblock before the children of Israel, to eat things sacrificed unto idols, and to commit fornication." – Revelation 2:13-14**

Our Lord warns the Pergamos church about failing to keep out false teachers. Although this church does not fully embrace false teachings, they are so busy "doing good" that they errantly allow heretics to work among them and seduce God's people into compromising with the world – especially in sexual sins.

False teaching causes a Pergamos church to subtly lose their doctrinal discipline and moral purity. We see these apostate characteristics today in the United Methodist Church (UMC). For example, though the UMC formally states that homosexuality is incompatible with Christian teaching, and even voted in 1984 to prohibit ordination of self-avowed, practicing homosexuals, these statements mean almost nothing in practice.[105]

As soon as the prohibition against homosexual ordinations went into effect, UMC bishops ordained sodomites in Colorado and California. The New York UMC Conference passed a resolution which said, "We deeply regret our denomination's continued oppression of homosexual persons . . . We look forward to the day when the church will accept gay and lesbian persons into full fellowship." [106]

Retiring UMC bishop Melvin Wheatley spoke to a body of the Metropolitan Community Churches (MCC) in Sacramento, California, in 1985, and said the MCC is "wonderful because you are mixing the gay and Christian experience." The MCC is a homosexual denomination. Wheatley said in 1983, "I clearly do not believe that homosexuality is a sin . . . Homosexuality, quite like heterosexuality, is neither a virtue nor an accomplishment. It is a mysterious gift of God's grace . . . His or her homosexuality is a gift – neither a virtue nor a sin." [107]

Many United Methodist churches have performed wedding ceremonies for homosexuals, and a number of homosexuals have been ordained to the ministry in the UMC. James Conn, pastor of a UMC congregation in Ocean Park, California, said, "The Gospel, as I understand it, is about the quality of the relationship, whether it is a homosexual or heterosexual one." Ignacio Castuera, of Hollywood First Methodist Church, said the church is under a moral obligation to bless gay requests for marriage ceremonies.[108]

In 1992, the UMC Commission on Christian Unity and Interreligious

Concerns declared itself open to the full participation of all people, including gays and lesbians, and the top judicial body of the UMC ruled that the agency was within its rights to make such a declaration. When Melvin Talbert was ordained head bishop for Northern California and Nevada in 1988, he stated, "I do not believe we know enough about homosexuality to make hard and fast rules. I would have hoped we could be more open and compassionate to people of different sexual orientations. I come with no prejudgments." That same year, the California Methodist Conference sponsored an "enrichment weekend" for homosexual couples.[109]

(3) A busy church without doctrinal discipline and moral purity risks sliding into the spiritual disorder of Thyatira, a church that appears to manifest love, faith, patience, and good works. However, all of these vital attributes will never substitute for sound doctrine and godly living.

The major fault that Jesus finds with the Thyatira church is that it entrusts positions of teaching leadership to *immoral* women, prophetesses who teach and mislead the people to follow them instead of Jesus:

> **"I know thy works, and charity, and service, and faith, and thy
> patience, and thy works; and the last to be more than the first.
> Notwithstanding, I have a few things against thee, because thou
> sufferest that woman Jezebel, which calleth herself a prophetess,
> to teach and seduce my servants to commit fornication, and to
> eat things sacrificed unto idols." – Revelation 2:19-20**

These female teachers stray away from the fundamental truth of the Scriptures and seduce the Thyatira church into committing fornication and idolatry by disguising carnality as spirituality. They stress "love" over doctrine and separation, and merge pagan practices and idolatry into Christian works and worship by morphing secular rituals into the authority of Scriptural doctrine.

We see these apostate characteristics today in the Presbyterian Church (USA), which is struggling with Biblical interpretation, particularly as it relates to homosexuality. In 2005, for example, a female Presbyterian minister in Pennsylvania came under scrutiny after performing a marriage between a lesbian couple, including infusion of Buddhist rites in the ceremony.[110]

Her case was to be heard by the church's court. Officially, this church does not prohibit clergy-performed blessing ceremonies for same-sex unions, as long as it clear that the blessing ritual is not a marriage ceremony. Spiritual confusion reigns over this denomination, where sexually-active gay people cannot officially serve as pastors, elders or deacons, but many Presbyterian scholars, pastors, and theologians are heavily involved in the debate over homosexuality.[111]

(4) A church that tolerates immorality risks becoming *superficial* in their faith, like the church at Sardis, which lacks any real spiritual substance:

> **"I know thy works, that thou has a name that thou livest, and art dead. Be watchful, and strengthen the things which remain, that are ready to die: for I have not found they works perfect before God." – Revelation 3:1-2**

This church was once strong, but its spiritual power is gone. The members profess to be Christians, but they are not truly born again. They only go through the motions of religion – a sad situation found in many churches today. Though they appear to be alive and impressive outwardly, the church is absolutely dead inside. Even their good works are driven by wrong motives. Bottom line: Jesus has nothing for which to commend Sardis.

(5) A spiritually dead church evolves into spiritual complacency, like the church at Laodicea, which is blinded by spiritual arrogance and self-satisfaction. Our Lord sternly warns them:

> **"I know thy works, that thou art neither cold nor hot: I would thou wert cold or hot. So then because thou art lukewarm, and neither cold nor hot, I will spue thee out of my mouth. Because thou sayest, I am rich, and increased with goods, and have need of nothing; and knowest not that thou art wretched, and miserable, and poor, and blind and naked . . ." – Revelation 3:15-17**

Spiritually, these people are neither frozen nor fiery. They are *lukewarm*, unenthusiastic, indifferent and apathetic. This church sits on the premises instead of standing on the promises, unexcited about anything, unalarmed by anything. They hinder the cause of Christ, because spiritual indifference and apathy turns many away from the Gospel.

But even worse, they are unaware of being in this terrible condition. They ignorantly think they thrill God's heart, but they actually sicken His stomach. They consider themselves wonderful, but God calls them a failure. They deserve pity rather than praise. They are rich in material things, but bankrupt in spiritual things. Instead of having a vision, they see visions.[112]

Discerning eyes can now recognize the apostate church of the False Prophet that is coming up around us:

- A very busy church that appears to do many good deeds, but is spiritually dead.
- A church that professes Christianity, but tolerates and even teaches immorality.
- A superficial church that is merged with the world, with no witness for Jesus Christ.

Unless this apostate church repents and returns to their relationship with the Lord, they will be led by the False Prophet into the ecumenical "harmony" of the interfaith movement. Interfaithism is tailored to spiritually compromise and politically integrate all the belief systems of the world into one religion that serves a "greater good for humanity" – the global system of the Antichrist.

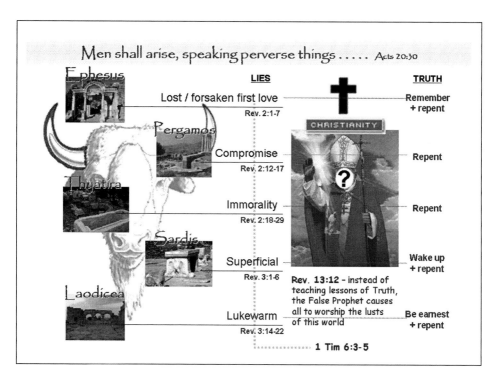

As John sees the False Prophet rising to power, note how he

147

repeatedly reminds us of the healing of the deadly wound – the reconstruction of the global economic system after it collapses:

> "to worship the first beast, *whose deadly wound was healed* ... to the beast, which had *the wound by a sword, and did live.*" – Revelation 13:12, 14

Under the False Prophet, the apostate church will blindly worship the Antichrist through religious ceremonies, global tithing, faith-based social programs, and other religious initiatives that will be used to help reconstruct his economic and political systems and heal the deadly wound.

But that's not all. For those few stragglers that remain skeptical of the interfaith movement, the False Prophet will deceive them through supernatural signs and wonders, absolute miracles that happen right before their eyes and "shock and awe" them into his web of destruction.

CHAPTER 11

Signs and Wonders

The rise of the False Prophet testifies how superficial religion is chained and bound to the judgmental pressure-cooker of the coming one-world political and economic system.

Can't you already sense that the world's system of living is evolving into a pressure-cooker for those people who profess to know the Lord, but don't really know Him? All around us, we see superficial religion boiling under political and economic pressures, secular stresses and anxiety. The harder it works to succeed within the secular system, the higher the heat rises. Superficial religion burns inside with restlessness, discontentment, fear and anger. Superficial religion lives under the bondage of the antichrist spirit – the bondage of busyness.

Busyness is the exact opposite of quiet. Continual busyness is not healthy. A continually busy life has no quiet time, no rest, no peace. The busier life becomes, the lesser fulfillment it contains. Busyness increases stress and anxiety. Stress and anxiety thrive under pressure, and John emphasizes that the boiler of secular stress and anxiety will explode when the world economic system collapses and the Antichrist rises to power through his uncanny abilities to rebuild the political and economic systems of the world.

A spiritual earthquake erupts when the global economy collapses. All at once, the superficial religion of the masses goes into meltdown when the financial calamity happens. When superficially religious people are consumed with accumulating wealth and power, work and possessions – not God – become their entire reason for existing. There is no real spiritual governance over their secular life. When the world's financial system collapses, their entire reason for existing is challenged. They lose everything that gives them meaning to their life – their job, their wealth, their sense of power over their personal sphere of influence.

Their loss of these secular expressions wounds their superficially religious attitude and motivation. Their very reason for being implodes. This is the real impact of the deadly wound: the loss of secular influence slices deep into the superficial religion of people, far beyond their financial and political calamity. The deadly wound bleeds a spiritual havoc that turns superficially religious people into depraved, rebellious, wounded animals.

In the midst of all this chaos, the Antichrist takes center stage. As he rebuilds all the regional political and economic operations into one system under his authority, the Antichrist fully understands that his new system will not function properly under the depravity and rebellion of a spiritual meltdown. His system risks total anarchy unless the people can be spiritually united to find some sort of inner peace from their rampant spiritual disorder, so the Antichrist relies on his False Prophet:

> **"And he doeth great wonders, so that he maketh fire come down from heaven on the earth in the sight of men, and deceiveth them that dwell on the earth by the mans of those miracles which he had power to do in the sight of the beast . . ." – Revelation 13:13-14**

To impose the secular politics and economics of the Antichrist inside the spiritual lives of people who are desperately searching for answers, the False Prophet will unite all of the religions of the world. He will overthrow and replace any remaining skepticism of the people about his spiritual power by *doing great wonders*. The term *wonders* here in the ancient Greek literally means "miracles that indicate or signify supernatural power." This immediately reminds us of our Savior's warning about the end times:

> **"For there shall arise false Christs, and false prophets, and shall shew great signs and *wonders*; insomuch that, if it were possible, they shall deceive the very elect." – Matthew 24:24**

Notice that Jesus prophetically speaks here of the Antichrist and the False Prophet using supernatural powers to deceive the *very elect*, i.e. those people in roles of religious authority who are spiritually intelligent.

Our Lord is explaining why all the people in the world, even those in respected positions of religious authority who should know better, will be deceived into believing that the Antichrist is the Messiah that has come to save them and their collapsing world. Blinded by deception, the masses will allow him and his False Prophet to assume totalitarian control over their lives.

This will be "shock and awe" on both a natural and supernatural scale never before witnessed by human eyes. Everyone will watch in total awe of the amazingly fast recontruction, absolutely successful organization, seemingly magical abundance of the global economic system built by the Antichrist. At the very same time, they will literally be shocked into believing he is the savior of the world by the spectacular miracles performed by his False Prophet.

John explains that the False Prophet will awe people with "*great wonders.*" This master magician will showcase his phenomenal supernatural power on a massive scale, even to the point of "making fire come down from heaven on the earth in the sight of men." In the ancient Greek, the term *fire* means "lightning," and the phrase *come down* means "to descend." In other words, the False Prophet will literally cause lightning to descend from the sky in front of everyone's eyes – certainly an awesome feat of power.

But that's not all, because "calling down lightning" reveals something much deeper than a mere streak of lightning that becomes visible to the human eye. The phrase *come down* also means "to cast down" or "fall down," the same term Jesus used to describe Satan falling from heaven *as lightning*:

"And He said unto them, "I beheld Satan as lightning fall from heaven." – Luke 10:18

When Lucifer, once a beautiful archangel of light, rebelled against Jehovah God, our Lord expelled (cast down) this angel of light from the spiritual realm of heaven. This supernatural ejection was manifested and seen in the natural world as a physical bolt of lightning (Satan) falling down out of the sky to signify that *all* demons are fallen angels who are subject to God's authority and power. No demon, not even Satan himself, has any supernatural abilities except those that are granted to him by Almighty God alone.

This again confirms that our Lord is in complete control of everything going on in His creation. Absolutely nothing can happen during the last days unless He alone allows it. This means the magic of the Antichrist and the False Prophet are only powers permitted by God Himself to be components of the strong delusion that our Lord sends to the unrighteous people in the world during the last days:

> "Even him, whose coming is after the working of Satan with all power and signs and lying wonders, and with all deceivableness of unrighteousness in them that perish; because they received not the love of the truth, that they might be saved. And for this cause God shall send them a strong delusion, that they should believe a lie: that they all might be damned who believe not the truth, but had pleasure in unrighteousness." – 2 Thessalonians 2:9-12

We must recognize and understand here that the depth of God's "strong delusion" transcends both the natural and supernatural realms. To fully delude people into believing that the Antichrist is the Messiah, God will allow the False Prophet to "call down lightning from the sky" before shocked human eyes in the natural world. But in the supernatural world that is invisible to the human eye, this lightning represents demons (fallen angels) that are being called down from the spiritual realm by the False Prophet to breed deeper deception among the people.

Under the influence of demons, in a world where real Christianity and the Truth of the Gospel have been removed during the Rapture, people will succumb to the spiritual foolishness and ignorance of the global interfaith system of the False Prophet. This religious system will foster disobedience and ultimately rebellion against the Lord. In this manner, the False Prophet is allowed to preach and proclaim his portrayal of the Antichrist as the coming Messiah prophesied by Jesus – by calling down lightning:

> "For as *lightning* cometh out of the east, and shineth even unto the west; so shall also the coming of the Son of Man be." – Matthew 24:27

By shocking the masses with extraordinary miracles in the natural realm, and confusing them through demonic influences in the supernatural realm, the False Prophet will spread the great delusion that the Antichrist is the Lord Himself, returning to restore His Kingdom.

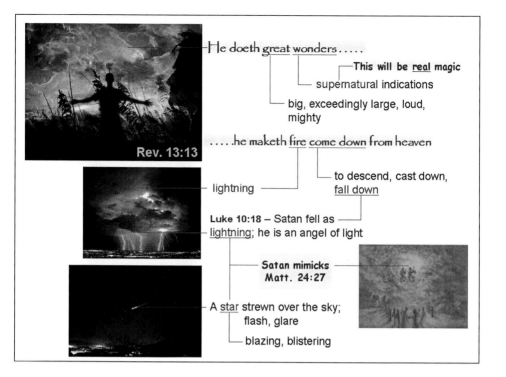

He doeth great wonders . . . . .

This will be **real** magic
supernatural indications
big, exceedingly large, loud, mighty

Rev. 13:13

. . . . .he maketh fire come down from heaven

to descend, cast down, fall down

lightning

Luke 10:18 – Satan fell as lightning; he is an angel of light

Satan mimicks Matt. 24:27

A star strewn over the sky; flash, glare
blazing, blistering

Could all of this really happen? It not only could, but it will, because we can already see the stage being set behind the scenes with the young people of our generation today. Most of these kids have largely grown up with no Christian background. Instead, they (along with many of their parents) have grown up being entertained by a world filled with the magic of books, movies, television and computer games seen in Harry Potter, the Lord of the Rings, Doom, Halo, WarCraft, Dungeons and Dragons, Star Trek, Twilight Zone, and volumes of other science fiction and horror movies. For many of them, entertainment and magic have subconsciously become one in the same thing.

For this reason, kids today could consider magic to be perfectly normal: they read about magic, talk about magic, watch magic, play games of magic, or play with toys about magic. Many of them already subconsciously accept that magic is real. You might say that, for them, *seeing is believing.*

These kids are being raised as a totally secular generation without any knowledge of the Lord, but with heavy cultural impressions of magic, sorcery, witchcraft and the occult. This generation will grow up being impressed by signs – by *things they can see.* Jesus speaks candidly about this generation:

153

> **"Then certain of the scribes and of the Pharisees answered, saying, Master, *we would see a sign from thee.* But He answered and said unto them, An evil and adulterous generation *seeketh after a sign . . .*" – Matthew 12:38-39**

Jesus is teaching us here that any generation that only has faith in what they can see and touch is spiritually vulnerable and weak, easily deceived. In other words, these people will mindlessly and selfishly follow a public display of supernatural power like a herd of cattle being led to slaughter.

Who are these people? They are the kids around us today, growing up inundated with all sorts of magical signs that thrill them in movies and computer games. They are many adults today who wander from church to church, seeking signs and wonders.

Notice that our Lord here is speaking to the Pharisees, who represent a shadow-in-type of the apostate church. When we consider what Jesus is saying here to the Pharisees about weak faith and doubt, we're immediately encouraged by what our Savior tells one of His disciples who had begun to doubt Him:

> **"Jesus saith unto him, Thomas, because thou hast seen Me, thou hast believed: *blessed are they that have not seen, and yet have believed.*" – John 20:29**

Our Lord is telling us that we who believe in Him by faith alone – not by any signs or wonders – are spiritually strong through His Grace and His Mercy. Hallelujah to the Holy One! Praises be to the Lamb that was slain! Glory to God our Father through Jesus our Lord! Just like Thomas, each of us calls Jesus Christ "my Lord and my God."

However, many of the young people around us today will be the secular humanists going through the spiritual meltdown of tomorrow, an evil and perverse generation that seeks a sign – and they get that and more from the False Prophet. They will readily accept the wonders performed by the False Prophet as real and, in doing so, will totally collapse under his power and join his interfaith religious movement.

As head of the interfaith religion, the False Prophet will exercise all the satanic power of the first beast. He will share all the same values, the same beliefs, the same worldview, the same economic, political and social policies as the Antichrist – and a lost generation of tomorrow will publicly adore him.

154

Consider the broader applications here. By sharing satanic power with the Antichrist, and leveraging his massive public support, the False Prophet will undoubtedly play a key role in bringing peace to the Middle East. His prominent appeals may even help the Antichrist craft the seven-year peace agreement between the Arab and Jewish people that will trigger the period of Tribulation. There is no question that he will build trust among everyone worldwide who watches his humanitarian efforts.

Most importantly, as the high priest of the apostate church, he will redesign and reconstruct all the religious rituals of the interfaith church by weaving witchcraft and mysticism into church liturgy. Newly created pagan rites will literally institute a spiritual depravity and rebellion that binds mankind to hell here on earth, because the ceremonies of the apostate church will reopen the "Days of Noah" that Jesus warns us about:

> **"But as the days of Noah were, so shall also the coming of the Son of Man be." – Matthew 24:37**

The interfaith religion will usher in an unprecedented New Age of witchcraft across the planet. Jesus prophetically explains how, during this time, absolute demonic wickedness will run rampant. Our Lord relates the magnitude of this wickedness to one other period in history: the days of Noah, a time when pure evil exploded on a scale so great that it grieved God to the point of destroying the world with the Flood:

> **"And God saw that the wickedness of man was great in the earth, and that every imagination of the thoughts of his heart was only evil continually. And it repented the Lord that He had made man on the earth, and it grieved Him at His heart. And the Lord said, I will destroy man who I have created from the face of the earth . . . for it repenteth me that I have made them." – Genesis 6:5-7**

Under the strong delusion of this evil sorcerer, the wickedness of people will be great in the earth. Every imagination of the thoughts of their hearts will be only evil continually. This describes the apostate interfaith church in the last days, growing in all its satanic glory.

Demonic activity and profound wickedness will return to an intensity not seen since the predeluvian days of Noah. Under the interfaith religion, the world will enter into unprecedented spiritual darkness. The interfaith "church" will evolve into a variety of pagan rituals and ceremonies

155

centered on the mystical doctrines of the False Prophet.

For example, since Wicca is openly accepted as part of the interfaith doctrine of the United Religions Intiative, magic and witchcraft will be publicly practiced in high places – displayed in front of the eyes of everyone.[113]

This will be a time when the public use of witchcraft and mysticism is no longer considered taboo. Instead, occult practices will become institutionalized, taught and marketed. The public displays of magic by the False Prophet will literally draw people into the pews, temples and mosques of the apostate church across the world.

These superficial people will be spiritually hurting, with no place else to turn, and they will all selfishly want magical powers of their own to redeem themselves and their lives. For this reason, religious manipulation will guide and direct the masses.

During this time, the apostate church will evolve into a completed Tower of Babel: traditional sermons will be replaced by astrology, the channeling of spirits, the casting of spells and other magic. Sunday school will be exchanged for classes that teach members how to use astrology to restore their finances, their health and their self-esteem.

During these modern Days of Noah, the apostate church will offer cell groups that teach members how to use fortune-telling to restore their business. There will be lessons on how to cast magical spells and use other witchcraft to help people restore or enhance their way of life.

That's not all. Today, we talk about applying Christian teaching to our daily walk, in all facets of our life. Tomorrow, consider how these occult teachings will apply to a person's daily walk, in all facets of their life:

Astrology will be used in their business, as a strategic planning tool that follows the planets to determine when to launch certain products, when to target specific advertising and marketing areas. Tarot cards and other fortune-telling devices will be used to determine when to hire and fire employees, when to raise prices, when to invest in specific stocks, when to sell other assets for profits. Magical spells will be cast by business executives on their competitors to ruin their companies and their product brands. Witchcraft will be used to fight lawsuits and handle other legal matters.

Society will become saturated with the occult as a way to "get ahead" within the system of the Antichrist. A pagan world will revert back to its ancient pagan heritage of the Pharaohs and their magicians, of witches, sorcerers, and mediums.

All of these
practice witchcraft
with magical wonders

Wonders –
• Channeling of spirits
• Astrology
• Predicting the future
• Casting of spells
• Magic

Genesis 41:8 – Egyptian magicians of Pharoah

Exodus 7:11-12, Exodus 8:7; 2 Timothy 3:8-9 –
Jannes, Jambres, magicians of Pharoah

1 Samuel 28:7-19 – Witch of Endor

Acts 8:9,13,18,24 – Simon, a Samaritan sorcerer

Acts 13:6 – Barjesus/Elymas, a Jewish sorcerer

Acts 16:16-18 – a medium in Thyatira

**Revelation 13:13-14 – The False Prophet of the
unholy trinity**

Witchcraft will be encouraged and used in formal events, led and performed by the False Prophet himself. For example, imagine him calling down fire one evening during a highly-publicized religious ceremony attended by the Antichrist and broadcast across the globe. As he stirs and excites the crowd with his passionate sermon, you can hear the False Prophet claiming to be the Elijah that Jesus said would return to renew and invigorate all facets of man's life here by quoting the Scriptures:

> **"And Jesus answered and said unto them, Elias truly shall first come, and restore all things." – Matthew 17:11**

Then, as he calls fire down from heaven just as Elijah did in the Old Testament, the False Prophet will continue the delusion by repeating Elijah's exact words:

> **"And it came to pass at the time of the offering of the evening sacrifice, that Elijah the prophet came near, and said, Lord God of Abraham, Isaac, and of Israel, let it be known this day that Thou art God in Israel, and that I am they servant, and that I have done all these things at Thy Word. Hear me, O Lord, hear me, that this people may know that thou art the Lord God, and that thou hast turned their heart back again. Then the fire of the Lord fell, and consumed the burnt sacrifice, and the wood,**

and the stones, and the dust, and licked up the water that was
in the trench. And when all the people saw it, they fell on their
faces: and they said, The Lord, He is the God; the Lord, He is the
God." – 1 Kings 18:36-39

The cameras will expose the shocked audience, falling on their faces in
awe of his power. There is nothing like "an experience" to convince people
that something must be true, is there? Think about the evangelism explosion
that this public display of magic will have on the world. Just as Jehovah God
uses His signs to authenticate Jesus and His Gospel, so Satan is allowed to
use these public displays to authenticate the beast and his message.

Why? Because wandering people – those who are spiritually blind
– look for a sign to follow, and here they are given one.

At that moment, the master deceiver will turn the platform over to
the Antichrist, who strolls up to the podium in all of his sinister pomp
and majesty, basking in glory as the crowd worships him as God. Playing
off the crowd's awe of the fire called down from the sky, the Antichrist
immediately portrays himself and his False Prophet as the two witnesses
of Revelation 11 by quoting excerpts from the Scriptures (he will try to
discredit the two *real* witnesses):

"And I will give power unto my two witnesses, and they shall
prophesy . . . these are the two olive trees, and the two candlesticks
standing before the God of the earth. And if any man will hurt
them, fire proceedeth out of their mouth, and devoureth their
enemies: and if any man will hurt them, he must in this manner be
killed." – Revelation 11:3-5

The son of perdition will portray himself as the loving Lamb of God,
possessing supernatural abilities to elevate the happiness of people who
are struggling with stress and pressure. But in reality, both he and his False
Prophet are dedicated to the complete spiritual destruction of all those
they have deceived. Their roles, indeed their entire lives, are a delusion:
they are both religious impostors, frauds who cause people to stray from
spiritual safety and truth, from virtues, from doctrinal orthodoxy or piety.

In other words, the entire mission of the False Prophet is to propagate
a lie about the fulfilling deliverance of the Antichrist and his system. His
teaching will expound upon a systematic discourse of religious ideas,
spiritual reasoning and rational logic that focus on the Antichrist alone as
the living God. He will proclaim that the system of the Antichrist is the

ultimate path to freedom, both here in this moment of life and for eternal peace in the future.

In fact, these public displays of supernatural power and miracles leave the people is such awe – their delusion becomes so strong – that the False Prophet actually convinces them to build and worship a statue of the Antichrist as their god:

> **"And deceiveth them that dwell on the earth by the mans of those miracles which he had power to do in the sight of the beast; saying to them that dwell on the earth, that they should make an image to the beast, which had the wound by a sword, and did live."**
> **– Revelation 13:14**

Here we see the lowest point ever in the history of mankind. The interfaith church is exposed in all of its apostate blindness, nakedness and weakness. Organized into a religious institution that is completely yielded to the power of the False Prophet in every facet of life, these apostate people proudly and publicly break the First and Second Commandments:

> **"Thou shalt have no other gods before me. Thou shalt not make unto thee any graven image, or any likeness of any thing that is in heaven above, or that is in the earth beneath, or that is in the water under the earth. Thou shalt not bow down thyself to them, nor serve them: for I the Lord they God am a jealous God . . ."**
> **– Exodus 20:3-5**

There will be absolutely no separation of church and state in the apostate church, as it becomes one in the same with the public marketplace. The experiences encountered in one resemble the same experiences of the other. The mystical signs and wonders used to succeed in the public marketplace will originate from the interfaith church. All will adhere to and work within the system of the Antichrist.

This means that religion, economics and politics will all have the same appearance, the same meaning, *the same purpose*. The center of worship and the affairs of the state will all intermix and merge together so transparently that they will even share the same *image*, a statue built in worship of their god – the Antichrist.

CHAPTER 12

Image Is Everything

"... to them that dwell on the earth, that they should make an image to the beast, which had the wound by a sword, and did live. And he had power to give life unto the image of the beast, that the image of the beast should both speak, and cause that as many as would not worship the image of the beast should be killed."
– Revelation 13:14-15

An *image* is a likeness that resembles that which it represents. The term *image* here in the ancient Greek points to an actual statue that will be physically constructed as an outward representation of the first beast.

The first beast represents a dangerous economic and political system driven by a destructive attitude of rebellion against God. The Antichrist, who is the evil leader and icon of this system, stands for the rebellious people that want independence from God. That means that this image, this statue, represents the icon of political and economic independence of those who are in rebellion against God.

Because rebellion is a form of spiritual disorder that begins in the heart, this statue, then, is ultimately a public symbol of the spiritual disorder inside the hearts of those in rebellion. In other words, before this statue is ever *physically* built, the image of the beast will have already been constructed *inwardly*, within the hearts of the people. In fact, we can see that this construction has already begun in the hearts of many of those around us.

For example, we see the image of the beast being built everywhere that has an "anything goes" attitude. We see the profile of the beast being chiseled out everywhere that irreverence towards the things of God exists.

We see the image of the beast being carved into Biblical standards that are compromised for the sake of "unity" or "political correctness."

Anywhere that sin is applauded, allowed, or made comfortable – particularly in the name of *love* and *forgiveness* – represents an outward manifestation of the image of the beast that exists inside the heart. Once the idolatrous heart condition completely resembles the image of the beast, then the outward physical statue will be constructed in the same likeness. The physical statue here in Revelation 13:14-15, then, is an outward representation of what the rebellious heart actually worships, what the sinful heart yields to.

This statue will resemble the physical likeness of the Antichrist himself, but at the same time it will also magnify the profile of the UN as his all-powerful global system. How will it do all of this?

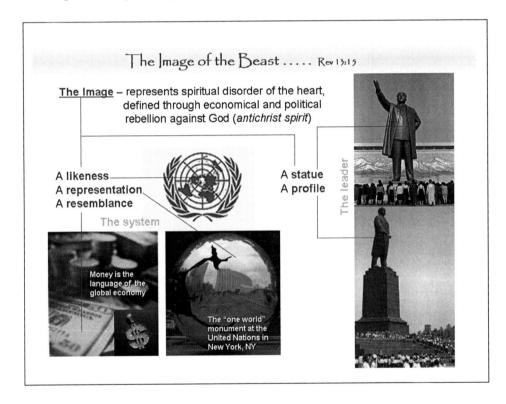

The Image of the Beast ..... Rev 13:15

The Image – represents spiritual disorder of the heart, defined through economical and political rebellion against God (*antichrist spirit*)

A likeness
A representation
A resemblance

The system

A statue
A profile

The leader

Money is the language of the global economy

The "one world" monument at the United Nations in New York, NY

The Old Testament provides us with some detailed prophetic insights into this question by pointing us back into ancient time, to the exaltation of another false god in another demonic system of religion, one whose worship represented a false salvation and delivery from death:

"Nebuchadnezzar the king made an image of gold, whose height was three-score cubits, and the breadth thereof six cubits: he set it up in the plain of Dura, in the province of Babylon. Then Nebuchadnezzar the king sent to gather together the princes, the governors, and the captains, the judges, the treasurers, the counselors, the sheriffs, and all the rulers of the provinces, to come to the dedication of the image which Nebuchadnezzar had set up.

Then the princes, the governors, and captains, the judges, the treasurers, the counselors, the sheriffs, and all the rulers of the provinces, were gathered together unto the dedication of the image that Nebuchadnezzar the king had set up; and they stood before the image that Nebuchadnezzar had set up. Then an herald cried aloud, To you it is commanded, O people, nations, and languages, that at what time ye hear the sound of the cornet, flute, harp, sackbut, psaltery, dulcimer, and all kinds of musick, ye fall down and worship the golden image that Nebuchadnezzar the king hath set up:

And whoso falleth not down and worshippeth shall the same hour be cast into the midst of a burning fiery furnace. Therefore at that time, when all the people heard the sound of the cornet, flute, harp, sackbut, psaltery, and all kinds of musick, all the people, the nations, and the languages, fell down and worshipped the golden image that Nebuchadnezzar the king had set up." – Daniel 3:1-7

King Nebuchadnezzar was the unprecedented ruler of the government of Babylon, unchallenged in political, economic and legal power over the people. The Antichrist will be the unprecedented ruler of the world government, unchallenged in political, economic and legal power over the people. Nebuchadnezzar was the icon of government authority and control, just as the Antichrist will be. Nebuchadnezzar constructed an image of gold for the people to worship him as their god. The Antichrist will build an image of himself for the people to worship him as their god.

All of these "back to the future" matches identify Nebuchadnezzar as an ancient shadow-in-type of the future Antichrist. As such, this ancient state ceremony that unveiled the statue of Nebuchadnezzar in Babylon over 2,500 years ago also prophetically reveals many details about the future image of the Antichrist and the absolute state power that it symbolizes behind the scenes.

First of all, note in Daniel 3 the astounding size of Nebuchadnezzar's statue of gold, which was three-score cubits tall and six cubits wide. A *cubit* measures from the elbow to the tip of the middle finger, approximately 18 inches, meaning this enormous statue was 90 feet tall and nine feet wide! To fully appreciate its size, consider that the average man today is around 5'10" tall. Men today are taller than they were only a few decades ago, even more so than those of 2,500 years ago. By assuming conservatively that the average man in Babylon was 5'9" tall, we can begin to grasp the immense magnitude of this statue.

This reveals that the image of the Antichrist will also be a gigantic statue, a revelation that has already been confirmed by recent history when we recall the huge 60' tall statue of Lenin (another shadow of the Antichrist) that was erected by the communists in Vilnius, Lithuania under the totalitarian atheistic state of the Soviet Union (another shadow of the beast).

The extraordinary size of this image relates to another prophetic truth of Jesus' words to the disciples about the last days:

> **"But as the days of Noah were, so shall also the coming of the Son of Man be."** – Matthew 24:37

Our Savior explains that He, the Son of Man, will return during the last days – a time that He compares to "the days of Noah." These "days" refer to the time of Genesis 6, when the entire heart of mankind was in total rebellion against God. Human wickedness was so perverted that demons literally left their first estate (the spiritual realm) and mated with rebellious human women. Their offspring were the *giants*, enormous and wicked partial-human/partial-demon creatures that began to dominate the world.

The giants of Noah's time were physical images created from the demon seeds of independence and rebellion against God that had mated with human hearts to birth spiritual disorder – just like the image of the beast. Because rebellion is a form of spiritual disorder that begins in the heart, these giants, then, were ultimately public symbols of the spiritual disorder inside the hearts of those in rebellion – just like the image of the beast. Before these giants were ever *physically* born, their images were already constructed *inwardly*, within the hearts of the people – just like the image of the beast.

This explains how the giants are Old Testament impressions of the image of the Antichrist:

- Both have colossal size that awes and intimidates humans
- Both are created by demons through humans
- Both symbolize a dangerous, perverted world in wicked rebellion against God

164

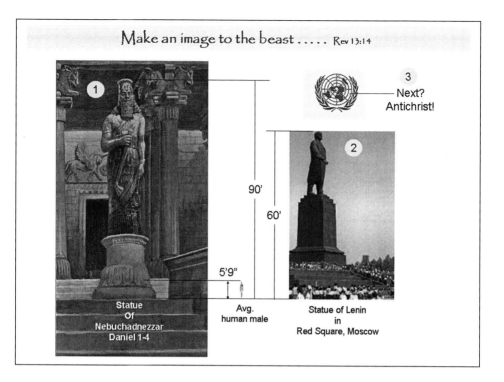

Make an image to the beast ..... Rev 13:14

1 — Statue Of Nebuchadnezzar Daniel 1-4

90'

60'

5'9" — Avg. human male

2 — Statue of Lenin in Red Square, Moscow

3 — Next? Antichrist!

Second, in Daniel 3 we note that the statue of Nebuchadnezzar is made of gold to symbolize political authority and economic wealth. This reveals that the image of the Antichrist will magnify the son of perdition as the symbol of ultimate political authority and unlimited economic wealth.

Next we see that Nebuchadnezzar sets up his statue in the plain of Dura, an easily accessible location that allows a vast number of people to view and worship the statue at the same time. Notice in Revelation 13:14 that the image of the beast will be viewable to "them that dwell on the earth" – it will be seen globally, *by everybody* on the planet, *from everywhere* on the planet. How will this be accomplished?

The advent of the Internet and the convergence of wireless technologies has transformed our world into a new "plain of Dura." We live in an Age of Screens that provides easy access to news, events or entertainment from any location on the planet. No matter where we go or what we do – homes, workplaces, cars, phones, televisions, computers, restaurants, office lobbies, theatres – there are one or more screens before our eyes, constantly televising some sort of information media.

In the new plain of Dura, Internet technology will bring the image of the Antichrist into full and constant view of the entire world, so that

165

everyone across the globe will have to worship it. It is not a coincidence that access and use of the Internet requires people to enter "<u>www.xxxxx. xxxx</u>," where *www* is the acronym for *w*orld *w*ide *w*eb and is normally used as the prefix, or first node of the Internet domain names, such as "<u>www.whatever.com</u>." This acronym prophetically relates the Internet to the Antichrist further down in our text:

"Here is wisdom. Let him that hath understanding count the number of the beast: for it is the number of a man; and his number is Six hundred threescore and six." – Revelation 13:18

The ancient Hebrew and Greek alphabets do not use separate characters or alphabets to represent numbers and letters. Letters are also used to represent numbers, so each letter is also a numerical value. The Hebrew equivalent of our "w" is the letter "vav" or "waw." The numerical value of *vav* is 6. So the English "www" transliterated into Hebrew is "vav vav vav," which is the numerical equivalent of 666. This means "www" *relates* to the number of the beast identified by the Apostle John, but it is not *the* number, as we shall see later on.[114]

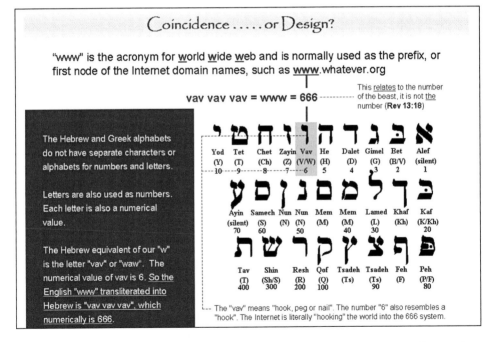

Furthermore, the term "vav" literally means "hook, peg or nail," and the shape of the number 6 actually does resemble a hook. This insight reveals that the Internet is literally "hooking" everyone in the world into accepting the future system of the beast.

The Internet has already created the new "plain of Dura" that the Antichrist will use to set up his image for worship, just as Nebuchadnezzar did before. But that's not all, because many of the screens in our lives are not just watched passively. We have already been hooked into using them interactively. We use converging communications technologies for all sorts of services at work and play (word processing, engineering design, production control, entertainment, online shopping, banking and financial services, travel arrangements, etc.) or for different forms of security and protection from terrorism and anarchy (cameras, embedded sensors, video alarms, etc.).

Today, all types of situations and events – public, private, intimate, secret – can now be viewed *by everybody* on the planet, *from everywhere* on the planet, all at the same time. All of the people, the nations, and the languages can link together to watch events on the global stage, with an unlimited variety of choices. In the Age of Screens, people have become more dependent on communications technology than ever before for their entire livelihood.

But behind the screens – behind the scenes – a technological paradox is evolving: the expanding integration of communications tools that serve people today will control them tomorrow.

Tomorrow, after the collapse of the global economy, the Antichrist will begin his reconstruction initiatives. One of those initiatives will be to seize absolute control of all communications and media broadcasting under the mandate of security from terrorism and anarchy in a world of chaos. Overnight, the same World Wide Web that was once used to *provide* services will be used to *control* services provided. At that moment, the Internet will be used to "peg" and scrutinize everyone in the world through the system of the beast.

It won't stop there. As the Antichrist institutes his new political and economic systems, communications technologies will be used on more personal levels to expand control over those who depend upon it for their work, their entertainment, their entire livelihood. All events – public, private, intimate, secret – *will* be viewed by everybody on the planet, from everywhere on the planet, all at the same time – regardless of whether the participants want them seen or not.

Ultimately, for the Antichrist to establish himself as God over the masses, the day is coming when his image will be seen on every screen, by everybody, from everywhere, at the same time – whether they want to see it or not. On that day, the Internet will be used to "nail" and bind everyone to the system of the beast. Welcome to the return of Babylon:

"And upon her forehead was a name written, MYSTERY, BABYLON THE GREAT, THE MOTHER OF HARLOTS AND ABOMINATIONS OF THE EARTH." – Revelation 17:5

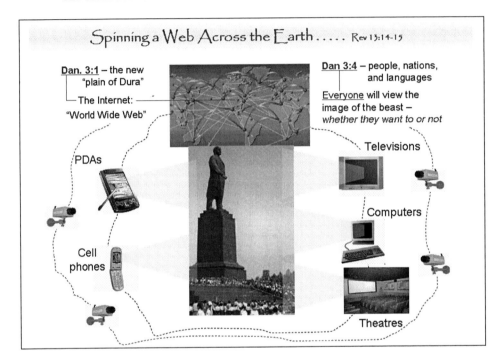

Also notice in Daniel 3 Nebuchadnezzar's public ceremony of prostration before the image. Here are all the political, judicial and public representatives of the state, conducting a religious ceremony for the image of their god – no different than what the False Prophet is doing for the image of the Antichrist here in Revelation 13:14-15.

Nebuchadnezzar calls together all of the principal officials of his kingdom to dedicate the statue. This assembly includes the highest officials of each province, plus any individuals that come into contact with every element of society. These men, representing the highest military, civilian, and judicial authorities in the land, are initiated and indoctrinated into the cult of the state so that they can return to their respective regions and enforce the new cult on the immediate population under their control.

The Scriptures are explaining here in Daniel 3 exactly how the global system of the Antichrist will fall in line. Check this out. In Daniel 3, seven classes of officials are specifically designated. Each class prophetically represents a position of authority within the beast (the United Nations). *Princes* in the Babylon under Nebuchadnezzar were his chief rulers, guardians, the watchers over major divisions of his empire. These ancient princes symbolize the globalist bankers who manage the International Monetary Fund (IMF), the World Bank and the Bank for International Settlements (BIS), and the globalist politicians who legislate the World Trade Organization (WTO) and the International Court of Justice.

Governors in Nebuchadnezzar's Babylon were the civil administrators over his provinces, those smaller areas within the major divisions of his empire. These ancient governors symbolize the globalist politicians who will manage the seven primary commercial trade alliances of the WTO: NAFTA, EU, APEC, OPEC, MERCOSUR, CIS and the African Union.

It is no coincidence that these bodies within the hierarchy of the UN under the Antichrist reflect the celestial hierarchy of demons under Satan that the Apostle Paul lists in the New Testament:

> **"For we wrestle not against flesh and blood, but against** *principalities*, **against** *powers*, **against the** *rulers of darkness* **of this world, against** *spiritual wickedness in high places.***"** – **Ephesians 6:12**

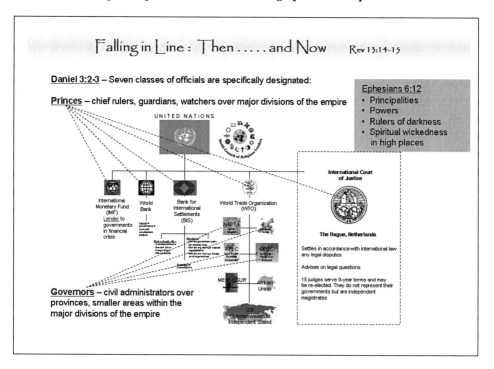

169

This means the globalist "princes" of the UN occupy the same position of authority in the natural world that the "principalities" do in the supernatural realm. In the same way, the globalist "governors" of the UN conform with the "powers" of the spirit world.

Judges in ancient Babylon were the judges, lesser judges, lawyers and guardians of the law. These ancient judges symbolize the judges who work in the International Court of Justice. They also represent manifestations of the "rulers of darkness" in the spiritual realm.

Captains were the ancient political and military commanders who exercised supreme authority over cities. They represent the officials who will enforce the laws in each of the seven primary commercial trade alliances in the WTO. As such, they also conform to "spiritual wickedness in high places" in the celestial world.

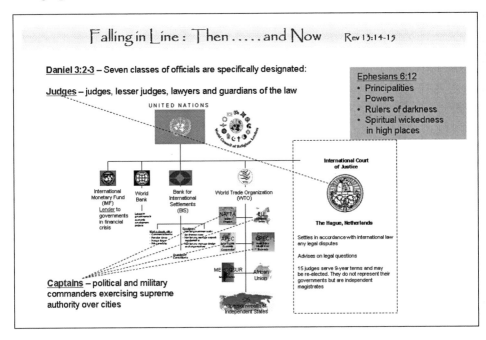

In Daniel 3, as soon as all of these dignitaries are assembled before the colossal statue, the spokesman for Nebuchadnezzar – his herald – makes a loud proclamation to unveil the purpose of the dedication ceremony. This dedication is to promote the cult of Nebuchadnezzar and his cult of the state – the same proclamation that the False Prophet makes concerning the Antichrist in Revelation 13:14-15.

In both situations, the assembly of state dignitaries represents the first step in making the worship of the image *mandatory* for *all* those who are watching. In Daniel 3, the purpose of this ceremony is made plain by the herald, the spokesman of Nebuchadnezzar, as he informs the leaders that this command is proclaimed over *everybody* in the kingdom – including themselves, those that are in positions of power. This is the exact same command that the image of the Antichrist proclaims when the False Prophet "gives it life" in Revelation 13:15.

Where Nebuchadnezzar uses a human spokesman to speak for him in Daniel 3, the image of the Antichrist itself actually speaks in Revelation 13: ". . . he (the False Prophet) had power to give life unto the image of the beast, that the image of the beast should both speak . . ." What exactly does this mean? Does the False Prophet really bring this statue to life?

In the ancient Greek, the term *power* means *to give, to deliver*. In other words, the False Prophet possesses supernatural abilities (power) to transfer (give) life to this statue. He also shares authority (power) over the global communications technology of the Antichrist to send (deliver) the message to every person on the planet that he has given this statue life.

The term *life* means *to breathe a spirit* (a demon, in this instance), and *breathe* means *emit a perception* or *expression*. Here the master magician uses his mystical ability to transfer a demon into this statue so that the image itself emits a perception of being alive. Then he authorizes all of the media to broadcast (emit) a graphical expression of this living statue across the globe for all to see.

The term *speak* means *to talk, to utter words*, and the term *utter* means *to publicly express an opinion or statement*. As such, the demon placed inside the statue talks to the public. Everyone will perceive that the statue itself is alive because it appears to be speaking. Think about that for a moment. Can you imagine the absolute shock and awe of seeing this gigantic statue come to life right before your eyes? People will, no doubt, be spellbound by this towering monstrosity, held captive by its words.

What does this demon statue say?

The living image becomes the state oracle of the Antichrist. It will publicly express, with authority and grandeur, its convincing support for the evil one and its approval of the political, economic and social systems he has reconstructed ("which had the wound by the sword, and did live"). It will praise the Antichrist as the messiah of the people, the savior of the world. It will proclaim that he is the one true god.

All of this adulation from the living oracle will be continually broadcast around the world until the airwaves, along with people's minds, become saturated with the propaganda. But that's only the beginning.

The opinions issued by the demon statue will begin to define how life must now change for everyone. A new day has arrived, a new kingdom is at hand, and the Antichrist is the absolute ruler. As the living image glorifies the sovereign power of the Antichrist and the safety and security of living under his system, it also announces that every person must now express their thanks to the Antichrist by worshipping him – or else face the consequences.

Pause for a moment and reflect on what is really going on here.

The False Prophet has supernaturally transferred a demon spirit into this statue, a creation formed by man. It appears to become a living soul. He "breathes a spirit of life" into this statue, and transforms it into an image of the Antichrist – the ultimate mockery of God when He created man in His own image:

> **"And the *Lord God formed man* of the dust of the ground, and breathed into his nostrils *the breath of life*, and *man became a living soul*." – Genesis 2:7**

Rather than desiring to worship God his Creator, fallen man is now forced to worship his own creation as a god. The demon statue orders all of the people in the world to fall under the authority of the Antichrist.

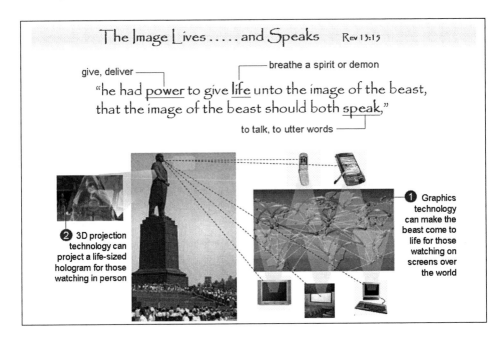

172

The False Prophet will, no doubt, use the most advanced 3D projection technology available to project life-sized holograms of the living image in front of everyone across the planet. Whether watching in person or from distant screens in faraway lands, all eyes will be glued to the ominous presence of the enormous living image of the Antichrist.

Drowning in the great delusion, all voices will declare that he is their god.

Daniel 3 prophetically emphasizes that this living image of the Antichrist will cause *everyone* to worship the son of perdition, with no exceptions: the command is given to *peoples*, which designates people by their racial heritage; the command covers all *nations*, which designates those people of differing geographical and political connections; and finally, the command universally transcends all *languages*, which designates people by their linguistic tendencies.

When the living image of the Antichrist speaks to the world, its words will be translated through communications technology such that they are clearly understood in all languages, even more smoothly and eloquently than the foreign broadcasts we watch today on our televisions. An effect will be created such that, when the demon image of the Antichrist speaks, its words will be the one language that reunites the world under the new Tower of Babel:

> "And the whole earth was of one language, and of one speech."
> – Genesis 11:1

This statue, filled with a demon spirit, speaking in the native tongues of the peoples, represents a satanic version of the Holy Spirit at the day of Pentecost:

> "And they were all filled with the Holy Ghost, and began to speak with other tongues, as the Spirit gave them utterance . . . Now when this was noised abroad . . . every man heard them speak in his own language."
> – Acts 2:4, 6-7

By demanding that "all of them that dwell on the earth" worship the Antichrist and none other, the living image mocks and defies the very Word of the Lord:

> "For as it is written, As I live, saith the Lord, every knee shall bow to me, and every tongue shall confess to God." – Romans 14:11

Daniel 3 also provides another prophetic insight into the future worship of the Antichrist when the herald informs the people that there will be an instrumental musical interlude that follows his speech, and every time they hear this particular song, they are to prostrate themselves and worship the golden image.

Notice that the different instruments listed include a cornet (or horn); a flute; a dulcimer (or bagpipe); a harp, sackbut, and psaltery (all stringed instruments). It is no coincidence that wind instruments and stringed instruments are the musical tools identified here.

This music is more than just a signal to worship, because a single, simple trumpet blast could do that. This music is designed to arouse the emotions of those that hear it, in ways that stir them to be much more willing to participate in the system of the Antichrist.

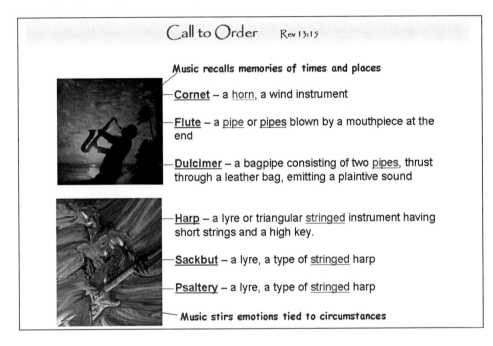

Call to Order   Rev 13:15

Music recalls memories of times and places

Cornet – a horn, a wind instrument

Flute – a pipe or pipes blown by a mouthpiece at the end

Dulcimer – a bagpipe consisting of two pipes, thrust through a leather bag, emitting a plaintive sound

Harp – a lyre or triangular stringed instrument having short strings and a high key.

Sackbut – a lyre, a type of stringed harp

Psaltery – a lyre, a type of stringed harp

Music stirs emotions tied to circumstances

Music is an "international" language that speaks directly to human emotions in ways that can eliminate intellectual, cultural, and religious barriers that may exist between people and divide them. It does this by instantly resurrecting those public and private events from the past that emotionally impacted human lives in one way or another, whether good or bad, intimate or not.

This emotional connection is how a certain song can immediately transport a person back to a specific place and time, identify an entire generation of people with an era in time, or unify a diverse body of people who otherwise have nothing in common.

Since one purpose of the state under the Antichrist is to provide a common, unifying interfaith religion for all of the diverse ethnic, national, and linguistic groups that comprise his kingdom, then music serves as the perfect tool to bring people together as a perfect compliment to his propaganda machine.

Because people tend to let down their guard when they hear music that appeals to them, it can be used to promote and advance virtually anything, including that which is evil. Today, the marketing arms of the media use music to enhance everything from automobile advertisements, feed-the-world campaigns, environmental agendas and animal rights to drug usage and pornography. Tomorrow, the music played by the marketing arms of the Antichrist will appeal to people of all ages.

Many times people can be persuaded to think, say or do things they might not otherwise accept if it is set to beautiful music. In other words, music can be a powerful tool used by the enemy to coerce people into destructive behaviors. The Scriptures explain how the power of music links the Antichrist to the power of the dragon, because Satan was once the choir director of heaven:

> "Thou hast been in Eden the garden of God; every precious stone was thy covering, the sardius, topaz, and the diamond, the beryl, the onyx, and the jasper, the sapphire, the emerald, and the carbuncle, and gold: the workmanship of thy tabrets and of thy pipes was prepared in thee in the day that thou wast created. Thou are the anointed cherub that covereth, and I have set thee so: thou wast upon the holy mountain of God; thou has walked up and down in the midst of the stones of fire. Thou wast perfect in thy ways from the day that thou wast created, till inquity was found in thee.
>
> "How art thou fallen from heaven, O Lucifer, son of the morning! How art thou cut down to the ground, which didst weaken the nations! For thou has said in thine heart, I will ascend into heaven, I will exalt my throne above the stars of God: I will sit also upon the mount of the congregation, in the sides of the north: I will ascend above the heights of the clouds; I will be like the most High.
>
> "Thy pomp is brought down to the grave, and the noise of thy viols ..." – Ezekiel 28:13-15; Isaiah 14:12-14, 11

Prior to his fall from heaven, Satan was named Lucifer (which means *morning star*), a perfect creature whose ancient beauty was emitted through the precious stones of his covering. It is no coincidence that these stones correspond with ten of the 12 stones in the ephod, the shoulder piece that was later worn as a spiritual covering of righteousness by the Jewish high priest in the worship of God.

The ten colorful stones that covered Lucifer reflected the precious emotions of joy that God feels when His Creation praises and worships Him, which is exactly what Lucifer was created to do. He led the angels each morning in the praise and worship of Almighty God with a musical talent that colorfully personified the emotional beauty being displayed in the throne room of heaven (the holy mountain of God).

Lucifer was truly the star of the morning service, a dynamic praise and worship leader that walked up and down the congregation of angels, stirring up passion (fire) for the Lord. His tambourine (tabret) music and beautiful melodies (pipes) must have launched emotional rainbows of color through the precious stones that covered him, filling the throne room with the beauty of God's joy.

But Lucifer became so proud of his own talent and beauty that he arrogantly attempted to ascend upon God's throne and replace the Almighty One, so that *he* would be exalted by all of heaven (I will be like the most High). This prideful archangel became the adversary of Jehovah God, convincing one-third of the angels in heaven to rebel against the Lord and overthrow heaven. But in the heavenly war that followed, God had the archangel Michael and his angels cast Lucifer and his followers out of heaven forever:

> "And his tail drew the third part of the stars of heaven, and did cast them to the earth . . . and there was war in heaven: Michael and his angels fought against the dragon; and the dragon fought and his angels, and prevailed not; neither was their place found any more in heaven. And the great dragon was cast out, that old serpent, called the Devil, and Satan, which deceiveth the whole world: he was cast out into the earth, and his angels were cast out with him."
> – Revelation 12:4, 7-9

The Lord cast His adversary out of heaven and renamed him Satan (which means *accuser* or *adversary*). Pride corrupted his original beauty and he fell from God's presence as an incomplete creature. The same ten stones that once emitted God's joy and pleasure through Lucifer now shed God's judgment upon Satan, a reminder to us that *ten* always represents the spiritual *testimony of law and responsibility*.

As such, those ten stones recall the precious emotional pleasure God enjoys whenever His creation praises and worships Him through responsible obedience to His Law. But they are also a testimony of the destruction of those who arrogantly fail their responsibility to abide by God's Law:

"Pride goeth before destruction, and an haughty spirit before a fall."
– Proverbs 16:18

Because of his arrogance and failure, this former angel of light and beauty was transformed into a hideous dragon of darkness, the same dragon that provides power to the Antichrist. Before pride took hold, his innocent beauty drew close to God through his musical talents. After pride set in, his repulsive arrogance fell away from God. But the emotional power tied to his musical legacy lives on.

Where God wants to recreate people into His image through Jesus Christ, Satan wants to coerce people into his image through the Antichrist. He does this by relying on his musical talents to manipulate their emotions.

For example, the enemy can arouse and control fires of emotional passion through wind instruments (saxophones, trumpets, flutes)

177

and stringed instruments (electric and acoustic guitars) that resonate throughout rock and roll – the same instruments used in Daniel 3. In this way, the evolution of rock and roll music over the last few decades has been a satanic composure orchestrated by the dragon to coerce our entire culture into destructive emotional behaviors.

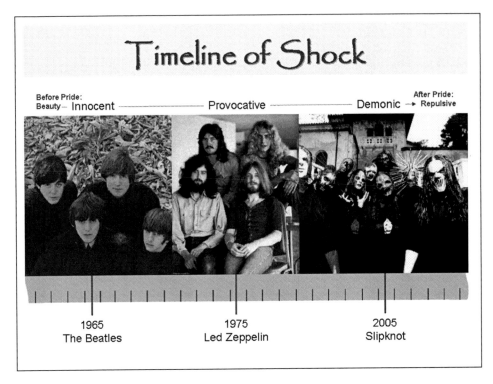

Timeline of Shock

Before Pride:
Beauty– Innocent ———————— Provocative ———————— Demonic → Repulsive

After Pride:

| 1965 | 1975 | 2005 |
| The Beatles | Led Zeppelin | Slipknot |

Consider that the early songs played by bands such as the Beatles were often light, beautiful melodies that reflected the behaviors of cultural innocence in the early 1960s. That innocence began to vanish as pop music evolved into the heavy metal sound created by groups like Led Zeppelin, whose behaviors grew more provocative. Now, as certain strains of heavy metal have evolved into blatantly demonic noise from bands like Slipknot, we are seeing the repulsive elements linked to that music bleed into the mainstream of our culture.

And the orchestra plays on. Today, at every public or private event where rock music is used to arouse emotional frenzy – parties, rock concerts, television programs, football games, wrestling matches, even political campaigns – the image of the Antichrist is already being worshipped in the hearts of the people. Tomorrow, this same form of music will be used to stir people into emotional frenzy around a physical image of the beast, such that they will worship the Antichrist they adore as a god.

This is the exact same indoctrination process that was followed by Nazi Germany in the 1930s. In a letter published by *The Times* of London on July 29, 1936, Baldur von Schirach, the head of the youth program in Nazi Germany, said, "If we act as true Germans, we act according to the laws of God. Whoever serves Adolf Hitler, serves Germany, and whoever serves Germany, serves God." [115]

Can't you hear the image of the beast speaking those same words to the brainwashed generation of tomorrow? "If we act as true members of our earth family, we act according to the laws of God. Whoever serves the Antichrist, serves his system, and whoever serves his system, serves God."

In Daniel 3, the sound of the music transcends into a command of loyalty to Nebuchadnezzar and his state:

> "And whoso falleth not down and worshippeth shall the same hour be cast into the midst of a burning firey furnace. Therefore at that time, when all the people heard the sound of . . . all kinds of musick, all the people, the nations and the languages, fell down and worshipped the golden image that Nebuchadnezzar the king had set up." – Daniel 3:6-7

This is no different than the command of loyalty to the Antichrist and his living image:

> ". . . that the image of the beast should both speak, and cause that as many would not worship the image of the beast should be killed." – Revelation 13:15

In either case, failure to fall down and worship the image is not only considered impious and irreligious, it also amounts to treason. Failure to worship the image represents a betrayal of trust in the god the people worship and the state he controls. And the penalty is death.

Those who obey the commands of the Antichrist show their blind allegiance to him. Indeed, they place the fate of their entire lives solely under the whims of the sovereign state that he rules, and they will be marked as being loyal members of his kingdom.

CHAPTER 13

The Mark of the Beast

In the dark world ruled by the Antichrist, there will be absolutely no separation of church and state. The satanic beliefs of the interfaith religion will be completely merged with the economic and political operations of the public marketplace. The intents behind religious sacrifices and business transactions will blur into the same thing.

Under the Antichrist, there will be no distinction between the world and the church. The marketplace and religion will both worship political power. They will both worship economic influence and materialism. They will both be servants of the Antichrist that kneel to their master: mammon. Jesus encountered this exact problem in the temple of Jerusalem:

> "And Jesus went into the temple of God, and cast out all them that sold and bought in the temple, and overthrew the tables of the moneychangers, and the seats of them that sold doves, and said unto them, It is written, My house shall be called the house of prayer; buy ye have made it a den of thieves.
>
> "No servant can serve two masters: for either he will hate the one, and love the other; or else he will hold to the one, and despise the other. Ye cannot serve God and mammon." – Matthew 21:12-13, Luke 16:13

As He addressed the prideful greed that had manifested inside this temple, our Lord foresaw the spiritual corruption that will mark the future world ruled by the Antichrist.

Jesus tells us that the *true* temple of Almighty God should be a house of humble prayer, a place of peace that goes beyond understanding, a place of rest for the soul. As true Christians, our lifestyles should be a reflection of our worship of Jesus in the temples *of our heart*.

We live a life of peace when we praise the Lord, for our God inhabits our praise of Him. For this reason, the last five Psalms all open with praise of the Lord – because five is the spiritual number of grace, and the stronger our praise is of Jesus Christ, the greater is the power of His grace over our lives. Meditate on that for a moment:

> "Praise ye the Lord. Praise the Lord, O my soul. Praise ye the Lord: for it is good to sing praises unto our God; for it is pleasant and praise is comely. Praise ye the Lord. Praise ye the Lord from the heavens: praise Him in the heights. Praise ye the Lord. Sing unto the Lord a new song, and His praise in the congregation of saints. Praise ye the Lord. Praise God in His sanctuary: praise Him in the firmament of His power."
> – Psalm 146:1, Psalm 147:1, Psalm 148:1, Psalm 149:1, Psalm 150:1

Can't you feel the power of God when you praise Him? When we praise the Lord, we can hear Jesus telling us that His grace is sufficient for every trial, every problem we encounter that makes us weary and weak:

> "And He said unto me, My grace is sufficient for thee: for My strength is made perfect in weakness." – 2 Corinthians 12:9

Now contrast the peace and rest provided by God's grace in the temple of the righteous heart with the disturbing oppression that engulfs the prideful heart under the Antichrist. The hearts of the people have become houses filled with greed, temples where business transactions take priority. Their temples are places of competitive unrest, where the soul is selfishly agitated.

We can relate this to life today, where the secular world and the apostate church are beginning to look more and more alike. It is obvious that temples of selfish greed are already under construction in many of the hearts of both secular and religious leaders and their followers. If we open our spiritual eyes, we can literally see the hardening idolatry *of the heart* – the hardening of mankind to the Gospel of Good News of Jesus Christ. Paul explicitly warns us against this idolatry:

> "Having a form of godliness, but denying the power thereof; from such turn away. What agreement hath the temple of God with idols? For ye are the temple of the living God; as God hath said, I will dwell in them, and walk in them; and I will be their God and they shall be my people. Wherefore come out from among them, and be ye separate, saith the Lord, and touch not the unclean thing; and I will receive you." – 2 Timothy 3:5, 2 Corinthians 6:16-17

The "unclean thing" in the hearts ruled by the Antichrist is the worship of *image*, because the False Prophet will guide the people into a dangerous world where the idol of image personifies everything in life. Under the direction of the False Prophet, both the secular people and the apostate religions worship idols of public image, personal image, and private image.

All of these idols are marked by the money they make and the assets they own – both of which reflect a vanity that is bound to and controlled by the system of the Antichrist. In order to make money and own assets, the False Prophet will teach the apostate religions to worship the image of the Antichrist and the system he operates.

But Jesus teaches us an exact opposite theme for living. He explains that we should never worry about money or things:

> **"And He said unto His disciples, Therefore I say unto you, Take no thought for your life, what ye shall eat; neither for the body, what ye shall put on. The life is more than meat, and the body is more than raiment. Consider the ravens: for they neither sow nor reap; which neither have storehouse nor barn; and God feedeth them: how much more are ye better than the fowls? And which of you with taking thought can add to his stature one cubit?**
> **"If ye then be not able to do that thing which is least, why take ye thought for the rest? Consider the lilies how they grow: they toil not, they spin not; and yet I say unto you, that Solomon in all his glory was not arrayed like one of these. If then God so clothe the grass, which is today in the field, and tomorrow is cast into the oven; how much more will he clothe you, O ye of little faith?**
> **"And seek not ye what ye shall eat, or what ye shall drink, neither be ye of doubtful mind. For all these things do the nations of the world see after: and your Father knoweth that ye have need of these things. But rather seek ye the kingdom of God; and all these things shall be added unto you. Fear not, little flock; for it is your Father's good pleasure to give you the kingdom.**
> **"Sell that ye have, and give alms; provide yourselves bags which wax not old, a treasure in the heavens that faileth not, where no thief approacheth, neither moth corrupteth. For where your treasure is, there will your heart be also." – Luke 12:22-34**

Our Savior explains that worry is directly related to the treasure of a person's heart – in other words, more worry reflects less spiritual trust in God. Less worry reflects more spiritual trust in God.

Now relate our Lord's insight to the image of the Antichrist and his system: a physical image that defies spiritual trust; the physical image of a heart corrupted by economical and political rebellion against God. Blinded by their own vanity, people will be absolutely amazed that this graven image, created by mere men, is given life to glorify the Antichrist for a moment in time.

The brief life given to this image will certainly be interesting, but it does not compare to the amazing promise that our Lord gives us. He states that Jehovah, the Almighty God, the Creator of *all* things, gives us *eternal* life through Jesus Christ, that we may *forever* glorify Him as the Ancient of Days:

> "These words spake Jesus, and lifted up His eyes to heaven, and said, Father, the hour is come; glorify Thy Son, that Thy Son also may glorify Thee. As Thou has given Him power over all flesh, that He should give *eternal life* to as many as Thou hast given Him. And this is *life eternal*, that they might know Thee the only true God, and Jesus Christ, whom Thou has sent." – John 17:1-3

In the last days under the Antichrist, the Apostle John explains that the worship of this graven image is mandatory for everybody in the world:

> "... and cause that as many as would not worship the image of the beast should be killed. And he causeth all, both small and great, rich and poor, free and bond, to receive a mark in their right hand or in their foreheads: And that no man might buy or sell, save he that had the mark, or the name of the beast, or the number of his name." – Revelation 13:15-17

Notice there are no exceptions, for the system causes *all* people to worship the Antichrist: everyone in the whole world. This includes anyone who is alive, from the (small) everyday common citizen to (great) public leaders, dignitaries, officials and celebrities. From those who are (rich) wealthy and possess many assets and influence to those who are (poor) financially distressed, down to beggars and paupers. All are bound under the Antichrist, even those (free) unrestrained citizens who would otherwise be exempt from obligations or liabilities.

In order to control all of these types of people, the Antichrist must use a "universal" language to communicate the same message across all of these diverse backgrounds, one that causes all of these people to worship him as a god.

Recall that in the kingdom of Babylon under Nebuchadnezzar in Daniel 3, music was more than just a signal to worship, because a single, simple trumpet blast could do that. Instead, the music was used – as it still is today

– to arouse the emotions of those that heard it, making them much more willing to participate in the behaviors dictated to them.

Daniel 3 explains how those people lived in fear of being thrown into a fiery furnace if they didn't worship the image of Nebuchadnezzar. His music in Babylon was used to evoke the emotion of *fear* – just as it will be under the Antichrist, where people will also live in fear of being killed if they don't worship his image.

However, along with music the Antichrist will also manipulate emotions through another universal language, one that communicates fear even deeper into the hearts of his citizens. He will treat *money* as more than just a tool to operate with and live on. Money – or more specifically, the *lack* of money – will be used to evoke the emotion of fear.

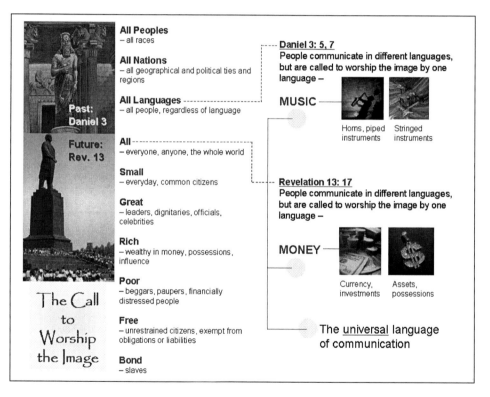

Under both Nebuchadnezzar in the ancient past and the Antichrist in the near future, people are cultural prisoners of fear. Their hearts are captive to their own self-defeating vanity, bound and yoked to the worship of the image. We can already see this same cultural prison of fear being constructed around us today, as the hearts of people fall captive to their own

185

self-destructive behaviors, bound by what others think of them, worshipping the idol of their own image through their love of money.

Music has universal appeal, but money arouses even deeper emotions in people of all ages. The love of money taps into people's public image, personal image, and private image in ways that nothing else can. Money, even more than music, can be used to persuade people to think, say or do things they might not otherwise consider. Money is the most powerful tool the enemy uses to coerce people into destructive behaviors:

> "For the *love of money* is the root of all evil: which while some coveted after, they have erred from the faith, and pierced themselves through with many sorrows." – 1 Timothy 6:10

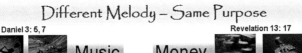

Different Melody – Same Purpose

Daniel 3: 5, 7   Revelation 13: 17

Music   **Money**

* Tends to eliminate intellectual, cultural, and religious barriers that exist between people and divide them.

* Since the purpose of the state here is to unify the diverse ethnic, national, and linguistic groups that comprise the kingdom, it serves as the perfect tool to bring people together.

* Causes people to let down their spiritual guard because it appeals to them.

* Used to promote anything and everything under the sun – including that which is evil or anti-Christian.

* Used to promote everything from automobile advertisements, feed-the-world campaigns, environmental agendas and animal rights to drug usage and pornography.

* Appeals to people of all ages – it is the perfect means to appeal to the masses.

* Can be used to persuade people to think, say or do things they might not otherwise.

* Can be a powerful tool of the enemy to coerce people into destructive behaviors.

In the future world under the Antichrist, music will be used to usher rebellion into the hearts of the masses, but money will be the ideal means of deeply manipulating their fears.

In fact, there is already such a heavy emphasis placed on money and finances in our lives that, at times, it can seem as if the entire world around us already lives in fear. But in those times when fear attempts to filter into our lives, we believers can take heart because we can hear our Savior whispering "fear not" to us:

Under the Antichrist, people will lead broken lives completely wrapped inside fear. They will have no trust in anything other than the money they can earn in the system of the Antichrist. For this reason, they will gladly take a mark from the son of perdition in return for his promise to allow them to survive within his system.

Exactly what is this mark, and how does it work? Here in Revelation 13:16-17, John provides some insights into the mark by explaining how this new world of disorder will operate in the last days.

First of all, John identifies three different classes of people (small and great; rich and poor; free and bond) that will receive (or take) this mark in either their right hand or forehead. Then he describes different representations of the mark, each characterized by its own level of authority within the system of the Antichrist. In other words, each representation of the mark appears to be linked with a certain class of people.

Using this approach, John relates how close the coming system of the Antichrist is to our lives today.

First, how does the ancient Greek term *mark* point to the system of the Antichrist from our modern world? The term "mark" means a *scratch* or *etching*, such as a *stamp* representing a *badge of servitude*. Consider the weird, sudden rise in the popularity of tattoos, which are etched (scratched) into the skin.

Tattoos were once were a statement about nonconformity, an image of rebellion. But over the last 15 years, the acceptance of tattoos has exploded into the mainstream. What does this mean? According to columnist David Brooks of the *New York Times*, we are getting a culture of *trompe l'oeil degeneracy*.[116]

In his column "Nonconformity is Skin Deep," Brooks explains that "people adopt socially acceptable transgressions – like tattoos – to show they are edgy, but inside they are still middle class. You run into these candy-cane grunge types: people with piercings and inkings all over their bodies, who look like Sid Vicious but talk like Barry Manilow. They've got the alienated look – just not the anger."[117]

Brooks continues, "And that's the most delightful thing about the whole tattoo fad. A cadre of fashion-forward types thought they were doing something to separate themselves from the vanilla middle classes, but

187

are now discovering that the signs etched into their skins are absolutely mainstream. They are at the beach looking across the acres of similar markings and learning there is nothing more conformist than displays of individuality, nothing more risk-free than rebellion, nothing more conservative than youth culture. Another generation of hipsters, laid low by the ironies of consumerism." [118]

In other words, our entire culture not only worships image, it worships the image of being rebellious, edgy, hip, counter-cultural – the image of the Antichrist spirit. Tattoos and piercing are the rebellious stamps of ancient paganism, practiced since the days of the Egyptians who served the Pharoahs.

As such, tattoos and piercing point to that coming day when every citizen will be stamped and accepted as a rebellious pagan, proudly tattooed with the badge of servitude to the Antichrist. It could be that, unlike the current tattoos that display a wide array of colorful imagery, the future badge will only be a tattooed symbol representing the emblem of the beast. In any case, the mark itself will display that the person receiving it is *owned* by the pagan system of the Antichrist.

Next, John explains that this mark will be placed in one of two places on the body: either the *hand*, an ancient Greek term meaning *power*, *means*, *instrument*; or the *forehead*, which actually translates to mean the *motivation of the mind*. Whereas the mark itself proves *ownership by* the system, these two locations of receiving it represent *operation within* the system.

In the hand, the mark is an instrument that represents the power the pagan citizen is given to operate within the marketplace, where any and all transactions are performed and controlled electronically through the Internet. "Power" also implies that the mark might be some sort of wireless device that communicates with the other converging digital technologies used in the system.

For convenience and security, this device could be a tiny microchip that is permanently inserted underneath the skin in the right hand of the citizen. By simply waving their hand over store scanners, the citizen could electronically record a purchase or sale. Smart tags could be embedded into cans of food, shoes, fabrics and other materials to track merchandise and replenish inventory.

Think this is far-fetched science fiction? Think again, because these technologies already exist today.

For example, in "Technology Gets Under Our Skin," author Arlene

188

Wright discusses the breakthrough development of Radio Frequency Identification (RFID) modules. "These are computer microchips like those used to track livestock, identify lost pets, and make highway toll payments more efficient. The surprising difference is that these microchips are now being implanted under our skin. Something like this was once possible only in science fiction, but is now becoming a reality," she says. [119]

Wright describes each microchip as being the size of a grain of rice with 64K of memory capacity. These implanted microchips can store and transmit encrypted personal information, such as fingerprints, name, date of birth, etc. to reduce identity theft and fraudulent access to credit card accounts. [120]

"VIP members of an exclusive club in Barcelona, Spain, can get now get an injectable microchip implant for €125. After shots of anesthetic, a microchip can be injected under the skin in a matter of seconds. Usually there is no pain or swelling, and apparently people soon forget the device is even there," explains Wright. "The Barcelona VIP members use themselves as bar codes when paying for their drinks without cash or credit cards. When passed through a scanner, the microchip is activated and emits a signal containing the individual's account number, which is then transmitted to a secure data storage site." [121]

Wright points out that the goals of this technology are to simplify life and make it more secure. A person can simply wave their hand with the implanted chip within 3 inches of a "reader" device to activate it and supply a password. The U.S. Food and Drug Administration gave hospitals approval to inject microchips into their patients so that doctors can more closely monitor health conditions. Wal-Mart and other retailers use them to purchase merchandise. [122]

That's not all. After the 9/11 terrorist attacks, Wright states that the U.S. began moving to issue so-called "E-passports" based on implanted microchips in a system designed to last ten years that is intended to deter passport theft, forgeries, and speed up immigration checks at airports and borders. Dozens of other countries are also considering developing a similar program. [123]

Wright concludes, "Despite their many potential benefits, some worry that microchip implants could also be used by governments and other groups with malicious intent to invade privacy and individual rights because implants could potentially allow someone to monitor your level of activity and your whereabouts." [124]

In other words, Wright sees the potential for control that the Antichrist will have over everyone in the near future, where only those citizens who possess this mark will be able to purchase, sell, and conduct business in the marketplace. The *mark replaces money* in the system of the Antichrist.

As such, all of the manipulative emotional power of money will be transferred to the mark. The love of the mark will tap into people's public image, personal image, and private image in ways that nothing else can. The mark will be used to persuade people to think, say or do things they might not otherwise consider. The mark will be the most powerful tool the Antichrist uses to coerce people into destructive behaviors.

Without the mark, no one can legally purchase food or water to survive. No one can legally sell their products or possessions to make a living. The person that does not have the mark will not only be rejected from the marketplace, they will be expelled from society altogether.

Fear will occupy the mind of every citizen and become the absolute motivation to possess the mark. More specifically, the fear of *not having* the mark will motivate people to take it so that they can live life within the system.

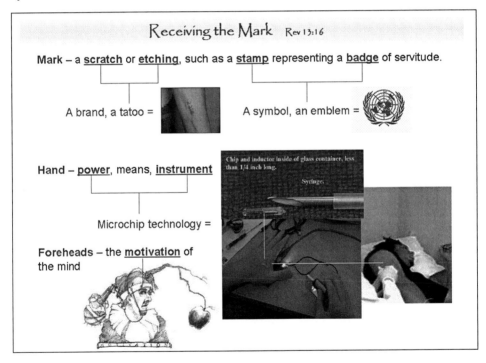

Receiving the Mark Rev 13:16

Mark – a **scratch** or **etching**, such as a **stamp** representing a **badge** of servitude.

A brand, a tatoo =

A symbol, an emblem =

Hand – **power**, means, **instrument**

Chip and inductor inside of glass container, less than 1/4 inch long.

Syringe.

Microchip technology =

Foreheads – the **motivation** of the mind

The power behind the mark cannot be overstated as a mechanism used by the Antichrist to divide his citizens into a hierarchy of three classes that will serve his system.

At the bottom is the largest number of people, the working class of the masses, consisting of everyday common citizens, beggars, paupers, and those who are financially distressed. These people will be tattooed with an emblem that brands them as a servant class citizen. As such, they will have some sort of wireless chip (the mark) implanted into their right hands, or possibly their foreheads, such that every move they make – public and private – is tracked and monitored by the system. These servants eventually lose all real control over their private lives and are reduced to mere slaves that exist under complete control of the system.

This enormous servant class will work under the local public leaders, dignitaries, captains, sheriffs, counselors and celebrities that are appointed to impose and police the regulations and controls of specific areas in each region in the system (each head of the beast).

These local officials will be tattooed with an emblem that brands their specific level of authority in the area of that region. They too will have some sort of wireless chip (the mark) implanted into their right hands, or possibly their foreheads, such that every move, every decision they make – public and private – is tracked and monitored by the system. Though they might have some appearance of autonomy, they are in fact nothing more than mid-level slaves that exist under complete dominance by the system.

These local leaders will, in turn, report to the regional authorities: the wealthy princes, governors, judges, treasurers and other globalists who freely roam the highest places of global authority within the system (the heads of the beast).

These regional rulers will be tattooed or implanted with a symbol/ wireless chip of the system (the name/number of the beast) that brands their specific level of authority over that region. This symbol will be tracked such that every move, every decision they make – public and private – is tracked and monitored through the system.

These authorities will totally succumb to their own lustful desires for wealth and power, allowing them to have more operational autonomy because of their loyalty to the system. They become images of their god, the Antichrist: pride totally suspends their minds; they are consumed by the unrestrained motivation to make more money than others, earn more power over others, run the system better than others, and gain direct access to the Antichrist himself.

191

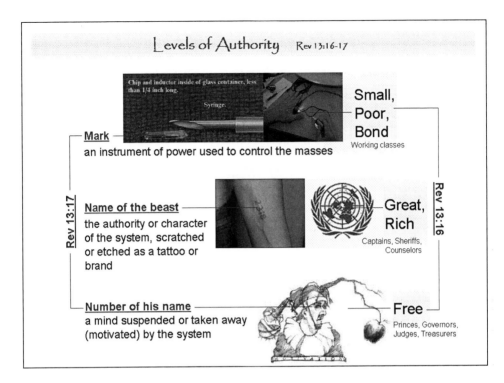

Levels of Authority Rev 13:16-17

Mark
an instrument of power used to control the masses

Small, Poor, Bond
Working classes

Name of the beast
the authority or character of the system, scratched or etched as a tattoo or brand

Great, Rich
Captains, Sheriffs, Counselors

Number of his name
a mind suspended or taken away (motivated) by the system

Free
Princes, Governors, Judges, Treasurers

Rev 13:17

Rev 13:16

Behind the scenes, the framework for using the mark of the beast – the condition of the human heart – is already being constructed all around us. Many troubling signs are now appearing that reveal how the dark system of the Antichrist is approaching faster than we think. For those who have the wisdom to understand what is really happening here, they can already see how the decadence of the human condition will announce his arrival through:

- the selfish worship of image
- the selfish love of money
- the divisive separation of people into financial classes
- the rebellious acceptance of tattoos and piercing, and
- the rapid breakthroughs in wireless technology

These signs, along with many others, point toward the great storm that is drawing near. Only those with wisdom will be able to avoid the destruction it brings.

WISDOM

666 – The Mystery of Inquity Revealed

Revelation 13:18

Here Is Wisdom

CHAPTER 14

The Number of a Man

"Here is wisdom. Let him that hath understanding count the number of the beast: for it is the number of a man; and his number is Six hundred threescore and six." – Revelation 13:18

The numeral 666 is a popular centerpiece of end-times prophecy, one of the most analyzed Scriptures in the entire Bible over the past 1900 years, and for good reason. This number points us to a person who the Apostle Paul describes as a man of complete evil:

"Let no man deceive you by any means: for that day shall not come, except there come a falling away first, and that man of sin be revealed, the son of perdition; who opposeth and exalteth himself above all that is called God, or that is worshipped; so that he as God sitteth in the temple of God, shewing himself that he is God." – 2 Thessalonians 2:3-4

Rational logic would suggest that being able to identify this evil individual is the same thing as being able to identify *the* Antichrist of the last days of time. Furthermore, to identify "the last days of time" implies that time is short for people to get their heart right with God. This association indicates that identifying the Antichrist should be a naturally strong tool for witnessing to others. This sort of logic makes sense, doesn't it?

Down through the centuries, people have used this logic to take the names of various leaders and attempt to compute and match the numbers of their names to the number 666 – the logic being that by identifying the Antichrist, the Truth of Scripture will be confirmed and people will give their hearts to the Lord right away because it points to the end of time.

However, there are several problems with this logic. The first problem – the most important one – is that the hearts of people are not supposed to focus so intensely on looking for the Antichrist. The hearts of people should *focus intensely on looking for Jesus Christ.*

In other words, if more people would spend more of their energy building a real relationship with Jesus, rather than wasting it on complicated mathematical tricks that "identify" who the real Antichrist is, the world would be a much better place. The bottom line here is this: the Antichrist is not a witness of the Gospel. Jesus Christ *is* the Gospel.

Furthermore, the Scriptures are very clear that believers who are taken up in the Rapture will never know (on this side) who the Antichrist really is:

> "Now we beseech you, brethren, by the coming of our Lord Jesus Christ, and by our gathering together unto Him, that ye be not soon shaken in mind, or be troubled, neither by spirit, nor by word, nor by letter as from us, as that the day of Christ is at hand ... for the mystery of iniquity doth already work: only He who now letteth will let, *until He be taken out of the way. And then shall that Wicked be revealed,* whom the Lord shall consume with the Spirit of His mouth, and shall destroy with the brightness of His coming." – 2 Thessalonians 2, 7-8

Paul is explaining here that the evil one will be revealed *after* the Holy Spirit is removed, wisking all Christian believers up into heaven with Him in the Rapture of the true church, as described by the Apostle John:

> "After this I looked, and, behold, a door was opened in heaven: and the first Voice which I heard was as it were of a trumpet talking with me; which said, Come up hither, and I will shew thee things which must be hereafter. And immediately I was in the Spirit: and, behold, a throne was set in heaven, and One sat on the throne." – Revelation 4:1-2

The Scriptures are clear that all true believers will be gone before the Antichrist is ever identified. This simple fact means that believers really shouldn't place so much emphasis on labeling the Antichrist from the perspective of witnessing to others. History proves that discussions *about* him can certainly be used as tools for witnessing, but using arithmetic games to *identify* him can produce some pretty wacky results.

For example, we studied earlier how the ancient Hebrew and Greek alphabets do not use separate characters or alphabets to represent numbers and letters. The first Hebrew letter is an aleph, Greek is alpha, and English is "A." The English alphabet originates from the Greek (alpha beta) and the Hebrew (aleph bet), whose letters are also used to represent numbers, so that each letter is also a numerical value.

The Hebrew equivalent of our "w" is the letter "vav" or "waw." The numerical value of *vav* is 6. So the English "www" transliterated into Hebrew is "vav vav vav," which is the numerical equivalent of 666. This means "www" *relates* to the number of the beast identified by the John, but it is not *the* number.[125]

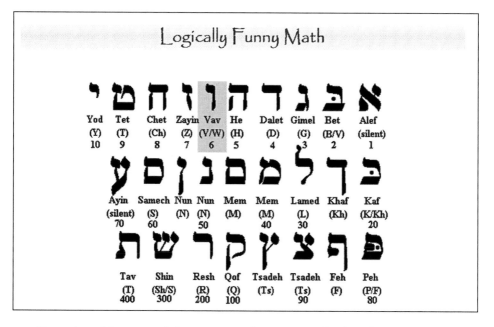

Logically Funny Math

Knowing this, one minister was curious as to whether the gematria (numerical values for each letter) would yield any interesting results. With the help of a friend of his who was more adept in computer programming, he wrote a computer program that would calculate the numerical value (gematria) for English.[126]

He limited the system only to the first 22 letters, as the ancients had done (Hebrew and Greek only have 22 letters). Once the program was written, he was able to type in all the names for all world figures past and present, calculating the gematria for each with computer accuracy. He had no expectations whatsoever for anyone when he started entering names. He did not, for instance, believe that Henry Kissinger, a man perceived to be the evil one by many people at that time, was the Antichrist.[127]

Upon entering the names of several high ranking leaders and popular figures, the computer calculated all sorts of numbers. But when this person entered the name "Prince Charles of Wales," the value displayed was 666! This meant Prince Charles was the Antichrist! [128]

It appears at first glance that a computer was able to solve the mystery, until the full name of Bill Clinton (William Jefferson Clinton) is entered. His name also adds up to 666. In fact, the same 666 results when entering different versions of the names of Franklin Delano Roosevelt, Anwar Sadat, Jane Fonda and other prominent figures from the past and present that people perceived to be "antichrists."

The wacky arithmetic games don't stop with matching names to the number 666, either. When John F. Kennedy received 666 votes at the 1956 Democratic convention, many claimed he was the Antichrist. Because president Ronald Wilson Reagan had six letters in all three of his names (666), others claimed he was the Antichrist.[129]

Rather than identifying the Antichrist, what is actually being established here is the problem of using "quick and dirty" logic that randomly misapplies the meaning of John's insight into the future. These errant games do more harm than good for the Christian cause, because they continually fail. And every time they fail, the unbeliever is ultimately challenged to question the authority of Scripture.

Logically Funny Math

The Gematria in English and Hebrew

Other recent "antichrists"

- Franklin Delano Roosevelt
  His name = 666

- John F. Kennedy
  Received 666 votes at the 1956 Democratic convention

- Ronald Wilson Reagan
  Had 6 letters in all 3 of his names

- William Jefferson Clinton
  His name = 666

Prince Charles of Wales = 666

Prince Charles is the antichrist

I do believe personally that the name of the actual Antichrist, whoever he is, will mathematically compute to the number 666. I personally believe that the Lord orchestrates that specific computation for all the logical people whose eyes will be opened too late, only to recognize that they have already been left behind in the last days.

During that scary period of time, I personally believe that someone will find a copy of a Bible, read the information that John makes known here in Revelation 13:18, and match the name with the man. But it will be too late then – and they will endure hardships and physical death to be saved.

Jehovah God does not want any person to live through the time of Revelation 13. For this reason, through the inspired writing of John, the Holy Spirit provides believers with spiritual intelligence so that we may apply practical caution to our hearts, our lives, and to the signs we see around us. This spiritual intelligence only comes from the thoughtful study of God's Word – and our Savior calls its *wisdom*.

This wisdom does not focus directly on mathematical tricks related to the number 666, but on how this number is a tool to discern signs and events that point believers directly to the blessed hope of the return of our Lord:

> "Teaching us that, denying ungodliness and worldly lusts, we
> should live soberly, righteously, and godly, in this present world;
> *looking for that blessed hope, and the glorious appearing of the great*
> *God and our Savior Jesus Christ*; Who gave Himself for us, that
> He might redeem us from all iniquity, and purify unto Himself a
> peculiar people, zealous of good works." – Titus 2:12-14

How in the world does 666 point believers to the coming of the Lord? I personally believe that the meaning of 666 goes much deeper than a simple math computation to identify a man. I believe 666 represents not only an evil man, but the eventual culmination of a one-world system of rebellious mankind, ultimately revealed through what Paul describes as *the mystery of iniquity*.

Paul explains that this mystery of iniquity is *already at work*. He also emphasizes that the Holy Spirit is the only Force capable of preventing this full culmination of evil, this complete depravity of mankind, from consuming our world. In other words, mankind is currently being spared by God's Grace – and only by His Grace, nothing else – from this evil destruction.

The power of the Holy Spirit not only provides our barrier of protection,

He also grants believers the wisdom to intellectually recognize and mentally understand how this evil rebellion is coming together around us, so that we can warn others before it's too late.

John explains that if believers *count* the number, we can reveal the mystery of iniquity already at work within this number 666. The Greek term *count* means much more than performing a mathematical equation. *Count* here refers to understanding the meaning of this number, discerning how it is derived and the significant content behind it – then applying this understanding and discernment to the past, present and future events of history.

In other words, "counting" the number of the beast is a way to compute the mystery of iniquity that Paul says is already happening around us, because once we understand the profile of the antichrist spirit and the related meaning of the events happening around us, believers can recognize how near we are to the second coming of Jesus – and we will all prepare for His return.

Now that we understand *what* "count the number" means, let's start *counting*.

We've already uncovered one equation to the mystery of iniquity, back when we were analyzing John's information regarding the False Prophet and his one-world religious system. Let's recount that equation for just a moment.

We saw earlier how John reveals that apostate Christianity will be the mantle of the interfaith religious component (the second beast) in the global system (the first beast) ruled by the Antichrist, as seen in the number 666 of the beast. The ancient Greek numerals in the number of the global system show that *six hundred* is represented by the symbol *chi* and threescore, or *sixty*, is represented by *xi*. However, a closer look at the numeral *six*, represented by the symbol *stigma*, reveals that the number *six* represents the *weakness of man*, the *evils of Satan*, and the *manifestation of sin*.

In the ancient Greek, the *stigma* is a mark incised or punched for recognition of ownership; a scar or *mark* of service that appears to look like a symbol representing a serpent. So the stigma represents the mark of the spiritually weak man who is scarred by the manifestation of sin inside, an evil person who serves and is owned by Satan himself.

Furthermore, when the *chi* is rotated 90 degrees clockwise, it bears a close resemblance to the cross used in the Episcopal Church today – a Protestant denomination, now synonymous with apostate Christianity

200

and spiritual disorder, whose liturgy closely resembles that of the Roman Catholic Church under the Pope, whose profile matches that of the False Prophet.

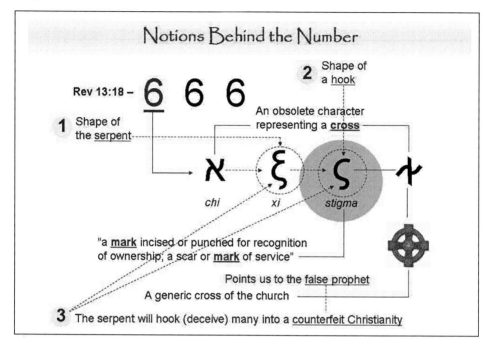

In other words, the number 666 equates to the manifestation of sin marked by the weakness of counterfeit Christianity, seen here in apostate man-made religions and cults that deceptively draw people into rebellion against God. The prophet Isaiah describes this deception in great detail through another equation of the mystery of iniquity:

> "Woe unto them that draw iniquity with cords of vanity, and sing as it were with a cart rope: That say, Let Him make seed, and hasten His work, that we may see it: and let the Counsel of the Holy One of Israel draw nigh and come, that we may know it! Woe unto them that call evil good, and good evil; and put darkness for light, and light for darkness, that put bitter for sweet, and sweet for bitter! Woe unto them that are wise in their own eyes, and prudent in their own sight! Woe unto them that are mighty to drink wine, and men of strength to mingle strong drink: which justify the wicked for reward, and take away the righteousness of the righteous from Him! – Isaiah 5:18-23

Here, Isaiah computes the way apostasy grows like a spiritual cancer from the inside out, multiplying through three stages that directly relate to the three numerals composing the number 666.

The first numeral of 666 is 6, which can be "counted" by multiplying 6 *x* 1. The numeral 6 represents the *weakness of man*, the *evils of Satan*, and the *manifestation of sin*. This equation emphasizes that apostasy originated with the first man, Adam, in the Garden of Eden – meaning apostasy is always birthed on a *personal* level, where evil can manifest itself in the weakness of pride (vanity). Isaiah warns us that vanity draws rebellion (*iniquity*) into the heart. In other words, pride is the personal root of rebellion against God.

This is the first stage of apostasy. People whose personal behaviors renounce their public profession of religious faith are being drawn into rebellion against God by the insecurities of their own vanity. The tidal wave of apostasy that is currently flooding mankind reflects a critical mass of individuals that are drowning in their own insecurities. Personal insecurity transforms the behaviors of those who profess faith into a mirror image of those who claim to have no faith.

The second numeral of 666 is 60, which can be "counted" by multiplying 10 *x* 6. The ancient Hebrew numeral 10 represents the *testimony of law and responsibility*. This equation points to the pride of man corrupting his responsibilities under the law. Isaiah warns us that rebellion is a testimony against God's Law, an unlawful behavior that breaks the Ten Commandments by treating *evil as good*, and *good as evil*. Vanity is the *darkness that replaces the light* in the heart of the apostate person who blindly clings to direction from man-made religions and cults that are *wise in their own eyes, prudent in their own sight*.

This is the second stage of apostasy, where unchecked rebellious behaviors blindly expand from personal experiences into the cultural phenomena of mainline denominations abandoning their spiritual principles and loyalty to God. We are now witnessing entire denominations of Episcopals, Presbyterians, Methodists and others publicly defect from the Word of God they once evangelized. They are attempting to alter the spiritual roots of our society from *sweet to bitter* by *rewarding wickedness*.

The third numeral of 666 is 600, which can be "counted" by multiplying 100 *x* 6. The ancient Hebrew numeral 100 represents *election by Grace* and *children of promise*. This equation points to the original apostasy being freely elected by Adam and Eve then passed down to their oldest son Cain, who then committed the first murder. This sequence established the continuing fulfillment of God's promise that the wickedness of a society will be magnified more intensely in the next generation and beyond:

"... that will by no means clear the guilty; visiting the iniquity of the fathers upon the children, and upon the children's children, unto the third and to the fourth generation." – Exodus 34:7

The Lord promises Moses here that those who elect to ignore God will raise children whose *righteousness is taken away* by the rebellious behaviors being passed down from their elders. These future generations become the evil children of lies that elect sin as their heritage.

This is the final – terminal – stage of apostasy, a cultural transition into rebellion and vanity as a way of life, where the mystery of iniquity is ingrained from one generation into another, passed from the past into the present and future, until the spiritual cancer finally reaches apostate self-destruction. Rebellious generations of children and grandchildren are being raised right before our eyes; the self-destruction of our civil society is at hand.

All of this shows how the number 666 ultimately computes the culmination of generational apostasy, an outline of the self-destruction of mankind. In other words, 666 is a profile of mankind consumed with rebellion against God, as portrayed through the three significant stages of apostasy described by Isaiah.

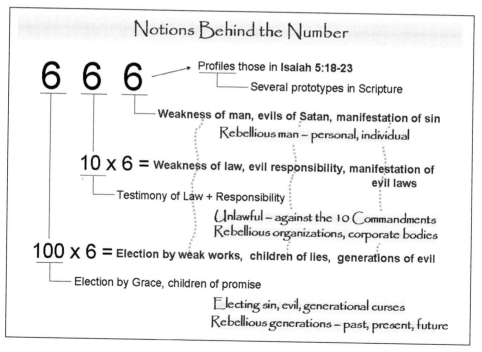

Notions Behind the Number

6 6 6 → Profiles those in Isaiah 5:18-23
└── Several prototypes in Scripture
└── Weakness of man, evils of Satan, manifestation of sin
Rebellious man – personal, individual

10 x 6 = Weakness of law, evil responsibility, manifestation of evil laws
└── Testimony of Law + Responsibility
Unlawful – against the 10 Commandments
Rebellious organizations, corporate bodies

100 x 6 = Election by weak works, children of lies, generations of evil
└── Election by Grace, children of promise
Electing sin, evil, generational curses
Rebellious generations – past, present, future

As a profile, 666 can be used to spiritually graph the character traits

203

of a human head or face of leaders – past, present and future – who *fit the profile* of the future son of perdition (without specifically naming him). By plotting these traits as points on the profile, the head or face of any prominent leader that matches the 666 profile represents a shadow-in-type of *the* Antichrist.

Furthermore, once a leader is identified as a shadow-in-type of the evil one, the events that happen around that leader reveal prophetic signs of future events that will actually occur around the coming Antichrist. The Bible graphs numerous characters and events against this 666 profile and provides several clear examples of leaders that are shadows of the Antichrist.

One early shadow-in-type is found in Cain, the oldest son of Adam and Eve. Their original rebellion against God was passed down to him (along with all of mankind) and manifested through Cain committing the first illegal sacrifice:

> "... Cain was a tiller of the ground ... Cain brought of the fruit of the ground an offering unto the Lord ... but unto Cain and to his offering He had not respect. And Cain was very wroth, and his countenance fell. And the Lord said unto Cain, Why art thou wroth? And why is thy countenance fallen? If thou doest well, shalt thou not be accepted? And if thou doest not well, sin lieth at the door. And unto thee shall be his desire, and thou shalt rule over him." – Genesis 4:2-3, 5-7

In the ancient Hebrew, the name *Cain* means *possess* or *own*, an accurate description of the heart that is selfishly consumed with materialism, possessions (symbolized by the "fruits" of the earth) and attaining personal wealth rather than sincerely serving God – character traits that match the profile of the Antichrist.

Cain's insincere fruit offering was rejected by God because his heart was corrupted with vanity: he presented God with an imperfect gift while keeping the better produce of the land for himself. Cain stole from the Lord and attempted to deceive Him with this offering.

By doing this, Cain made the sacrifice illegal, abhorrent, detestable, and utterly repulsive to God – an abomination that points to the future abomination of desolation that Jesus explains will be committed by the Antichrist:

> "When ye therefore shall see the abomination of desolation, spoken of by Daniel the prophet, stand in the holy place ..."
> – Matthew 24:15

Jesus was referring to a vision of events surrounding the future Antichrist that was given to the prophet Daniel by the archangel Gabriel:

> "... they shall pollute the sanctuary of strength, and shall take away the daily sacrifice, and they shall place the abomination that maketh desolate ... and from the time that the daily sacrifice shall be taken away, and the abomination that maketh desolate set up, there shall be a thousand two hundred and ninety days." – Daniel 11:31, 12:11

Cain's illegal sacrifice began the abominations predominantly associated with heathen idols and false gods that are detestable to the one true God. Just as this illegal sacrifice defiled Cain, who should have been a living temple inhabited by God, the future abomination of desolation will be an idolatrous act that will defile the Temple in Jerusalem.

The evil disposition in Cain's heart eventually provoked the first human jealousy, anger, and murder – more character traits that match the profile of the Antichrist:

> "And Cain talked with Abel his brother: and it came to pass, when they were in the field, that Cain rose up against Abel his brother, and slew him." – Genesis 4:8

Cain slew Abel because he was jealous that his brother's faithful sacrifice was received by God. Cain foolishly committed murder because of his defiant anger of being rejected by God.

As punishment, the Lord banished Cain from His Presence. Cain eventually builds the first city, a godless world economic system constructed upon material possessions and organized to guard wealth – shadows of the coming global economic system of the Antichrist:

> "And Cain went out from the presence of the Lord, and dwelt in the land of Nod, on the east of Eden ... and he builded a city, and called the name of the city, after the name of his son, Enoch." – Genesis 4:16-17

The corruption in Cain's heart was passed down through his children and exposed by his grandchild Lamech, the first person to break God's marriage vows of by taking two wives:

> "And Lamech took unto him two wives: the name of the one was Adah, and the name of the other was Zillah." – Genesis 4:19

There is no coincidence that one wife's name started with an "A" and the other with a "Z," the first and last letters of the English alphabet.

This polygamy began all of the destructive elements of the dysfunctional family: from women treated as sexual objects to marital adultery, from sexual perversions to illegitimate children and everything in between – all traits that match the profile of the Antichrist.

Another early example of the Antichrist was Nimrod, who is discussed at length in Chapter 5. Nimrod rose to become the key prophetic player in the grand scheme of the pagan system. His story in Genesis 11 reveals many prophetic insights into the future workings of the Antichrist: he constructs the first world economic system after The Flood; he builds the first temple and first world religious system; he merges the worldly marketplace with religious worship; and he places himself before God.

The story of Pharoah in Exodus 1-14 is a profile from 2500 BC that prophetically matches the Antichrist. The Scriptures describe this Egyptian's violent persecution of the Jewish people, his pagan authority over the world economic and religious system, his merging of the worldly marketplace and religious worship, and his placing of himself before God for worship – all traits that match the profile of the Antichrist.

The tale of Nebuchadnezzar in Daniel 1-4 is another example of the Antichrist. His story is analyzed in detail in Chapter 12. In 600 BC, this Babylonian king pursued violent persecution of the Jewish people, organized a world economic and religious system, merged the worldly marketplace and religious worship, and placed himself before God for worship – all traits that shadow the Antichrist.

Another prominent profile that matches the Antichrist is the Biblical account of Antiochus IV Epiphanes, given in a vision to the prophet Daniel by the archangel Gabriel:

> "The rough goat is the king of Grecia . . . Now that being broken, whereas four stood up for it, four kingdoms shall stand up out of the nation, but not in his power. And in the latter time of their kingdom, when the transgressors are come to the full, a king of fierce countenance, and understanding dark sentences, shall stand up. And his power shall be mighty, but not by his own power: and he shall destroy wonderfully, and shall prosper; and practise, and shall destroy the mighty and the holy people. And through his policy also he shall cause craft to prosper in his hand; and he shall magnify himself in his heart, and by peace shall destroy many: he shall also stand up against the Prince of prince; but he shall be broken without hand." – Daniel 8:21-25

These Scriptures prophesied how, after the death of Alexander the Great (the rough goat), the Greek empire would divide into four territories (kingdoms) governed by his four generals. Seleucus was the general who became king of the eastern provinces, which are now modern Afghanistan, Iran, Iraq, Syria, and Lebanon, together with parts of Turkey, Armenia, Turkmenistan, Uzbekistan, and Tajikistan. This kingdom was, like the empire of Alexander, actually the continuation of the empires before: the Assyrian, Babylonian, and the Achaemenid Empire.[130]

Count the Number

Gen. 4 – Cain v. 3,5: Commits illegal sacrifice – Matt. 24:15, Dan. 11:31, 12:11

v. 8:   Introduces violence, murder   Undated

v. 17: Builds the first city – first world economic system, material possessions, guarding of wealth

v. 19: Evil grandchildren – Lamech breaks marriage vows – takes two wives

---

Gen. 10: 8-9, 11 – Nimrod   Undated

v. 11:1: World economic system

v. 11:4: Builds the first temple – first world religious system

v. 11:4: Merges worldly marketplace and religious worship

v. 11:4: Places himself before God

Antiochus IV Epiphanes was a Syrian king that came to power about 175 BC as an evil forerunner of the Antichrist. He was one of the Seleucids who succeeded Alexander the Great and built a realm in Syria and adjacent lands. He forced Greek culture and manners on the Jews and attempted to end the Jewish religious community.[131]

He required all citizens honor him as their god. In 168 BC, Antiochus IV Epiphanes occupied Jerusalem, entered the Holy of Holies, desecrated the sanctuary by offering unclean animals upon the altar of burnt-offerings, polluted the whole building by sprinkling it with water in which flesh had been boiled, dedicated the Temple itself to Jupiter Olympius, erected a statue of Jupiter and plundered the temple treasures.[132]

This "abomination of desolation" on the altar of the Lord in the inner court of the Temple blatantly foreshadows the future defilement of the Temple in Jerusalem by the Antichrist in the last days.

Two other examples of more recent leaders that match the profile of the Antichrist are the notorious Roman emperor Nero in 60 AD, and Adolf Hitler, the leader of Nazi Germany during the 1930s and 1940s. Both of these men repeated the familiar cycle of violent persecution of the Jewish people, creating new economic and religious systems, merging the worldly marketplace with religious worship, and placing themselves before God.

In one way or another, every detail that John shares about the two beasts in Revelation 13 relates back to these profiles, situations and events. Every detail teaches us to recognize specific spiritual problems of this world – and to separate ourselves from them. Every detail emphasizes that our Christian walk should be all about immediate preparation – right now!

Count the Number

Ex. 1-14 – Pharoah   2500 BC

Violent persecution of the Jewish people

World economic + religious system

Merges worldly marketplace and religious worship

Places himself before God

Daniel 1-4 – Nebuchadnezzar   600 BC

Violent persecution of the Jewish people

World economic + religious system

Merges worldly marketplace and religious worship

Places himself before God

How do we prepare? By following the model of Jesus that is found throughout the Scriptures. Through deep study of the Bible, our Savior instructs us how to use our mental intellect to lovingly separate and combat the growing hatred of Christians and Christianity. He shows us how to fight the power and authority of evil that is so popular among unbelievers. Through Him, we can counter the growing blasphemy against the one true God and the war against believers by exposing the secular deception of the enemy.

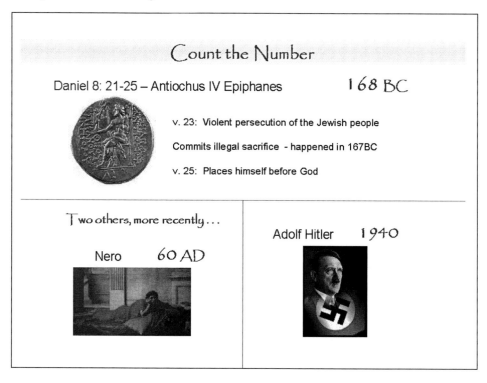

Count the Number

Daniel 8: 21-25 – Antiochus IV Epiphanes   168 BC

v. 23: Violent persecution of the Jewish people

Commits illegal sacrifice - happened in 167BC

v. 25: Places himself before God

Two others, more recently . . .

Nero   60 AD

Adolf Hitler   1940

Our Lord provides us with spiritual discernment to identify and support those circumstances, situations and events in our daily lives that make people more important than products. His Holy Spirit will guide us away from pride in personal programs, plans and successes so that we will never compromise God's Will and Word in our lives.

In this way, believers become living testimonies of Jesus Christ in their lives: they do what is right, no matter what the cost. They are involved in businesses that provide worthwhile products or services instead of things that feed the world's desires. And they *always* consider people above the making of money.

Counting with Wisdom   Rev 13:18

Use our **mental intellect to** separate and combat –	Use our **spiritual discernment to** identify and support –
• Hatred of Christianity	• Always make people more important than products
• Hatred for Christians	• Stay away from pride in personal programs, plans and successes
• Power + authority of evil	• Never compromise God's Will and Word
• Popularity among unbelievers	• Do what is right, no matter what the cost
• Blasphemy against God	• Be involved in businesses that provide worthwhile products or services – not things that feed the world's desires
• War against believers	
• Secular deception	• Always consider people above the making of money

Take a moment to meditate on this, and listen to the Lord speaking to us about being prepared:

> "... prepare to meet thy God, O Israel. For, lo, He that formeth the mountains, and createth the wind, and declareth unto man what is His thought, that maketh the morning darkness, and treadeth upon the high places of the earth, The Lord, The God of hosts, is His Name." – Amos 4:12-13

God is telling all believers to prepare themselves for our Rapture into heaven with our Lord. He is telling us that to "count with wisdom" is to purify ourselves from the sins of this world. To "count with wisdom" is to cloth ourselves with His fine linen, white and clean. To "count with wisdom" is to mount one of His white horses. To "count with wisdom" is to become a member of the army of God. To "count with wisdom" is all about deliverance from evil and salvation from destruction.

CHAPTER 15

The Good News

Here is the Good News of the Gospel: believers won't be here when the Antichrist takes power and his terrible destruction begins.

As believers, we should not fear the troubles that are brewing behind the scenes in the form of the two beasts. In fact, Jesus explains that we should be excited and not afraid, for these storms are nothing more than prophetic signals from God Himself to us, announcing that the Lord, our Redeemer, is coming soon to take us home *before* His devastating judgment begins:

> **"And when these things begin to come to pass, then look up, and lift up your heads, for your redemption draweth nigh." – Luke 21:28**

All believers – we who are the true bride of Christ – will be raptured out of this world before the perfect storm begins. Hallelujah! Believers will never know who the Antichrist or False Prophet is, though these evil men are probably already alive. We will never experience the deep insecurity – the consuming fear – forged by their awful global systems, though we can already see them being constructed all around us.

Until the Lord comes to take us home, however, our Savior tells all believers to stand fast, arm ourselves as soldiers in His army, and wage the good fight of faith:

> **"Fight the good fight of faith, lay hold on eternal life, whereunto thou art also called, and hast professed a good profession before many witnesses." – 1 Timothy 6:12**

How do we do enlist in His army? By faithfully cleansing and

211

purifying our hearts; by repenting of our sins; and by building our trust in Jesus alone, through the absolute Truth of His Word.

As believers, the growing signs of trouble we see should fast forward our hearts toward that exalted day when Jesus Christ will return, in all of His unmatched glory, to pronounce judgment on the evil global system of the Antichrist that the Apostle John has presented in Revelation 13:

> **"And I saw heaven opened, and behold a white horse; and He that sat upon him was called Faithful and True, and in righteousness He doth judge and make war. His eyes were as a flame of fire, and on His head were many crowns; and He had a Name written, that no man knew, but He Himself. And He was clothed with a vesture dipped in blood: and His Name is called The Word of God.**
>
> **And the armies which were in heaven followed Him upon white horses, clothed in fine linen, white and clean. And out of His mouth goeth a sharp sword, that with it He should smite the nations: and He shall rule them with a rod of iron: and He treadeth the winepress of the fierceness and wrath of Almighty God. And He hath on His vesture and on His thigh a Name written, KING OF KINGS, AND LORD OF LORDS."**
> **– Revelation 19:11-16**

Satan is a defeated foe. In Isaiah 54:17, the Scriptures promise that no weapon formed against us shall prosper. The second coming of Jesus Christ will break all of the chains of spiritual bondage that have held mankind in sin since Adam and Eve originally fell in the Garden of Eden.

But that's not all. The Good News of the Gospel proclaims that because Jesus Christ is The Living Word of God, no one has to wait for His second coming and judgment. We serve a Living God, for He lives in and through the Bible. You can be free *right now*! Hallelujah!

By sincerely asking the Lord to forgive you of your sins, by truly repenting and accepting Him into your heart, and by thoughtfully studying His Living Word, Jesus will lift and remove the burdens of this world from you. He will enter into your life, cleanse all of your sins, and replace your insecurity with His Hope. Jesus will replace your fear with His Love. Your Savior will replace your darkness with His Light. The Lord will replace your impurity with His Righteousness. God will replace your evil with His Holiness. Jesus will wash you clean, set you free, and you will be free indeed:

> **"If the Son therefore shall make you free, ye shall be free indeed."**
> **– John 8:36**

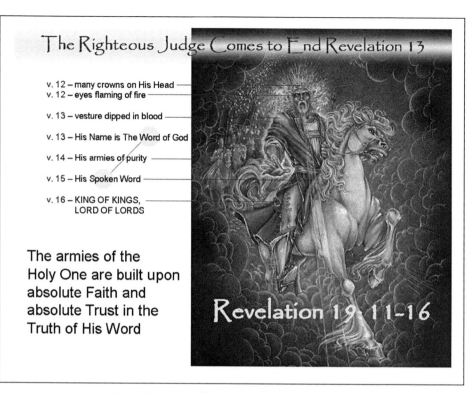

Through His Living Word, God will judge and destroy the influence of a fallen world within you. Through His Living Word, His precious blood – shed on the Cross of Calvary almost 2,000 years ago – will wash away your sin such that it will pass away from your life as a vapor locked in time. Through His Living Word, your Savior will carefully reconstruct your heart into an eternal home in heaven with Him:

> **"Let not your heart be troubled: ye believe in God, believe also in Me. In My Father's house are many mansions: if it were not so, I would have told you. I go to prepare a place for you. And if I go and prepare a place for you, I will come again, and receive you unto Myself; that where I Am, there ye may be also." – John 14:1-3**

By truly accepting Jesus Christ as the Lord over your life, you can all start over right now, fresh and new. Through His Living Word, you will be spiritually cleansed and protected from the satanic influences of the enemy. You will become a living testimony of that day when God's entire Creation will be cleansed and protected once and for all:

> "And I saw the beast, and the kings of the earth, and their armies, gathered together to make war against Him that sat on the horse, and against His army. And the beast was taken, and with him the false prophet that wrought miracles before him with which he deceived them that had received the mark of the beast, and them that worshipped his image. These both were cast alive into a lake of fire burning with brimstone . . . And the devil that deceived them was cast into the lake of fire and brimstone, where the beast and the false prophet are, and shall be tormented day and night for ever and ever." – Revelation 19:19-20, 20:10

Just as the Lord can fully restore His authority right now in people who sincerely repent of sin, who accept Him into their lives and study His Word, one day soon He will fully restore His authority by positioning all believers to reign with Him:

> "And I saw thrones, and they sat upon them, and judgment was given unto them: and I saw the souls of them that were beheaded for the witness of Jesus, and for the Word of God, and which had not worshipped the beast, neither his image, neither had received his mark upon their foreheads, or in their hands; and they live and reigned with Christ a thousand years." – Revelation 20:4

On that glorious day, after our Savior completes the physical and spiritual redemption of His creation, God will usher all believers into our new homes that reside in a new heaven and new earth:

> "And I saw a new heaven and a new earth: for the first heaven and the first earth were passed away; and there was no more sea. And I John saw the holy city, new Jerusalem, coming down from God out of heaven, prepared as a bride adorned for her husband. And I heard a great Voice out of heaven saying, Behold, the tabernacle of God is with men, and He will dwell with them, and they shall be His people, and God Himself shall be with them, and be their God. – Revelation 21:1-3

Out with the Old, In with the New

Revelation 19: 19-20
Beast of the Earth
- false prophet

Revelation 20: 10
The dragon
- satan, the devil

Beast of the Sea
- antichrist

The New Jersusalem
Revelation 21: 1-3

Source: Revelation Illustrated by Pat Marvenko Smith

The bottom line is this: where is your eternal home going to be? Perhaps you are reading this right now and do not know the Lord Jesus Christ as your Savior. If the Rapture has not yet occurred, that's Good News, because you don't have to go through the coming turmoil of the last days. Accept Jesus into your heart right now and the Lord will save you!

If the Rapture has already occurred, you may be experiencing the darkness of the evil one and the horrors of his system. Don't be weary, because there is Good News for you too. You don't have to die and go to hell for eternity. Refuse the mark of the beast, accept Jesus into your heart, and the Lord will save you as well!

In either case, say this prayer with sincerity from the depths of your heart, and Almighty God will save you:

> **"Dear Jesus, please forgive me for all of my sins. I'm sorry for all of the wrongful things I've done. Jesus, I recognize you as the Lord of my life. Please enter into my heart right now and save me, for you are my God. I love you. You alone, Lord, are worthy of all my praise, and I give it to you now, in Jesus' precious Name, Amen."**

If you have said that prayer and accepted Jesus into your heart, He has saved you:

> **"If thou shalt confess with thy mouth the Lord Jesus, and shalt believe in thine heart that God hath raised Him from the dead, thou shalt be saved. For with the heart man believeth unto righteousness; and with the mouth confession is made unto salvation . . . Whosoever shall confess that Jesus is the Son of God, God dwelleth in him, and he in God." – Romans 10:9-10; 1 John 4:15**

Heaven is now your eternal home – don't allow the enemy steal it from you. Jesus Christ alone is your eternal God – don't allow the enemy to scare or confuse you into thinking otherwise.

This story has a happy ending. Keep looking up, for your redemption is drawing near. Hallelujah! That's the Good News for all mankind.

REFERENCES

1. Directory of Health Savings Accounts Administrators, HSA for America, 2261 Shawnee Court, Suite 101,Fort Collins, CO 80525, August 26, 2006.

2. "Identity Chip Raises Privacy Concerns," Matthew Broersma, ZDNet UK, CNET Networks, Inc., July 3, 2001, accessed at news.zdnet.co.uk/ hardware/chips/0,39020354,2090580,00.htm on August 26, 2006.

3. "Digital Angel Named One of Four 'Cool Products' in Fortune Magazine's Cool List 2001," Applied Digital Solutions press release accessed at www.yahoo.com, www.adsx.com on August 26, 2006.

4. "Revelation 13: Closer Home Than We Think," David A. DePra, The Good News, 197 Tusseyville Road, Centre Hall, PA 16828, March 2004, accessed at www.goodnewsarticles.com/Mar04-2.htm on August 26, 2006.

5. Ibid.

6. Ibid.

7. "The Menorah from a New Angle," Eliezer Ben Moshe, adapted from a talk by the Lubavitcher Rebbe (Likutei Sichos, Vol. XXI, Terumah), accessed at www.jewish-holiday.com/menorah on October 6, 2006.

8. "Revelation 13: Closer Home Than We Think," Ibid.

9. "En Route to Global Occupation," Gary H. Kah, Huntingdon House Publishers, P.O. Box 53788, Lafayette, LA 70505, 1992, pp. 6-7.

10. Ibid.

11. Press Release from www.house.gov/paul, December 7, 2004, accessed on August 28, 2006.

12. Ibid.

13. Ibid.

14. "Global Banking: The Bank for International Settlements," Patrick Wood, The August Review, October 19, 2005, accessed at www. newswithviews.comWood/patrick4.htm, on September 3, 2006.

15. Ibid.

16. Ibid.

17. Ibid, Patrick Wood reference to BIS, Statutes of the Bank for International Settlements Article 3 [as of January 1930, text as amended on March 10,2003], Basic Texts (Basle, August 2003), p. 7-8.

18. Ibid, Patrick Wood reference to Baker, The Bank for International Settlements: Evolution and Evaluation, (Quorum, 2002), p. 20.

19. Ibid.

20. Ibid, Patrick Wood reference to IMF web site, accessed at www.imf.org, on September 3, 2006.

21. Ibid, Patrick Wood reference to World Bank web site, accessed at www.worldbank.org, on September 3, 2006.

22. Ibid, Patrick Wood reference to Baker, op cit, p. 141-142.

23. Ibid.

24. Ibid.

25. Ibid.

26. Ibid.

27. Ibid.

28. "Comparison with Other Regional Blocs," with reference to the CIA World Factbook 2005 and the IMF WEO Database, Wikipedia Encyclopedia, Wikipedia, Inc., accessed at www.wikipedia.org/wiki/NAFTA, on September 20, 2006.

29. Ibid, accessed at www.wikipedia.org/wiki/.EU, www.wikipedia.org/wiki/Asia-Pacific_Economic_Cooperation, www.wikipedia.org/wiki/ASEAN, www.wikipedia.org/wiki/African_Union, www.wikipedia.org/wiki/Mercosur on September 20, 2006.

30. Ibid, accessed at www.wikipedia.org/wiki/CIS, www.wikipedia.org/wiki/OPEC on September 20, 2006.

31. "En Route to Global Occupation," Kah, p. 30, with reference to Dr. John Coleman, The Federal Reserve Bank, Greatest Swindle in History, pp. 26-27.

32. Ibid, pp. 30-31.

33. Ibid, pp. 36-37.

34. Ibid, p. 35.

35. Ibid, p. 45.

36. Ibid, p. 46.

37. Ibid, p. 38.

38. Ibid, p. 40.

39. Ibid.

40. Ibid, pp. 40, 42.

41. "Silent Weapons for Quiet Wars," excerpted from Behold A Pale Horse, William Cooper, Light Technology Publishing, 1991, accessed at http://phoenix.akasha.de/~aton/swfqw.html on October 3, 2006.

42. "What I Believe About Conspiracy Theories," John W. Ritenbaugh, October 20, 1997, Tape 9709, accessed at http://bibletools.org/index.cfm/fuseaction/Library.show/CT/TRANSCRIPT/k/434 on October 3, 2006.

43. Ibid.

44. Ibid.

45. Ibid.

46. Ibid.

47. "Fed Chief Warns of Entitlement Collapse," The Patriot Post, Publius Press, Inc., accessed at www.patriotpost.us on October 6, 2006.

48. "Economy And Dollar Balancing Act," Michael Pento, Delta Global Advisors, Inc., 19051 Goldenwest, #106-116, Huntington Beach, CA 92648, accessed at www.DeltaGlobalAdvisors.com on October 7, 2006.

49. Ibid.

50. Ibid.

51. Ibid.

52. "Europe Forsakes Christianity for Islam?" Dale Hurd, CBNNews.com, The Christian Broadcasting Network, Inc., accessed at www.cbn.com/cbnnews/world/060206a.aspx on November 17, 2006.

53. "Revelation 6: Revelation Times," A Bible Study by Jack Kelly,

Gracethrufaith Inc., accessed at www.gracethrufaith.com/revelation-times/revelation-6 on January 22, 2007.

54. "Revelation 13: Closer Home Than We Think," Ibid.

55. "Barna Responds to Christianity Today Article," September 17, 2002, George Barna, The Barna Group, Ltd., 1957 Eastman Avenue, Suitte B, Ventura, CA 93003, accessed at www.Barna.org on February 25, 2007.

56. "Media and Worldviews," Kerby Anderson, Probe Ministries, 1900 Firman Drive, Suite 100, Richardson, TX 75081, accessed at www.probe.org on February 25, 2007.

57. Ibid.

58. Ibid.

59. "UN Religious Summit Speakers Decry Efforts at Conversion," September 8, 2000, Tom Strode, Baptist Press, The Southern Baptist Convention, 901 Commerce Street, Nashville, TN 37203-3699, accessed at www.worthynews.com on March 12, 2007.

60. Ibid.

61. Ibid.

62. Ibid.

63. Ibid.

64. Ibid.

65. Ibid.

66. Ibid.

67. Ibid.

68. Ibid.

69. Ibid.

70. "Interfaithism: The Religion of the New World Order," Eddie Sax, Endtime Magazine, July/August 1999, Endtime Ministries, Inc., PO Box 461167, Garland, TX 75046-1167, www.endtime.com, accessed at ryanj1678.tripod.com/christianity4today/id39.htm on March 14, 2007.

71. Ibid.

72. Ibid.

73. Ibid.

74. Ibid.

75. Ibid.

76. Ibid.

77. "About the World Council," The World Council of Religious Leaders, Empire State Building, 350 Fifth Avenue, Suite 5403, New York, NY 10118, accessed at www.millenniumpeacesummit.com, on March 17, 2007.

78. Ibid.

79. Ibid.

80. Ibid.

81. "Interfaithism: The Religion of the New World Order," Sax, Endtime Magazine, July/August 1999, www.endtime.com.

82. "Christianity, Islam, Hinduism, Chinese folk religion, Buddhism," Wikipedia Encyclopedia, Wikipedia, Inc., accessed at www.wikipedia. org/wiki/Christianity, www.wikipedia.org/wiki/Islam, www.wikipedia. org/wiki/Hinduism, www.wikipedia.org/wiki/Chinese folk religion, www.wikipedia.org/wiki/Buddhism, on March 27, 2007.

83. "Pope: Total and profound respect for Muslims," Alessio Vinci, CNN Rome, Cable News Network, accessed at www.cnn.com/2006/ WORLD/europe/09/25/pope.muslims/index.html?section=cnn_ topstories, on March 29, 2007.

84. Ibid.

85. "Vatican City," Wikipedia Encyclopedia, Wikipedia, Inc., accessed at www.wikipedia.org/wiki/Vatican City, on March 29, 2007.

86. Ibid.

87. "What is the Roman Catholic Pope?" August Cline, About: Agnosticism/Atheism, About, Inc., The New York Times Company , accessed at http://atheism.about.com/od/popesandthepapacy/p/ PopesPapacy.htm, on March 24, 2007.

88. "Rome," Wikipedia Encyclopedia, Wikipedia, Inc., accessed at www. wikipedia.org/wiki/Rome, on March 30, 2007.

89. "Greek Dictionary of the New Testament," The New Strong's

Exhaustive Concordance of the Bible, James Strong, LL.D., S.T.D., Thomas Nelson Publishers, 1990, p. 78.

90. "Episcopal Church in the United States of America," Wikipedia Encyclopedia, Wikipedia, Inc., accessed at www.wikipedia.org/wiki/Rome, on April 4, 2007.

91. "About the World Council," The World Council of Religious Leaders, Empire State Building, 350 Fifth Avenue, Suite 5403, New York, NY 10118, accessed at www.millenniumpeacesummit.com, on March 17, 2007.

92. Ibid.

93. "The National Day of Prayer National Prayer Service, September 14, 2001, Faith in Christ – or Interfaith, in "isms"?," Catherine Millard, Christian Heritage Tours®, P.O. Box 797, Springfield, VA 22150, accessed at www.christianheritagetours.org/contact.htm, on April 14, 2007.

94. Ibid.

95. Ibid.

96. Ibid.

97. Ibid.

98. "The Deity of the Mother of God," Fr. Malcolm L. Broussard, Jr., The Order of Saint Charbel, MWOA Pty. Ltd., October 21, 2002, accessed at www.shoal.net.au/~mwoa/documents/deity_of_mary.html, on April 12, 2007.

99. Ibid.

100. "Section 2, Sub-part C: Saints and others . . . Verifying the Dogma: There is No Salvation Outside of the Roman Catholic Church," accessed at http://immaculata-one.com/section_2.html, on April 12, 2007.

101. Ibid.

102. "Pope John Paul's Travels in 1993: Apostolic Voyage 57," accessed at http://travel-write.com/travel_articles/general/farewell_pope_john_paul/93-94.htm, on April 13, 2007.

103. "Do Catholics Think Non-Christians are Saved?" David MacDonald,

CatholicBridge.com, accessed at http://davidmacd.com/catholic/are_
non-christians_saved.htm, on April 13, 2007.

104. "Declaration on the Relation of the Church to Non-Christian Religions,"
Nostra Aetate, Proclaimed by His Holiness Pope Paul VI, October 28,
1965, accessed at www.vatican.va/archive/hist_councils/ii_vatican_
council/documents/vat-ii_decl_19651028_nostra-aetate_en.html, on
April 13, 2007.

105. "The United Methodist Church and Homosexuality," Methodist Church,
Way of Life Literature©, David Cloud, 1701 Harns Road, Oak Harbor,
WA 98277, accessed at BibleBelievers.Net at www.biblebelievers.net/
Apostasy/kjcmethd.htm, on May 2, 2007.

106. Ibid.

107. Ibid.

108. Ibid.

109. Ibid.

110. "Homosexuality and Presbyterianism," Wikipedia Encyclopedia,
Wikipedia, Inc., accessed at http://en.wikipedia.org/wiki/
Homosexuality_and_Presbyterianism, on May 2, 2007.

111. Ibid.

112. "The Church at Laodicea, Revelation 3:14-22," Sermons by Ken
Trivette from Revelation, the Living Word, Temple Baptist Church,
Chattanooga, TN, accessed at www.thelivingwordtbc.com/rev12.htm,
on April 14, 2007.

113. "Wicca and Nature Spirituality," Religions & Traditions, United
Religions Initiative,1009 General Kennedy Avenue, San Francisco, CA
94129, www.uri.org.

114. "Is "www" in Hebrew equal to 666?" Terry Watkins, Dial-the-Truth
Ministries, accessed at www.av1611.org/666 on May 31, 2007.

115. "The Coin," a sermon from St. Clement's Anglican Episcopal Church,
Prague, Klimentska 5, Prague 1, Czech Republic, accessed at www.
anglican.cz on May 25, 2007.

116. "Do You Like Tatoos?" Aaron Menikoff, Third Avenue Baptist Church,
1726 South Third Street, Louisville, KY 40208, www.thirdavenue.org,
August 27, 2006.

117. Ibid.

118. Ibid.

119. "Technology Gets Under Our Skin," Arlene Wright, accessed at www.vivapinoy.com, on June 1, 2007.

120. Ibid.

121. Ibid.

122. Ibid.

123. Ibid.

124. Ibid.

125. "Is "www" in Hebrew equal to 666?" Terry Watkins, Dial-the-Truth Ministries, accessed at www.av1611.org/666 on May 31, 2007.

126. "The Prince Who Is To Come," Monte Judah, YAVOH, He is Coming newsletter, November 2001, Lion and Lamb Ministries, P.O. Box 720968, Norman, OK 73070, 405-447-4429, Fax: 405-447-3775, accessed at www.lionlamb.net/Yavoh/2001/Nov2001.htm, on June 7, 2007.

127. Ibid.

128. Ibid.

129. "The Antichrist: Have You Seen This Man?" Todd Strandberg, Rapture Ready, www.raptureready.com.

130. "Antiochus IV Epiphanes," Jona Lendering©, Livius, Articles on Ancient History, accessed at www.livius.org, on June 29, 2007.

131. "Antiochus IV Epiphanes," Jay Atkinson, The Latter Rain Page, accessed at latter-rain.com, on June 29, 2007.

132. Ibid.